# THE GARLAND OF LETTERS

*Essays on Tantra/Mantra Śāstra*

## THE SELECTED WORKS OF SIR JOHN WOODROFFE (ARTHUR AVALON)

**The Dance of Shiva:** *Fourteen Indian Essays*

**The Garland of Letters:** *Essays on Tantra/Mantra Śāstra*

**The Great Liberation:** *Mahānirvāṇa Tantra*

**Hymns to the Goddess and Hymns to Kali:** *Karpūrādi Stotra*

**Introduction to Tantra Śāstra**

**Is India Civilized? :** *Essays on Indian Culture*

**Kamakalavilasa**

**Mahamaya:** *Cti-Shakti or Power as Consciousness*

**Principles of Tantra**

**The Serpent Power:** *Shat-Chakra-Nirūpana and Pādukā-Panchakā*

**Shakti and Shakta**

**The World As Power**

# THE GARLAND OF LETTERS

*Essays on Tantra/Mantra Śāstra*

SIR JOHN WOODROFFE
*(Arthur Avalon)*

New Age Books

THE SELECTED WORKS OF SIR JOHN WOODROFFE
(ARTHUR AVALON)

THE GARLAND OF LETTERS

ISBN: 978-81-7822-400-8
First NAB Edition: Delhi, 2013



**Library of Congress Cataloging-in-Publication Data**
Woodroffe, Sir John
The Garland of Letters: Essays on Tantra, Mantra Sastra/
Sir John Woodroffe—Ist Ganesh & Company edition
ISBN 978-81-7822-400-8 (pbk.)

*Published by*
**NEW AGE BOOKS**
A-44 Naraina Industrial Area, Phase-I
New Delhi (India)-110 028
E-mail: nab@newagebooksindia.com
Website: www.newagebooksindia.com

*Printed and published by*
RP Jain for New Age Books
A-44, Naraina Industrial Area
Phase-I, New Delhi-110 028. India

# PREFACE

This book is an attempt, now made for the first time, to explain to an English-knowing reader an undoubtedly difficult subject. I am therefore forcibly reminded of the saying, "Veda fears the man of little knowledge, since injury may be received from him" *(Bibhetyalpaśsutād-Vedo māmayaṁ prahariśyate)*. It is natural, given this difficulty and the mystery which surrounds the subject, that strangers to India should have failed to understand Mantra. They need not, however, have then (as some have done) jumped to the conclusion that it was "meaningless superstition." This is the familiar argument of the lower mind which says "what I cannot understand can have no sense at all." Mantra *is*, it is true, meaningless to those *who do not know its meaning*. But there are others who do, and to them it is not "superstition." It is because some English-educated Indians are as uninstructed in the matter as that rather common *type* of Western to whose mental outlook and opinions they mould their own, that it was possible to find a distinguished member of this class describing Mantra as "meaningless jabber." Indian doctrines and practice have been so long and so greatly misunderstood and misrepresented by foreigners, that it has always seemed to me a pity that those who are of this *Puṇyabhūmi* should, through misapprehension, malign without reason anything which is their own. This does not mean that they must accept what is in fact without worth because it is Indian, but they should at least first understand what they condemn as worthless.

When I first entered on a study of this Śāstra I did so in the belief that India did not contain more fools than exist amongst other peoples, but had on the contrary produced intelligences which (to say the least) were the equal of any elsewhere found. Behind the unintelligent practice, which doubtless to some extent exists amongst the multitude of every faith, I felt sure there must be a rational principle, since men on the whole do not continue throughout the ages to do that which is in itself meaningless and is therefore without result. I was not disappointed. The Mantra-Śāstra, so far from being rightly described as "meaningless superstition" or "jabber," is worthy of a close study which when undertaken, will disclose elements of value to minds free from superstition, of metaphysical bent and subtle-seeing *(Sūkṣmadarśin)*. A profound doctrine, ingeniously though guardedly set forth, is contained in the Tantras of the Mantra-Śāstra or Āgama. This is an auspicious time in which to open out the secrets of this *Adhyātmika* science. For here in this country there has been a turn in the tide. The class of Indian who was wont to unite with the European critic of his Motherland in misunderstanding and misrepresenting Her thoughts and institutions, is to Her good fortune, gradually disappearing. Those who are recovering from the dazzle produced on its first entrance by an alien civilization are able to judge aright both its merits and defects as also to perceive the truth of the saying of Schiller: "Hold to your dear and precious native land; there are the strong roots of your strength *(Ans Vaterland ans teure schliess dich an. Da sind die starken Wurzeln deiner Kraft.)*" Again in the West there is a movement away from the Materialism which regarded that alone as "real" which is gross sensible matter; and towards that standpoint whence it is seen that thought itself is a thing which is every whit as real as any external object. Each is but an aspect of the one conscious Self whence both Mind and Matter proceed. This self or *Cit* is the Soul of the Universe, and the universe is *Cit* which has become its own object. Every being therein is Consciousness, that is, *Cit* manifesting as the multiple forms of Mind and Matter which constitute the universe. This Western movement is called by its adherents "New Thought," but its basal principles are as old as the Upaniṣads which proclaimed that all was Feeling-Consciosuness *(Cit)*, and therefore what a man thought, that he became. In fact thought counts for more than any material means whatever. I am not however here entering upon a general defence of so immense a subject, for this cannot be compassed in a work such as this. In any case—and this is what I am concerned to show— the Mantra Śāstra is not the mere senseless rubbish it has been supposed to be.

This book is, as the sub-title states, a Collection of Studies in, or Essays upon, particular subjects in the Mantra-Śāstra, a term which is commonly applied to the Tantra-Śāstra. It is practically composed of two parts. After Chapter 1, which deals with the "Word," Chapters 2-9 treat of the Principles of the general doctrine of *Śabda*. I am much indebted in the preparation of these Chapters to my friend, Professor Pramathanātha-Mukhopādhyāya. Chapters 10-21 are elucidations of some subjects in the Tantra-Śāstra which adopt the Mīmāṁsā doctrine of *Śabda* with some modifications to meet its doctrine of Śakti.

Chapters 12, 28 and 29 deal with the Mantras "Om" and the Gayātrī. An understanding of such terms as Śakti, Nāda, Bindu, the Causal Śaktis of the Praṇava, Bīja-mantras and so forth, is essential for those who would understand the Śāstra in which they appear Hitherto knowledge of these matters has been confined (where it exists at all) to the Gurus and Sādhakas. This does not mean that my information has been gathered from oral sources only. On the contrary, the substance of it may be found in the Tantras. These are however generally unknown. The definitions must be sought for in many Śāstras. When found they must be explained by the aid of general Śāstric knowledge and of *Upāsakas* who possess the tradition. As regards technical terms I refer my readers to other books which I have published, in particular to "Śakti and Śākta," "The Serpent Power," and the volumes of the series called "The World as Power" describing the chief concepts of Indian Philosophy and Religion.

Chapters 10-21 and 14 are reprinted from the Journal the *Vedānta-Kesarī*. Chapters 22-23 on *"Om"* and the "Necklace of Kālī" appeared in *East and West,* and Chapters 28-29 on *Mantrasādhana* and the *"Gāyatrī"* in the Introduction to my edition of the Mahānirvāṇa Tantra, which is now superseded, as regards the Introduction, by the fuller account of the Tantras and Tāntrik ritual given in my volume, "Śakti and Śākta," and as regards the Text, by another and more correct edition which I have in preparations. Chapter 30 on the "Gāyatrī as an exercise of Reasoning" is a reprint of a paper read by me before the Indian Rationalistic Society at Calcutta

and has been previously published in its Bulletin. Ten of the papers dealing with general principles were delivered by me in 1919 as Extension Lectures at the instance of the National Council of Education, Bengal.

As I write the concluding lines of this preface heard by the ancient and desolate Temple to the Sun-Lord at Konāraka in Northern Orissa, a continuous rolling sound like that of the Mahāmantra is borne to me from afar. I heard the same sound many years ago at the Pemiongchi monastery when some hundred Buddhist monks rolled out from the depth of their bodies the mantra *Om*. Their chant then suggested the sea, as the sea now suggests the Mantra. Here where the sound is heard are green woods, bushes of jasmine, cactus in bloom and the rose and yellow of the Karavīra and Kalikā flowers. Travelling however whence it comes some two miles seaward, the eye surveys a wide wild waste of land, with here and there sparse clumps of Ketaki, stretching from the world famous Temple of the "Lord of the Universe" in the south to the Golra jungle on the North. On the Eastern edge the surf of the Bengal Ocean in great waves, marbled with foam with creaming crests, whipped into filmy vapour by the wind, ceaselessly beats upon lonely shore. The waves as all else are Mantra, for Mantra in its most basal sense is the World viewed as—and in its aspects of— sound. But as I have explained in the Text we must distinguish between Natural Name in its pure sense as the sound of the constituent forces of a thing and the sounds made by the thing when so produced. All sounds and therefore movements form the "Garland of Letters," which is worn by the Divine Mother, from whose aspects as *Om* or the General Sound *(Sāmānyaspanda)* of the first creative movement all particular sounds and things come. For all things may be rendered in terms of sound. The Universe is movement The Letters are the sound of particular movements. These are audible as the gross letters which Kāli, the Source of movement, wears as a garland round Her neck. I record this note on a scene which I have known and enjoyed for many years, since I may now be seeing it for the last time. If (as I hope not) this be so, then I bid farewell to my old friend the Sādhu Jagannātha-Dāsa and to this place set in an air of magic of which the Kapila-Saṁhitā (Ch. VI) says:

*Maitreyākhye vane puṇye rathayātrāmahotsave*
*Ye paśyanti narā bhaktyā te paśyanti tanu raveḥ.*

**J.W.**

# CONTENTS

## Chapter 1

# VĀK OR THE WORD

The word 'Vāk' (in Latin Vox) comes from the root 'Vac' which means "to speak". The feminine noun 'Vāk' therefore means literally both voice and the word it utters, as also the sound of inanimate objects. It has the same sense therefore as *Śabda*. *Artha* is meaning or object. *Pratyaya* is mental apprehension. All things have a threefold sense, supreme (Parā), subtle (Sūkṣma), gross (Sthūla) Parā-Vāk is the Causal Stress which, in terms of Pratyaya, is the Cosmic Ideation (Sṛṣṭi-kalpanā) of Īśvara. This is the Divine "Word". But Vāk is also an effect, either subtle or gross. Paśyanti Vāk is Vāk actually going forth as Ikṣaṇa (Seeing), producing or manifesting, as Sūkṣ ma Madhyamā-Vāk, or Hiraṇyagarbha Śabda which is the Mātṛkā state of Śabda as it exists in man prior to its gross manifestation as the Varṇas in spoken speech (Vaikharī-vāk). In the Ṛgveda, Sarasvatī (V.43-11) is called Pāviravi or daughter of the Lightning, that is, of the great Vajra which sustains the worlds, which according to Sāyaṇa is *Mahyamikīvāk*. (See Muir O.S.T.—V.337 ff.) Spoken speech (Vaikharī) is manifested to the ear by the gross physical sound or Dhvani produced by the contact of the vocal organs on the surrounding air by the effort (Prayatna) to speak. In the transcendental quiescent Brahman (Paramātmā) or Paramaśiva there is neither Śabda (Aśabda), Artha (Nirviṣaya) nor Pratyaya. There is therefore neither name (Nāma) nor form (Rūpa). In this Infinite Calm there arises a metaphysical Point of Stress or Bindu or Ghanībhūta-Śakti, which stirs forth (Prasarati) as the multiple forces of the universe. This energising is the cause of, and as Jivātmā is, the World experience with its duality of subject and object. This play of Śakti takes place in the Ether of Consciousness (Cidākāśa) in such a way that the latter is neither effaced nor affected when the second condition appears, which last is that of both Transcendence and Immanence. This is creation (sṛṣṭi) or, more properly, seeming development (Pariṇāma), since the English word "creation" does not truly express the process. Creation, in the Christian sense, excludes the notion that God is a material cause, creation being neither out of pre-existing matter nor out of God's own substance. Cration also involves an absolutely first appearance. With this reservation the term "creation" is used. More accurately the Brahman Itself, in the form of its Power (Śakti), goes forth (Prasarati). This Sṛṣṭi enduses a while (ṣ thiti) that is far a day of Brahmā, which there is according to some, a complete disolution (Mahāpralaya). Others say that there is no such Mahāpralaya, but that there is always existing some universe, though one or another may disappear. In Mahāpralaya the second state is potentially contained in the undifferentiated unmanifest Māyā-Śakti. Śabdabrahman as an Ullāsa of Śiva sinks as it were into the eternally existing Calm, just as the rising wave breaks itself and sinks upon the ocean, or as the spray of a fountain falls again into the waters which feed it. This notion of the "Word" is very ancient. God "speaks" the word and the Thing appears. Thus the Hebrew word for Light is "Aur". Genesis says, "God said: let there be Light (Aur) and there *was* Light (Aur)". The Divine word is conceived of in the

Hebrew Scriptures as having creative power. A further stage of thought presents to us the concept of an aspect of the Supreme or Person who creates. Thus we have the Supreme and the Logos, Brahman and Śabdabrahman. In Greek, Logos means (as does Aparaśabda) thought, and the word which denotes the obejct of thought. To Heraclitus, Logos was the principle underlying the universe. (See J.N. Heinze, Die Lehre vom Logos in der Griech, Philosophie). To the Stoics it was the "Worldsoul" the uniting principle of all rational forces working in the world. According to Plato, the Logoi were supersensual primal images or patterns (Jāti) of visible things. The Alexandrian Philo, influenced by Platonism and other philosophies of Hellenism, combined the two conceptions and read into the Old Testament and Jewish Theology a Being intermediate between It (that is *ho on*) and the manifold universe. This intermediate Being was the Logos. According to Philo, Ideas moulded matter. God first produced the intelligible world of Ideas which are types (Aparajāti) of the physical world. Though in Itself nothing but the Logos, the latter is the author of the ideal world. Just as an architect projects in his mind a plan of a town (Polis) and then produces the real town according to the ideal, so God acted when He created the world, this Megalopolis (Brahmāṇḍa). The Author of the Fourth Gospel took up these ideas but gave them expression in such a way as to serve Christian theological needs. (See J. Réville, *La Doctrine du Logos dans law quatriéme Evangile et dans les Aeuvres de Philon)*. It has thus been said that John's adoption of the notion was not a mere copy, but a free adaptation of the Philonian *Logos* and a Christianising of it. According to the Evangelist, the Logos is a Person who was before creation and Himself God. It is the Potency of the external Wisdom proceeding from the unmainifest Godhead for the purpose of world activity, and in the world. It is the *Logos Endiathetos* or immanent divine wisdom (See Moeller, Hist. Ch. Church I, 92-222). The Logos through whom the world was created became flesh (Avatāra), that it was manifested in man *(Verbum caro factum est).* He is the Son who is Jesus Christ, He who in the heavenly pre-existence is called the Logos and after His incarnation the man Jesus who is the Christ, who is neither prophet nor superman but Pūrṇāvatāra of God. The Logos is the perfect self-presentation of God in the Son. In Jesus there was identity of being with God. The fourth Gospel opens grandly, "In the beginning was the Word and the Word was with God, and the Word was God." These are the very words of Veda. *Prajāpatir vai idam āsīt:* In the beginning was Brahman. *Tasya vāg dhvitīyā āsīt;* with who was Vāk or the Word; (She is spoken of as second to Him because She is first potentially in, and then as Śakti issues from Him); *Vāg vai paramam Brahma;* and the word is Brahman. Vāk is thus a Śakti or Power of the Brahman which is one with the Possessor of Power (Śaktimān). This Śakti which was in Him is at the creation with Him, and evolves into the form of the Universe whilst still remaining what It is – the Supreme Śakti.

It is always possible that human thought may develop similarly and yet independently. It is not improbable also, seeing the influence of India on the West, that the philonic and Neo-platonic and Johannean conceptions were, in part at least, indebted for their origin to India. Nevertheless there are, with general points of similarity, others of difference, for which accuracy demands attention. Thus, the Brahman is the material cause of the world which the Christian Logos is not. For Christianity is dualism. Vāk is no Person in a Trinity. Vāk is Herself the Mother of the Trimūrti who are Brahmā, Viṣṇu and Rudra. For She is the Supreme Śakti, one with Brahman. The full incarnation is a concept of Hinduism, yet, in the form of Jīva, Vāk is incarnated not in one historic person only but in all men, beings and things. The Word as Vāk became flesh, not on one particular date in one particular place and in one particular historic person. It appeared and now appears in the flesh and other forms of matter of all limited beings or Jīvas, each of who may through Veda directly realise the Bṛahman whose Śakti is the word of Vāk. Jesus alone was God in human form others were not, are not and never can become God. Vāk manifests Herself in every man and is knowable and known as She is in Herself— that is Brahman, in that spiritual experience which is Veda.

The universe is the outcome of the Divine Desire (Kāma) or Will (Icchā). Kāma on the physical plane denotes among other things, sexual desire. In the highest sense it is the first creative impulse of the One to be many, whereby It begets Itself as all creatures. Earthly desire and self-reproduction are but limited manifestations of that first impulse. The Divine Will is continually and presently working through the individual sexual desire for the continued creation of the universe. This Divine Kāma is eternal and the origin of all things. And so Parmenides speaking of Eros or Love, said *Prōtision mén érōta theōn nélīsato pañton.* ("He devised Eros, the first of all the Gods"). This is the Divine Eros through whom things are; (See Plato Symp. 5-6). The Daughter of Kāma is Vāk. The latter as the Divine Will speaks the Divine Word upon which the Thing is. In the Atharvaveda (IX-2) Kāma is celebrated as a great Power superior to all the Devas. The

Daughter of Kāma is named "The Cow which sages call Vākvirāt," that is Vāk in the form of the universe.

In the "beginning" there was Brahman and with It was Vāk. In the Veda (Śatapatha-Brāhmaṇa VI. 1-1-8) it is said, "this Being (Puruṣa) Prajāpati willed 'May I be many', 'May I be propagated,' He energised *(So śrāmyat sa tapo' tapyata).* Vāk was His, She was produced from Him *(Vāg evā sya sā sṛjyata)* and pervaded all which exists." Then on the issue of Vāk, "By his mind he united with Vāk (Śa. P. x.6-5-4; Orh. Ar. Up. Roer p.50) and thus (Śa. P.VI. 1-2ff) became pregnant *(Garbhi 'abhavat')."* In the Kāṭhaka it is said (XII-5 and XXVIII-1) "Prajāpati only was then this *(Prajāpatir vai idam āsīt). Vāk* was a second to Him *(Tasya vāg dvitīya āsīt).* He united with Her *(Tāṁ maithunaṁ sambhavat)* and She became pregnant *(Sā garbhaṁ ādhatta).* She went out from Him and produced these creatures *(Sā asmād apākrāmat sā imaḥ prajāḥ asṛjata)* and again re-entered Him *(Sā prajāpatiṁ eva punaḥ prāviśat)."*

Again in the Pañcaviṁśa Br. (XX-14-2) it is similarly said: "Prajāpati alone was this universe. He had Vāk too as His own, as a Second to Him. He thought, 'let me now put forth this Vāk. She will traverse and pervade all this That, is, the Brahman or Śiva first willed to be many and His Śakti, which was one with Him, issued as His Word." The Union of Will and Word was the potency of creation, all things being held in undifferentiated mass in the Great Womb (Mahāyoni) of the Mother of all (Aṁbikā). This potency became actual as the manifested universe, and at its dissolution Śakti, as such universe re-entered Brahman and remained one with It (Cit) as Cidrūpiṇī. Meanwhile She pervades, as immanent Spirit, both Mind and Matter which are Its temporal forms for as the Bṛhadāraṇyaka-Upaniṣad says (pp. 50-53), Ed. Roer: "By that Vāk and that Ātma He created all things whatsoever, the Vedas, Metres, Sacrifices and all Creatures" *(Sā tayā vācā tena ātmanā idaṁ sarvaṁ asṛjata ad idaṁ kiñca ṛco yajūṁṣi sāmāṃśi chandāṁsi yajñān prajāḥ paśūn)*. "First was produced the sacred Vaidik science" (Ś.P. Br. VI. 1-18). In the Mahābharāta, Sarasvatī as Vāk is called the "Mother of the Vedas" (Śāntiparva, V.12, 920) and the same is said of Vāk in the Taittirīya-Brāhmaṇa (II. 8-8-5) where (and in the preceding parva IV) She is also said to contain within Herself all words and to have been sought with Tapas by the Ṛṣis who put forth the Vedic Hymns *(Ṛṣ aya mantrakṛtaḥ)*. In the Bhīṣmaparva of the Mahābhārata (v. 3019) Acyuta (Kṛṣṇa) is said to have produced Sarasvatī and the Vedas from His mind; and in the Vanaparva (V.13, 432) the Gāyatrī is called the Mother of the Vedas, for Gāyatrī Devi is a form of Vāk. Vāk is the Mother of the Vedas and of all things which their words denote Vāk in the form of Veda is Vedātmikā Vak (See Sāyaṇa and other citations given in Muir O.S.T. I-325ff where, as in other volumes, some of the Texts concerning Vāk are collected). The substance of the whole world is Vāk (*Jagat Vāṅmaya)* for as previously stated the world (Jagat) is Śabdaprabhāva.

The Ṛgveda (X.125-5) says: "I (Vāk) make him whom I love formidable, him a Brāhmaṇa, him a Ṛṣi, him a Sage", It is this Vāk which entered the Ṛṣis, and has thus made Herself known to men "By sacrifice they followed the path of Vāk and found Her entered into the Ṛṣis" (Ṛgveda, X. 71-3). The Ṛṣis called their Hymns by various names, amongst others Vāk for they are manifestations of Vāk. Vāk is one with Brahman for Śiva and Śakti are one. In the Bṛhadāraṇyaka-Upaniṣad it is said (Ed. Roer, 688),

"By Vāk, O Monarch, the Brahman is known. Vāk is the Supreme Brahman" *(Vāchaiva saṁrād Brahma jñāyate vāg vai saṁrāt paramam Brahma)*. The Mahābhārata (Śāntiparva V. 12,920), says: "Behold Sarasvatī, Mother of the Vedas abiding in me *(Vedānaṁ mātraṁ paśya mātraṁ paśya matsthāṁ devīṁ Sarasvatīṁ)*. She, this great Śakti, is one with Maheśvara. And so in the Maṅgalācaraṇa prefixed to the Commentaries on the Ṛk Saṁhitā and Taittirīya Saṁhitā by both Sāyaṇa and Mādhava it is said: "I reverence Maheśvara the hallowed abode of sacred knowledge, of whom the Vedas are the breathings and whom from the Vedas formed the whole universe." *(Yasya niśvasitaṁ vedāh ya vedabhya' khilaṁ jagat, Nirmame taṁ ahaṁ vande vidyatirthaṁ Maheśvaraṁ)*. The Taittirīya-Brāhmaṇa (III, 39-I) says that Vāk is imperishable, the first-born of Ṛta, Mother of the Vedas and centre-point of immortality *(Vāg akṣarām prathamāja ṛtasya vedānāṁ mātā amṛtasya nābḥ)*. The Śatapatha-Brāhmaṇa says (VII, 5-2-21): "Vāk is the unborn." It was from Vāk that the Maker of the Universe (Viśvakarmā) produced creatures *(Vāg vai aja vāco vai prajāḥ viśvakarmā jajāna)*. Various texts associate the Lord of creatures (Prajāpati), called Paśupati in the Śaiva śāstra, with his Śakti Vāk, as to which see Weber, Indische Studien, IX, 477 ff. and Muir's Original Sanskrit Texts, V. 391.

Śaṁkarācārya (Sūtra 1-3, 28) quoting 'By His mind He united with Vāk,' says that by this and other Texts the Veda in various places declares that creation was preceded by the Word from which the whole universe of Devas and organic and inorganic earth-life are produced. But it is said that the world was produced from Brahman. How then was it produced from the Word? Creation was preceded by the

Word. He says that when any man is occupied with any end which he wishes to accomplish, he first calls to mind the word which expresses it and then proceeds to effect his purpose. Using this as analogy he says that before creation the words of Veda were manifested in His mind and afterwards he created the objects which resulted from them: Thus, the Vaidika text which says "Uttering Bhūḥ (earth) he created the earth (Bhūmi)" and so forth, means that the different worlds and the beings therein were manifested or created from the word "Bhūḥ" and so forth manifested in His mind. These distinctions of "before" and afterwards and so forth are Vyāvahārika. Human analogies are necessarily imperfect. In Īśvara as causal body what (as manifested) are called Pratyaya, Śabda, Artha are one and identical (and therefore, as manifested, co-ordinate) though for the purposes of exposition we may say that His Sṛṣṭi kalpanā is a fraction of the Pratyaya which He has of his own Ānandamaya causal body, and included therein the subtle and gross bodies His Paraśabda involves as effects all Aparaśabdas, and His Artha is the first stressing mass of Prakṛtiśakti in which are experienced all elements (Vikṛti) and things which are compounded of them For Īśvara has direct and immediate apprehension of the three bodies, Hiraṇyagarbha of the second and third, and Virāt of the third, Parā-Vāk is therefore what has been previously spoken of as Paraśabda, and Vāk (simple) as Śabda in its subtle form as Mātṛkā (Madhyamā-Vāk) and gross form (Vaikharī-Vāk). The latter is that of the spoken letters (Varṇa) which the Mantras are made. There is but one Cause of speech, as also of all the things in the universe which it denotes and also, of the mental apprehension (Pratyaya) or "going towards" the object of the mind. That cause is the Supreme Devī Sarasvatī,

Mother of the Vedas and of the Worlds,. manifesting as the name (Nāma) and form (Rūpa) which is the Universe. She is thus the Supreme Śakti to whom a title is given, taken from one of Her productions, the manifested word of speech. The musical instrument (Vīṇā), which Sarasvatī holds, denotes all sounds (Śabda), of which She is the Mother White are Her garments and transparent whiteness is the colour of both Ākāśa and Buddhi. Her name denotes "flow" or "motion" (Saras). She is such, in the Supreme sense, as being the activity (Śakti) of the unmoving Śiva or Brahman. She is again such as the play in the manifested World of the dynamic Śaktis in and around the rigid Ether, "Haṁ" and then stood still as the steady framework on, and in which the whole universe flows or moves. According to Science, Ether has no such imperfections as we associate with matter. It is the property of the latter to grow old, to decay, to wear out. But such as exists in the Ether remains unchanged. It is this rigid, unwasting enduring Ether which is Vajra, the hard, stable, lasting unwasting Vajra, the static manifestation of the static Brahman, in which the Dynamic Brahman as Sarasvatī flows or moves. The former is Śūnya, the void of space, in which all movement takes place. Just as in Brāhmanism Ākāśa is transferred to the Brahman idea as Cidākāśa: so this Ethereal Śūnya in Northern Buddhist Monism as sTongap-nyid (Śūnyatā) stands for the Ultimate beyond all categories (See the Demchog Tantra published as the seventh Volume of my "Tantric Texts as sTongap-nyid)" Sarasvatī, the Dynamic Brahman with Her "consort" the static Brahman as Brahmā is borne upon the Haṁsa which is no material "bird" but the natural name of the vital function manifesting as the expiring (Haṁ) and inspiring (Sah) breath or Prāṇabīja in all breathing creatures (Prāṇī).

She again is the Divine in the aspect as Wisdom and Learning, for she is the Mother of Veda, that is of all knowledge touching Brahman and the Universe. She is the Word of which it was born and She exists in that which is the issue of Her great womb (Mahāyoni). Not therefore idly have men worshipped Vāk or Sarasvatī as the Supreme Power.

## Chapter 2

# ARTHA, PRATYAYA AND ŚABDA

The One Supreme Consciousness (Cit) which is the Changeless Principle of all experience evolves by, and from out of, its Power (Śakti), which is both Cit-Śakti and Māyāśakti – the duality of subject and object, mind and matter. In Parasaṁvit or Saccidānanda the experience is unitary and devoid of every species of duality. I have dealt in my book "Śakti and Śākta" with the various possible English renderings of the untranslatable word 'Cit' which subject to the reservations there made, may be called Feeling-Consciousness or with less liability to misunderstanding the Changeless Principle of all changing experience. Through the operation of Śakti the homogeneous Unity becomes the Many or universe of subject and object, mind and matter. The Perfect Experience, without ceasing to be such, involves Itself in mind and matter and thus becomes the imperfect or limited experience. As all is the one Self, this apparent dichotomy means that the Self which manifests as a limited subject sees (though it is unaware of it) itself as object.

Cit is without motion (Niṣpanda), without action (Niṣkriya), without mind (Amanaḥ) and without Śabda

(Aśabda). It is neither subject nor knows any object other than Itself as Cidrūpiṇī-Śakti. Creation commences by an initial movement or vibration (Spandana) in the Cosmic Stuff, as some Western writers call it, and which in Indian parlance is Saspanda Prakṛti-Śakti. Just as the nature of Cit or the Śiva aspect of Brahman is rest, quiescence, so that of Prakṛti is movement. Prior however to manifestation, that is during dissolution (Pralaya) of the universe, Prakṛti exists in a state of equilibrated energy (Sāmyāvasthā) in which there is Sarūpapariṇāma. It then moves (Virūpapariṇāma). This is the first cosmic vibration (Spandana) in which the equilibrated energy is released.

The approximate sound of this movement is the Mantra Oṁ. Dualism with all its varieties is thus produced. There is thus a bifuracation of Consciousness into Mind and Matter which therefore constitute a parallelism of common origin. The mind as subject has apprehension (Pratyaya) of objects (Artha), and names those objects by word (Śabda) or language. In man Śabda, Artha, and Pratyaya are connected but distinct. Like everything else they are three effectual manifestations of the movement (Spanda) which is the common Causal Stress. At the stage of Causal Śakti however the three are one; so that then Śabda=Artha= Pratyaya = Spanda, the last being not, as in manifestation, a common denominator but the equivalent of Śabda, Artha, Pratyaya. The state is one of logical unity. Īśvara's Spanda is His Śabda, is His Artha, is His Pratyaya. Doubtless in projecting our standpoint as existence into Divine Being we cannot help using the analogy of aspects. And so we speak of Cit and the Causal Stress (Śakti) of Śiva and Śakti as two aspects and so on. Nevertheless we must not understand that there is any distinctness in the midst of relationships or even of unity which expresses our idea of aspects. Ultimately the relation of Śabda, Artha and Pratyaya is an identical equation and not a ratio, that is a fraction with a numerator and a denominator. Whilst on the absolute plane which is the Cosmic Causal body the three are one, there is, on and with the manifestation of the subtle body, a divergent descent of the three, retaining, as they always do, their mutual connection. The causal aspect is Śabdabrahman, the Stress or Creative Śakti giving rise to motion and bodies produced by it which are forms of the subtle and gross Śakti. What was a simple stress in quiescent and unaffected consciousness with unitary experience becomes bifuracated as mind and matter. It is here most important to remember (for it is the key to that which follows) that the nature of a process in which the One becomes Many involves this: – the essential substance (Spirit) of both Mind and Matter remains the same, and the Śakti elements and the motion of both are similar. Hence, they are mutually connected with a natural relation. Feeling and object of feeling are correlated. Thus sensation through the eye and Manas, and colour as an object which is perceived, are at base the one Ātmā thus dually manifested. The sensation of sight and the colour are both again products of Tejas-Tanmātrā. The Indriya is Sāttvikaṁśa of the Apāñcīkṛta-Tanmātrā, and the object seen is the Tāmasikāṁśa of the same. In Sāṁkhya, and commonly in the Śākta-Tantras, both are products of the same Ahaṁkāra. Sensation and its object are two aspects of one and the same thing. The vibration of the object (Artha) and of the Vṛtti or modification of mind by which apprehension (Pratyaya) it had of it are the same, and the natural (Śabda) of an object (Artha) is the sound produced by the forces which constitute it. There exists all this parallelism because our postulate is that mind and matter are but twin aspects of the one undivided Self. So, when an object (Viṣaya, Artha) affects the senses (Indriya), being attended to by that function of mind which is called Manas, there arises in the mind a modification (Vṛtti) of its substance which is an exact counterpart of the external object. In passing I may observe that this is a fundamental principle on which all Tāntric-Sādhanā by way of Upāsanā rests. By worship and meditation or Japa of Mantras the mind is actually *shaped* into the form of the object of worship and is made pure for the time being through the purity of the object namely, Iṣṭadevatā, which is its content. By continual practice (Abhyāsa) the mind becomes full of the object to the exclusion of all else, steady in its purity, and does not stray into impurity. So long as mind exists it must have an object and the object of Sādhanā is to present it with a pure one.

Before proceeding further it is necessary to have clear notions as to the meaning of Mind, Matter, Pratyaya, Śabda and Artha. Everything is "material" according to the Vedānta which is not Pure Transcendent Spirit (Anupāhita-Cit). Immanent of Upāhita-Cit is that which is associated with mind and matter. The Cit with Upādhi is either Para = Śuddha-sattva-pradhāna = Utkṛṣṭopādhī = Samaṣṭi, or Apara = Malina-sattva-pradhāna = Nikṛṣṭopādhi = Vyaṣṭi. In each of these there are the three bodies causal (Kāraṇa), subtle (Sūkṣma) and gross (Sthūla). This Upādhi is Śakti as Māyā or Prakṛti-Śakti as that term is used in Advaitavāda. As Prakṛti-Śakti is "material" not as being scientific "matter" but as the subtle material cause of all things, all its effects (Vikṛti) are necessarily of the same character as their cause and are material. These Vikṛtis may be divided into the two parallel group of Mind (Antaḥkaraṇa) and its outer instruments or senses (Indriya), and matter of Pañca-bhūta derived from the more rudimentary forms of infra-sensible "matter" which are the Pañca-Tanmātrās. These are beyond the threshold of sensation of the ordinary Jīva.

What then is Mind? It follows from the above that it is a manifestation of Śakti or Power in the form of force, which is Power translated to the material plane, and is as much a material (Bhautika) substance as is matter (Bhūta) itself. Thought (for, except in Samādhi, mind is never free of thought) is from the creative standpoint a passing thought and matter a lasting thought. Matter is a dense and gross form of the more subtle and tenuous form of the common Prakṛti-Śakti. Mind is Bhautika because it is according to Vedānta composed of the Sāttvika part (Sāttvikāṁśa) of the Tanmātrā. According to Sāṁkhya it is Ahaṁkārī. According to Vedānta, Mind is not Vibhu that is all-spreading, unlimited and indivisible into parts: nor is it Aṇu or atomic, that is limited and indivisible into parts. It is Madhyama-Parimāṇa, that is limited and divisible into parts and thus takes the form of its objects. Mind has parts in the sense that is divisible into parts, that is one part of the mind can attend to one thing and to another at one and the same time. As it also takes the shape of the object perceived, it spreads or shrinks with it. It pervades the whole body whether in the waking (Jāgrat) or dreaming state (Svapna), but in deep sleep (Suṣupti) it is withdrawn as all else into the causal body and according to one account is then absorbed in the Nāḍī.

What then is the nature of knowing by the mind? According to the Naiyāyikas who hold that the mind is atomic (Aṇu), it does not go forth, or transform itself into the shape of the object. Jñāna is a Guṇa of Ātma which is produced by the association of Mind (Manas) and Ātma.

According to Vedānta, Jñāna is a transformation (Pariṇāma) of the Antaḥkaraṇa or Mind which is a Tattva of Madhyama-Pariṇāma. Jñāna is of two kinds, *viz.*, Jñāna Svarūpa and Jñāna Vṛtti. The former is Brahmasvarūpa of Perfect experience or Cit. The latter is knowledge of objects or the ordinary worldly imperfect Experience. Opinion varies as to the mode of operation in the case of the Mind and Jñānavṛtti. According to some, light from the eye goes forth. Hence, the eye is called Tejas. Mind going forth with the light of the eye impinges upon and takes the shape of the object. Mind is called "transparent" (Svaccha) because it can take the shape of the object presented to it. Ātma is ever illuminating the mind and when there is a particular Vṛtti, Ātmā illuminates it so that it is present to the limited conscisouness.

Knowledge is true or false (Mithyā). Right knowledge or Pramā is defined as *Tadvati tat prakārakajñānaṁ* which means apprehension of an object according to its true nature, that is, in its own class or Jāti. The mind not only perceives a particular thing (Vyakti) but also the genus or class (Jāti) to which it belongs; for this Jāti is not merely a subjective thing but is inherent in the Vyakti as its nature (Prakāra) and both are perceived in right knowing, as when in the case of Ghaṭa (jar) its Jāti or Ghaṭatva (jarness) is perceived. Where however a rope is mistaken for a snake there is Mithyā-Jñāna. The particular rope excites knowledge, but it is false knowledge, because through a defect (Doṣa) in the percipient subject, the rope is not perceived under its Jāti but under that of a serpent. In short in right perception there is true conformity of thought with its object. To perceive on the other hand a rope where there is Ghaṭatva is false perception.

What then is Artha or object (Viṣaya)? This is the object which constitutes the mind's content. Object is manifold as the various forms (Rūpa) which make the universe. It is the "other" which the Self as mind perceives. These forms are constituted of the five Bhūtas – Ākāśa, Vāyu, Tejas, Āp, Pṛthivī representing various densities of Prākṛtika substance. Just as the mind is a form of motion (Spandana) of that substance, so the five Bhūtas are five forms of motion of the same Prakṛti which in the Tantras are symbolised by figures denoting the forms of the vibration namely a circle with openings (Chidra) shown as points on it denoting the interstitial character of Ākāśa; a circle denoting Vāyu; and a triangle, crescent and cube-square denoting Tejas, Ap, and Pṛthivī respectively. The direction of the vibration also varies as being in all directions at an acute angle to the line of the wave (Tiryag-gamanaśīla), upwards, downwards and "in the middle" where the forces are equilibrated and matter becomes stationary. These again are space-giving, general movement (Calanapara), expansion, contraction, cohesion, stimulating the sense of hearing, touch and feel, (not all forms of contact), sight or colour and form, taste, and smell respectively, the centres of which in the Piṇḍāṇḍa are the Cakras from Viśuddha to Mūlādhāra. The Bīja Mantras of these are Ham, Yam, Ram, Vam, Lam, the meaning of which is later explained when dealing with natural name. They seem like gibberish to the uninitiated. Hence, even the common Bengali expression "What Hayaralava is this?" These Bhūtas derive from the Tanmātra commencing with Śabda-Tanmātra or infra-sensible sound; which by addition of mass becomes Ākāśa, the Guṇa of which is sensible sound which generates Vāyu-Tanmātra from which comes Vāyu Bhūta and so on with the rest, though the mode of derivation is not always given in the same terms. The substance of it is that Bhūta or gross sensible matter is derived from a subtle form of the same which is not sensible by the gross ear but mentally apprehensible by the Yogī. Hence it is said *Tāni vastūni tanmātrādīni pratyakṣ-aviṣayāṇi* (that is to Yogīs). Object (Viṣaya) is thus not limited to the gross obejcts seen by the senses of ordinary men. There are also subtle objects which may be perceived through the senses or the mind by the possessor of "Powers" (Siddhi) which are merely extensions of natural faculty. These are hidden from ordinary men whose powers vary. Some can perceive more than others. By scientific instruments which can see (microscope) and hear (microphone) things beyond the capacity of the highest natural power of the senses. Is that the end? No, because as we perfect these auxiliaries of natural instruments we see and hear more. Once the microscope gave only a magnification of a few diameters. Now, it is of thousands. At each stage more is known. A point however is reached at which "seeing" takes place not through the gross senses but by the mind. Everything may be an object which is not the Asaṅgabrahman or Brahmasvarūpa that is the Supreme Self or Spirit as It is in Itself. This is not known by either sense or mind or by the Śabda-Pramāṇa or Veda here fails. Because Brahman as It is in Itself (Svarūpa) is never an object, being the true nature of the cognising Self. As such it is beyond mind and speech. The latter can only give an indication (Lakṣaṇa) of it. Higher objects beyond the reach of the senses (Atīndrīya) are only perceived by the heightened powers of the mind of Yogis. Mind, for instance, is Atīndrīya for it cannot be sensed. Yet Yogis can "see," that is, mentally apprehend the mind of another which becomes an object for their apprehension. In such cases his mind takes the form of that other, when everything which was in the latter mind namely its modification (Vṛttis) or thoughts are known to him. And so the experience of objects becomes more and more subtle and inclusive until the state of Supreme Experience Itself is attained when there is neither subject nor object. This is Brahma-svarūpa. This apprehension or image which one has of an object (Artha) evoked by a word (Śabda) is called Pratyaya. The third form of divergent descent of the Śabda-brahman, namely Śabda, will be the subject of the following chapters.

## Chapter 3

# AŚABDA AND PARAŚABDA

Indian doctrine revolves round the two concepts of Changelessness and Change. As these propositions cannot be logically predicated of the same substance, recourse is had to the doctrine of aspects. According to this, Brahman as It is in Itself (Brahmasvarūpa) or Śiva does not change, but Brahman as the Power (Śakti) from which the world evolves does, as Māyā, change. It is perhaps more simple to say that Brahman produces and exists as the world without derogation to Its own unchanging unity. How this can be is, like other ultimates, inconceivable. But its truth is said to rest on two established facts, namely the daily experience of the world of the many on the one hand, and the ecstatic (Samādhi) experience of the One on the other. Both are facts of experience though *how* they can be so is a mystery.

When we come to deal with the Mantra-Śāstra the same doctrines are expressed in the language of the subject with which it is occupied, namely Śabda, of which Mantras are forms. Śabda or Sound exists only where there is motion or Spanda. If there is no Spanda there is not Śabda. If there is Śabda there is Spanda. But the transcendent Brahman or Cit (Brahmasvarūpa) is quiescent and changeless. Therefore, it is said to be without motion (Niṣpanda) and without Śabda (Aśabda). From out of this

Cit (for there is but one) but without affecting its own changelessness, there arises a creative stir or stress which evolves into the universe. This is the work of the active Brahman or Īśvara. Just as the Parabrahman is Aśabda, Īśvara is Śabdabrahman or Paraśabda. As the former is Niśabda, the latter, as Māyā Śakti, is with motion (Saspanda). Paraśabda, Parā Vāk or Śabdabrahman are each names for the Brahman as the cause of the manifested Śabda Paraśabda is the causal body of sound. Śabdatanmātra is the subtle body of the sound, Ākāśa is the gross body of sound which (though a Guṇa of it) is only apprehended through the medium of air, the sound waves which strike the ear. Through the latter and mind the sensation of sound is experienced. Śabdatanmātra is pure natural sound as apprehended by Hiraṇyagarbha or Yogis who share his experience. Gross sound is of two kinds namely Vaidika sound (Śrautaśabda) or approximate natural sound either primary or secondary, and Laukika Śabda, the speech of the ordinary average mortals other than Vaidika Śabda. Taking "cognizance" to mean 'direct apprehension,' Īśvara has cognizance of all kinds of Śabda, (Paraśabda, Śabda Tanmātra, Śrauta Śabda, Laukika Śabda), Hiraṇyagarbha or Sūtrātma of the last three, Ṛṣis of the last two and ordinary men of the last only. From Paraśabda or Parā-Vāk therefore proceed in their order Śabdatanmātra, Śrauta-Śabda and Laukika Śabda.

Dealing nextly with Pratyaya, Artha and Śabda in their cosmic and individual aspects, – in the Īśvara stage (*i.e.* in so far as there is the causal body) Pratyaya is the Īśvara consciosuness of His own body of Bliss (Ānandamaya) and the cosmic ideation (Sṛṣṭi-kalpanā whereby He projects the world. This Sṛṣṭi-kalpanā against it the stressing mass of Prakṛti or Māyā and Avidyā śakti, and this it the Paraśabda or Parā-Vāk, involving (as the cause involves its effects) the various kinds of Apara-Śabda including the Mātṛkas, Varṇas and Mantras. The approximate representation of the causal (Para) Śabda as a whole to the Ṛṣi-ear is "om." It is however to be noted that Īśvara's whole Pratyaya is Sṛṣṭi-kalpanā, His Artha is the stressing mass of Prakṛti. It is further to be noted that, in Īśvara, Pratyaya, Śabda, and Artha are one and not distinct though co-related, as in Hiraṇyagarbha, Virāt and the individual Jīva. What we may call the elements of the universe namely the Apañcīkṛta Bhūtas or Tanmātras, the Indriyas, Prāṇas, Antaḥkaraṇa and Sthūla Bhūtas are evolved directly by Īśvara as Īśvara. This is Bhūtasṛṣṭi.

He then, as Hiraṇyagarbha, evolves Bhautika-Sṛṣṭi. The elements themselves must be traced directly to the causal body, but as Hiraṇyagarbha he compounds them. Hence, Hiraṇyagarbha's Sṛṣṭi-kalpanā refers to Bhautika-Sṛṣṭi, that is the compounding of the elements which have been already provided by Īśvara as Īśvara. Śabda in the Hiraṇyagarbha aspects is Śabda-tanmātra involving the lower or derivative forms. His Artha is everything except the Samaṣṭi causal body.

Bhautika-Sṛṣṭi may relate either to Sūkṣma or Sthūla elements, the former being everything except the latter; so that theoretically the creative operation may be divided between Sūtrātma and Virāt. But the Śāstra does not in fact contemplate such a division. Virāt is Cit associated with the created whole -- a *natura nturata* as it were, to borrow Spinoza's term. Causal activity does not appear to be extended to this. However, if we provisionally leave the compounding the the Sthūla elements to Virāt, then its Pratyaya too may be called Sṛṣṭikalpanā. His Śabda is various grades of sound, gross and subtle, extending to, but not including, Śabda-tanmātra. His Artha is everything except the Samaṣṭi causal and subtle body.

Sūkṣma and Sthūla are relative terms and admit of grades, hence between the limits of Śabda-tanmātra and average gross sounds there will be more and more subtle sounds– all apprehended by Hiraṇyagarbha; all save the Tanmātra being apprechended by Virāt as Virāt. If we define Sūkṣma as what is of the order of the Tanmātra as the superior limit, then Cit associated with this whole series of Sthūla is Virāt. The latter identifies Himself with Samaṣṭi Sthūla-Deha. It is however a long way from the Ananamaya Kośa of average perception to the Prāṇanamaya Kośa which comes "next" in order of fineness and which is a modification (Rājasika) of the Tanmātras. What the Śāstra calls Annamaya-kośa is therefore really a graded series. The gross body is made up of visible cells: those of microscopic granules; those of still finer corpuscles; and so on. The five Kośas are therefore only five broad landmarks in a series consisting of innumerable gradations as are the seven colours of the ranbow. Hiraṇyagarabha and Virāt are also the types corresponding cosmically to our experiences of certain distinctive forms, in a really innumerable series of forms. So that instead of three we may say that there are innummerable creative Cit-śaktis. If the numbers are given differently there is no essential discrepancy. Īśvara, Hiraṇyagarbha, and Virāt are three forms of creative manifestation corresponding cosmically to the Suṣupti, Svapna and Jāgrat. But the truth-seers, as compared with the system-makers, salute Him as the Many-formed (Namaste bahurūpāya). Īśvara has direct apprehension of all three collectively, causal, subtle, and gross. The cause involves the effects. As Hiraṇyagarbha, He apprehends directly the second and third (Svapna, Jāgrat), and as Virāt he apprehends the third (Jāgrat).

We pass now to the individual (Vyaṣṭi) aspect. Corresponding with Īśvara and with Māyā we have Prājña with Avidyā. The Pratyaya of Prājña is the Vyaṣṭi counterpart in Suṣupti of the Ānandamaya consciousness which Īśvara has of His own causal body. Some English writers misunderstand the statement in the Upaniṣad that the Jīva in dreamless sleep is Brahman to mean that the experience in slumber is that of Īśvara, or of the Supreme Brahman. Of course this is not so, for the Prājña's experience then is associated with Avidyā whereas Īśvara's is free of all Avidyā. The comparison is made by way of analogy. For just as in Suṣupti the Jīva loses the sense of duality, since all objects as separate thing disappear in slumber, so in Īśvara there is no sense of separateness. All things are conceived as in and as Himself. The Śabda of Prājña is Paraśabda-Viśeṣa. This is no sound to him but that "part" of the causal stress which is the causal body of the particular Jīva. His Artha is the Vyaṣṭi causal body, that is, the temporary equilibrium in Suṣupti of the Stress which makes the Jīva. As in the Samaṣṭi experience, Pratyayā, Artha and Śabda are one. Saṁskāras are latent and all Vṛttis are withdrawn into the Kāraṇa-Deha. The forces of all subsequent Jīva-processes are there. Hence, the experience of this fund of causal energy corresponds to Īśvara Pratyaya of His causal body. Sṛṣṭikalpanā of Īśvara is not the whole Pratyaya of Īśvara. For though in Pralaya the former is not there, Īśvara has Pratyaya still, namely the Ānandamaya consciousness of His own causal body. The prājña Pratyaya corresponds to this. The Śābdika counterpart of this is Para-śabdaviśeṣa while in Īśvara it is the Paraśabda whole involving all Viśeṣas. The Paraśabda in Jīva is no sound. Artha here is, as stated, the Vyaṣṭi causal body which is the temporary equilibrium of the Stress constituting the Jīva.

Passing to Taijasa, corresponding to Hiraṇyagarbha as Prājña does to Īśvara, his Pratyaya is experience of Sūkṣma-Deha or subtle body in sleep (Svapna). His Śabda is that which is not expressed by the vocal organ, being the mental image of articulate or inarticulate sound pushing up in Yoga to the Tanmātras. His Artha is the Vyaṣṭi Sūkṣma-Deha. The Pratyaya of the Sūkṣma Deha is either pleasurable of painful. Hiraṇyagarbha's Pratyaya includes two parts, *viz.*, *(a)* experience of cosmic (Samaṣṭirūpa) Sūkṣma elements as well as Sthūla elements and *(b)* Sṛṣṭi-kalpanā referring to the compounding of these elements already evolved by Īśvara. In Taijasa there is *(aa)* experience of the Jāgrat-vāsanārūpa Svapna or Vyaṣṭi Sūkṣma-Deha but not quite of the Jāgrat of Vyaṣṭi Sthūla-Deha, *(bb)* Sṛṣṭi-kalpanā manifesting as a compounding activity as regards various dream forms.

On comparison it is found that the parallelism between Hiṛaṇya and Taijasa is not complete, a fact due to an important distinction between the two Īśvara, Hiraṇyagarbha and Virāṭ are Para or Utkṛṣṭopādhi; the Upādhi *(i.e.,* Māyā-śakti) is preponderatingly Sāttvika. Hence as regards the relative scope of Śabda, Artha, Pratyaya, the three aspects may be represented by three concentric circles of which Īśvara is the outermost and Virāṭ the innermost. Hence Īśvara's Pratyaya, Artha and Śabda include those of Hiraṇyagarbha; those of Hiraṇyagarbha, include those of Virāṭ. It must not be thought that the Śabda, Artha, and Pratyaya of Īśvara, Hiraṇyagarbha, and Virāṭ are exclusive or ejective. The Sāttvika character of their limitations implies the concentric arrangement of the three circles. But Prājña, Taijasa and Viśva have Upādhis which, though Sāttvika, are impure and coarse (Malina). Hence practically as regards, Śabda, Artha and Pratyaya we have:

in lieu of

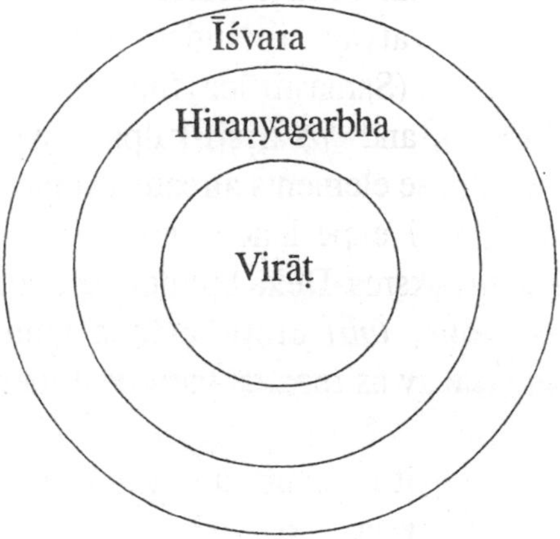


In other words they are practically ejective circles. Hence, the first Pratyaya is practically confined to Śuṣupti, his Artha to the Vyaṣṭi causal body and Śabda to Paraśābda section. Taijasa experiences Svapna and Sūkṣmadeha, but is practically ignorant of Prājña's state and Viśva's state. So with Viśva. But though their experiences apparently exclude one another, the causal unity between them is not in fact wanting.

Taijasa's Artha is Sūkṣma-deha-vyaṣṭi which contains the seeds of Jāgrat. His Śabda is the subtle form of the gross sound. The mental image of a sound becomes apparent of Prātibhāsika sound during the dream state (Svapna); higher sounds even may be heard during this The Yogika state is a voluntary refining and deepening of this state; and hence Dhyāna is called Yoga-nidrā. With the perfecting of the Yogika state one may rise to Śabda-tanmātra; or even in Samādhi to Para-śabda and Aśabda. The former is the cosmic Suṣupti and the latter the Turīya state from which, when regarded as the supreme state, there is no return.

Of the individual Viśva, corresponding to the cosmic or collective Virāṭ, Pratyaya is the experience or Vyaṣṭi Sthūla-Deha; Śabda is the gross sound articulate (Varṇa) or inarticulate (Dhvani) emitted by men, animals and natural objects. The Artha is the gross body (Sthūla Deha) and its processes and the gross environment and its processes. The Jāgrat-Sṛṣṭikalpanā here manifests as feelings of bodily movements caused by Saṁskāra and Icchā Śakti. But as Virāṭ is rather the created (Kārya) than the creative (Kāraṇa) aspects of the whole, so is Viśva the Kārya aspect rather than the Kāraṇa aspect of the section, that is the finitized centre of consciousness of Jīva.. The Artha is gross body and its processes together with the environment of that body and its processes. The Śabdas are the sounds emitted by the vocal organs of men and animals or otherwise produced by natural objects. This is Vaikharī sound which is a development from Paraśabda, through Paśyanti and Madhyamā sound. Paraśabda or Parāvāk is Bindu, Paśyanti is Īkṣaṇa or creative thought and action by that Bindu which is the causal body of Śabda. From this arises the subtle body of Śabda which is Tanmātra and

Mātṛkā which evolves into the gross body of sound which is the letters (Varṇa) uttered by the vocal organs which are made up into syllables and words (Pada) and then into sentences (Vākya). Mantra, so uttered, is a form of the gross body of Śabda. And this applies both to Bījas and other Mantras.

Śabda-Tanmātra or Apañcīkṛta Ākāśa is Apañcikṛta-Tanmātra. This is sound as such, that is ideal sound or the cognition of sound as such, that is ideal sound or the cognition of sound apart from conditions such as ear, brain and other material conditions such as air, water, earth, whereby sound is transmitted. In the case of Śabda-Tanmātra, sound is known as an object of the higher mind apart from these conditions. Therefore,. Śabda-Tanmātra is Śabda not conditional to varying perceptive faculties. It is not sound which is heard by this individual or that, on this plane or that; but it is sound as heard by the Absolute Ear and as uttered by the Absolute Tongue It is invariable and Apauruṣeya. Similarly Rūpa Tanmātra is form unconditional, as seen by the Absolute Eye. By "Absolute Ear" is meant the power (Śakti) of apprehending sound in itslef or as such without subjection to the varying conditions of Time, Place, (*i.e.* Plane) and Person. The Stress by which a thing is generated and sustained is the basis of all the five Tanmātras. It is Śabda-Tanmātra as apprehended by the Absolute Ear, Rūpa Tanmātra as apprehended by the Absolute Eye, and so on. From the gross standpoint Śabda is not the Guṇa of Ākāśa alone. In order to be manifested to the human mind and ear sound requires not only gross Ākāśa but Vāyu and the other Bhūtas. For the transmission of sound to the limited ear there must be a material medium for its transmission whethere as air, water of solid body. Virāṭ sound in short assumes the existence of the whole material universe.

To sum up– There is the unmanifest Lord (Avyakta Īśvara) and the manifest Lord (Īśvara). Both are Śiva-Śakti because there is never Śiva without Śakti not Śakti without Śiva, whether in creation or dissolution. Only in the latter there is nothing but Consciousness (Śakti being Cidrūpiṇī,) and in the former She assumes the form of the universe. For this reason the supreme state may be called Śiva-Śakti and the manifest state Śakti-Śiva to denote the preponderance of the Cit and Māyā aspects respectively One state is motionless (Niṣpanda), the other with motion (Saspanda). One is soundless (Aśabda) the other manifests as sound (Śabda). In one is the Unmanī-Śakti, in the other the Samanī Śakti. The manifest Īśvara displays itself in three forms– causal, subtle, gross. The causal form is Paraśabda, Parāvāk, or Śabdabrahman. This is Īśvara. The rest is Aparāvāk. The subtle form is Madhyamā vāk, which is Hiraṇyagarbha sound, which develops into Virāṭ Śabda or Vaikharī vāk. The sound is accompanied by movement. That of the causal body first projecting the manifold universe from out of itself is general movement or Sāmānya Spanda, the Śabda of which is the Praṇava or "Om." From Om all other Mantras are derived. Hiraṇyagarbha Śabda is accompanied by special motion (Viśeṣa Spanda) and Virāṭ Śabda is clearly defined movement (Spaṣṭatara Spanda) manifesting in man as articulate speech, and therefore as the gross or uttered form of Mantra.

## Chapter 4

# PARAŚABDA, CAUSAL ŚABDA

Śabda which comes from the root *Śabd* "to make sound" ordinarily means sound in general including that of the voice, word, speech and language. It is either lettered sound (Varṇātmaka śabda) and has a meaning (Artha), that is, it either denotes a thing or connotes the attributes and relations of things; or it is unlettered sound and meaningless (at any rate to us) and is mere Dhvani (Dhvanyātmaka-Śabda) such as the sound of a rushing torrent, a clap of thunder and so forth. I say "to us" because every sound may have a meaning for Īśvara. This Dhvani arises from the contact of two things striking one another. So lettered sound is manifested through the contact of the vocal organs with the outer air. As elsewhere more fully explained, Śabda is, and exists as, four Śaktis namely Parā, Paśyantī, Mādhyamā and Vaikharī. These are referred to in connection with Vāk or Devī Śarasvatī, another synonym for Śabda.

Śabda again is either immanent in its manifestation as sound, or transcendent. The first is threefold: (a) From an average point of view it means sound of either of these classes as heard by ears and sounds whose capacity (Śakti) is that of the normal or average plane. (b) From the Yogika point of view it means subtle sound, that, is, subtle sound as apprehended by ears and minds which are supernormal and therefore whose Śaktis rise above the average plane. But these capacities can be greater or less and therefore admit of grades, one person's capacity being greater than that of another, just as is the case with individuals in the ordinary plane, some of whom can hear better than others. (c) From the standpoint of the" Absolute Ear" that is a capacity to apprehend sound unconditionally such as exists in the case of the perfect Yogi, it means pure sound or Śabda-tanmātrā. This is apprehended by the perfect Yogi in its purity. All these are effects (Kārya). Transcendent Śabda means creative movement or Causal Stress itself, that is, it is not, the effect or manifestation *(i.e.* sound) to either the relative ear (a and b) or the "absolute ear" (c) but the cause (Kāraṇa) or Manifesting Fact itself. This in the Śāstra is Śabda-Brahman, that is, the source of all Śabda or name (Nāma) and of all form (Rūpa), the universe being "Name and Form" (Nāmarūpātmaka). This we rise step by step starting from average experience to supreme experience; from projections and manifestations to the Thing Itself which is Causal Stress or Śabda-Brahman. The term Śabda is throughout retained, though the connotations enlarge and deepen as we proceed upwards. This is in conformity with the concrete way in which Hindu thought has developed and by which the all-pervading and all-manifesting power of the Divine Śakti is shown. In teaching, it is the Arundhatīdarśananyāya, according to which a husband shows (or rather used to show– for, is Arundhatī sought now?) his newly wedded wife the tiny star Arundhatī, emblem of constant chastity, by drawing her attention first to some neighbouring big star. "You see this, now look to the left you see this, well next to it you see Arundhatī." So a Guru deals with his disciple (Śiṣya) in a way suitable to the latter's intelligence. He cannot learn what is the highest all at once. He must make his way upward to it. "Brahman is this; no it is that; no it is this;" and so on until the highest notion of It is capable of being given. Thus the Guru in Śruti says "Annam Brahma," that is Brahman is the food which the disciple eats as also matter generally. Then as the latter's knowledge deepens, the Guru changes the connotation of the word Brahman but retains the term itself. The disciple then consecutively learns that life is Brahman (Prāṇāḥ Brahma), Intelligence is Brahman (Vijñānam Brahma) and finally Bliss is Brahman (Ānandaṃ Brahma) where at last experience rests. Here there are five connotations of "Brahman," each more comprehensive and deeper than the foregoing, gradually evolved as the spiritual life of the Śiṣya unfolds and perfect itself. The connotations of most of the important philosophical terms have been evolved in this way. Thus there are different meanings of Prāṇa, Ākāśa, Vāyu and so forth. Śabda also has the four meanings stated which thought progressively evolves in the manner above stated. Some may think that from the standpoint of pure logic this state of things is unacceptable. We have however to deal with the matter practically. And what life wants is generally not that which pure logic demands. But apart from that the method and the statements are true. For Brahman is all things as Śakti, though the Brahman in itslef (Brahmasvarūpa) is beyond them all. If those, before whom all connotations of Brahman are at once placed, complain of ambiguity, this is due to the fact that they have not mastered their subject. And because the subject must be gradually mastered the Guru takes his Śiṣya gradually upwards to the point where all aspects are seen in relation to the whole (Pūrṇa) whose aspects they are.

For the present Chapter 1 will start at the beginning namely Causal Śabda or Śabda-Brahman. Śiva has two aspects namely Niṣkala (without parts), Nirguṇa (without attribute), Sakala (with parts) and Saguṇa (with attribute). The first is the unmanifested transcendent Supreme and the second the manifested and immanent creative Lord (Īśvara) or Ruling Mother (Īśvarī). The first is Niṣpanda, without movement, for it is the eternal changeless Brahman. It is Aśabda which here means the same thing, for being unmanifest there is neither Śabda as effect nor Śabda as cause. The latter means that there is then no Causal Stress. The other aspect is called Śabda-Brahman which appears at creation from out of Brhaman which is the equilibrated condition of Śakti. From the Śabda-Brahman all particular Śabdas as Mantras or otherwise appear. Śabda-Brahman is in Itself Avyakta (unmanifest) Śabda, Artha and Pratyaya and which uprises from the form of Bindu on the differentiation of the Supreme Bindu due to the prevalence of Kriyā-Śakti in Prakṛti.

*Kriyāśakti pradhānāyāḥ śabda śabdārtha kāraṇaṃ,*
*Prakṛterbindurūpiṇyāḥ śabdabrahm̐ābhavat paraṃ.*
*Śāradā-Tilaka* 1-12.

In other words the unmanifest potentiality of power which subsequently appears as Śabda and therefore as Artha and Pratyaya becomes manifest through its activity, manifesting in Prakṛti in the form of Bindu which is the undifferentiated Śiva-Śakti. With such activity Bindu becomes threefold as Śabda, Artha, Pratyaya. Avyakta-Rava is the Principle of sound as such (Nāda Mātra) that is undifferentiated sound not specialised in the form of letters but which is through creative activity the cause of manifested Śabda and Artha which are Its forms.

*Tena śabdārtha-- rūpa-viśiṣṭasya śabda-brahmatvaṁ avadhāritaṁ-- (Prāṇatoṣinī* 13).

It is the Brahman considered as all-pervading Śabda undivided and unmanifested whose substance is Nāda and Bindu, the proximate creative impulse in Paraśiva and proximate cause of manifested Śabda and Artha. *Sṛṣṭyunmukha- paramaśiva- prathamollāsamātraṁ akhaṇḍo-vyakto nādabindumaya eva vyāpako brahmātmaka śabdaḥ* (See *Prāṇatoṣini* 10. *Rāghava Bhaṭṭa Com on* v. 12, Ch. I, *Śāradā-Tilaka).*

The creative Brahman is called Śabda-Brahman. It may be asked why is this so, since the Saguṇa-Śiva (which Śabda-Brahman is) is the cause not only of all Śabda but of all Artha (Rūpa) and Pratyaya. This is so but the Śāstra uses the term Śabda-Brahman because it is here considering the origin of Śabda. But Śruti in explaining creation is impartial as between Śabda, Artha or Pratyaya. Now, it says "creation is out of Śabda" (Śabda-prabhāva) regarding the universe as constituted of Śabda (Vāṅmaya) in its causal sense. Now, it says that creation is out of Pratyaya using that term in the sense of creative ideation (Sṛṣṭikalpanā). Now, it says "Creation is out of Artha" that is the supreme Artha, the cosmic "Stuff" or cosmic "Matter" which is Prakṛti-śakti. What is done in such a case is to take an effect (Kārya) known to us, and to refer it to the one cause of all effects, giving that cause however the name of the particular effect which is subject of consideration. Moreover, the Śabda aspect of Brahman is of the highest importance for it is in this aspect that It is Veda.

But what is the sense in which Śabda is used in the term Śabda-Brahman? This has been already indicated in the quotation above cited. Śabda here does not mean either gross or subtle sound. To begin with these are both effects (Kārya) and we are dealing with their cause (Kāraṇa). Manifested sound is a Guṇa of Ākāśa. But in what sense? It is not merely a quality of Ether and thus not anything else; that is the term Śabda is not limited to the Guṇa of Ākāśa. If it were, it would not be possible to explain the well-known scientific experiment (which in early days was supposed to "demolish" all Hindu theories) in which a ringing bell creases to be heard in a closed vessel from which the Air has been pumped out, but in which Ether still remains. If Śabda were the Guṇa of Ākāśa only and unconnected with anything else it could not be said that sound increases and decreases, appears and disappears with Vāyu. Hence, the term Śabda is not limited to sound, gross or subtle. It is the Causal Stress or Spanda which inheres in the stressed condition of Cit-Śakti and Māyā-śakti which manifests first as the Śabda Tanmātra to the absolute "Ear," as more or less subtle sound to a Yogic (though not perfect) ear according as the fundamental Ākāśa Spanda is adapted to its relative capacity through other more or less dense media; and which finally appears as average human sound when the fundamental Spanda is adapted to the capacity of the human ear through a medium of such density as the common air. The air therefore like the ear is one of the factors of the manifestation of the fundamental Spanda which is Śabda as the original creative Causal Stress or agitation in the body of Prakṛti-Śabda. Śabda is the Cosmic Stress itself which takes place in the Primary Ether or Saspanda-Śakti which produces the Śabda Tanmātra which evolves into Ākāśa Bhūta and then into the Vāyu and other Tanmātras and Bhūtas. These according to Vedānta are Pañcīkṛta; that is, each Tattva has four parts of its own element and one of each of the four other. Through the Bhautika-Sṛṣṭi or indirect causation or Hiraṇyagarba there takes place the combination of the Tattvas produced by the Bhūta-Sṛṣṭi in direct causation (Sākṣātkartṛtvam) of Īśvara producing the gross world of the human senses which is Virāt. Thus, the one initial Stress is communicated as and throughout the chain of its effects. To distinguish this Śabda it is called Para-Śabda and the manifested Śabda is Apara-Śabda or commonly Śabda simply. The latter is subtle and gross sound, the first being supersensible to the normal mind and sense and the latter sensible or what we call in its compounds discrete matter. Paraśabda is thus not sound but a state of agitation in the Cosmic Śakti when, on the ripening of the Saṁskāras the hitherto existing equilibrium (Sāmyāvasthā) of Prakṛti is broken. There is then a disturbance (Kṣobha) or general movement (Sāmānyaspanda) in Śakti and this Cosmic Stress which is Paraśabda or Parāvaka reveals itself in manifested Śabda (Apara). This once stress, which is the potency of all in which it reveals itself, manifests in man as Artha, Pratyaya, Śabda, in the objects (Prameya) of which he as knower (Pramātri) has apprehension (Pratyaya) and in the names by which he thinks of them as an "after-construction in relation to the intuitive experience of life" as Professor Pramathanātha Mukhopādhyāya has well put it. The primordial Śabda or Parāvaka (corresponding in some ways to the Logos) is the cosmic predisposition to an precondition of creative evolution. The agitation in the primary Substance projecting itslef into the sensuous plane becomes audible as Dhavni or sound, but is itself only the possibility and substratum of Sound. Creation is said to be Śabda-prabhāva, that as it proceeds from, and is a manifestation of, the Stress or Cosmic Śakti. In this sense every movement or process in the universe in Paraśabda. Aśabda Jagat is a contradiction in terms. Whilst the stress or constituting force is one, It manifests Itself differently to the different sense-organs. The Causal Stress when striking the ear and mind produces sound, when striking the eye and mind it produces colour and form, and when striking other sense organs it produces other kinds of sensation it is to be noted that of the five Bhūtas, Ākāśa and Vāyu belong to the formless (Amūrtta) division and the remaining three to the form division (Mūrtta). The first is sensed by hearing. Śabda as lettered sound is vibration for the ear as name. Tejas the head of the second division is sensed as form (Rūpa). Artha is thus vibration to the eye (mental or physical) as form. It is because the one Power rays itself forth in threefold form that Śabda, Artha and Pratyaya as such have a natural and inseparable relation to one another. It is again because the Vaidika-Śabda is assumed (a matter which I will later discuss) to constitute the natural name of, and therefore to be in complete correspondence with, the Arthas denoted, that it is held to be eternal. Śruti says that the world is born of Śabda (Śabda-prabhāva) and that creation (Sṛṣṭi) is Śabda-pūrvaka, that is Śabda is the antecedent condition of creative process, which cannot be if Śabda be taken to be only that manifestation to the ear and mind (natural or Yogika) which is sound (gross or subtle). This manifestation is a subsequent and consequent fact and is to be distinguished from the antecedent and primordial condition of creation as such. The primordial condition is Causal Stress; that is, in the finite ether of consciousness, homogeneous, quiescent, there is a moving – a stir. Paraśabda is the name for that causal stress as it arises and before it manifests as the universe.

To sum up: In the creative process three stages are to be noted: (1) the transcendental quiescent condition immanent in the others, though veiled, which is Aśabdaṃ, Asparśam, Arūpam and so forth as Śruti negatively describe it; (2) the condition of cosmic stress which is

Śabda-Brahaman. The stress is a play of Śakti in the Cidākāśa in such a way that the first condition is not effected when the second appears. The Śabda-Brahman is Veda. After manifestation and at the conclusion of the cycle it is wrapped up as potential Māya-Śakti, when according to some, in Mahāpralaya the trancendental condition alone is. The human parallel is Suṣupti; (3) Śabda-Brahman reproduces itself gradually and partially as countless finite centres of varied finite experiences of Nāma and Rūpa. Hence forms together with sounds, sights and so forth vary as do the Śabdas. The sound which represents the above mentioned primordial functioning of the Brahmaśakti is the Mahābīja "Om" or Praṇava-- *Omityekaraṅga brahma tasya vācakaḥ pranavaḥ*. The nature of this great Bīja which is the source of all other mantras will be the subject of the future chapter after we have discussed what is meant by "natural name" which I have more fully dealt with in the chapter bearing that title.

## Chapter 5

# ŚAKTI AS STRESS

The cosmic state of Sṛṣṭi, Sthiti and Laya, together with the transcendental Parama-Śiva state as also Turīya and the Vyaṣṭi states of Jāgrat, Svapna, Suṣupti, must all be ultimately explained (so far as this can be) by the dynamical theory of Śakti as Stress giving rise to moving forms of Herself. For this purpose it is neccessary to investigate counditions of equilibrium and movement.

What is Stress? Let us suppose that two things A and B are attracting each other. The name for the total mutual action is "stress" of which the respective actions of A and B are the elements, partials, or components. Thus, there may be Stress for three or four things and so on. Ultimately we reach Universal Stress which is an infinite system of correlated force. A particular thing may be defined as a partial experience of this infinite system. Professor Pramathanātha Mukhopādhyāya to whom I am indebted in the preparation of this and some of the following papers has given it the appropriate name of "fact-section." The infinite system is however never really finitized by these partials. When the stress between one such partial and another touches the normal of consciousness in either or both, we may have, under circumstances and within certain limits, sensation of sound in either or both. The stress is Śabda and the sound is

Dhvani. There may be several stages from the one to the other. It is stress or Śabda which constitutes a thing. Whether this Śabda is followed or accompanied by a certain Dhvani or not will depend firstly upon the magnitude of its action in relation to a percipient, and secondly upon the conditions of the percipient's perceptive organs. Hence in order that a sound may be heard the rates of vibration of the air must be such and such, the ears and brain must be such and such, and so on. Beyond these limits there are no sounds. Thus, most objects of experience though influencing us do not express themselves in sounds to us such as the earth, sun, moon, stars and so forth. In the transcendental Paramaśiva or Turīya state which is Nirvāṇa, all Stress is dissolved and Śakti is then nothing but Cit, Cidrūpiṇī, Cinmātrūpiṇī. This may be illustrated by the case where causal stress being constituted by a number of forces, all these severally vanish and are each therefore separately zero so that the resultant is zero. This is the Transcendent Niṣkala state in which there is no Sṛṣṭi-Kalpanā, no Artha and no Śabda (Aśabda). In the case of Cosmic Suṣupti we need not take into consideration an external system, for nothing is external to the Cosmos. In this case we have only the static condition where each term is not separately zero, but where each of the forces constituting the Stress balances one another with the result that there is a state of equilibrated energy. There is the state of the Guṇas in Sarūpa-pariṇāma which, with loss of equilibrium in creation, is Virūpapariṇāma. Vyaṣṭi Suṣupti may be due to sets of facts. Either the forces constituting this state, without each being separately zero, yet have that resultant, in which case there is equilibrium in the Vyaṣṭi, causal body provided the external cosmic system does not disturb this internal equlibrium of the Vyaṣṭi system; or these forces result in something but this resultant is exactly counterbalanced by the action of the external system. Thus, this something which would otherwise be the Vyaṣṭi stress system practically vanishes and equilibrium is established in this last mentioned system. In the first case the external system has no action on the given internal system but it has action on other Vyaṣṭi systems. Thus, the world is not asleep because the individual is so. In the second case the external system has action on the given internal system but this action is just negatived by the reaction of the internal on the external. In both cases the external system is an actual stressing attitude. In Svapna and Jāgrat Avasthā the equilibrium of the Samaṣṭi and Vyaṣṭi Suṣupti or causal body is lost, and in Sṛṣṭi there is a system of kinetic stresses which again in Laya lapse into a state of potential stresses. The world process is thus divided into the three stages of Sṛṣṭi (creation), Sthiti (maintenance), and Laya (dissolution) which is a passing from a state of homogeneity (Laya) to one of heterogeneity (Sṛṣṭi and Sthiti) and back to homogeneity again in an unending series of evolution with periods of rest between. The growth of the universe is thus a pulsing forth of the Bindu holding potentially within Itself, as massive (Ghaṇībhūta) Śakti, all into which is subsequently evolves. This great Universe dies down again into that from which it sprang. Through we thus speak of three stages it cannot be properly said that there in Sṛṣṭi, that when it stops there is Sthiti, and then ultimately there is Laya. Evolution (Sṛṣṭi) and involution (Laya) are going on even during Sthiti. There is always, for instance, molecular birth and death. Each of these terms is employed according as one aspects or the other is emphasised. During Laya the stresses are potential. That is actual movements cease, so that the stresses are due simply to the configuration of relative positions of the units determined by their Karmas up to the time of Laya. There is for instance, stress in a stringed bow though the string may not be in actual movement. The nature of Īśvara experience as the ultimate Fact is as such logical and therefore human categories, if stretched to the fact, will inevitably lead into paralogisms and antinomies. In the same way creation is an unresolved riddle. Why should the spell of cosmic Suṣupti be broken and in what way does the Will of God infleunce it? Ultimately these questions are unanswerable in all faiths. We may say that Īśvara during Laya has experience of the casual body. The absolute "ear", "tongue", "eye" which God possesses are reabsorbed into a massive consciousness of Bliss (Ānanda) as is partially the case with the Jīva in Suṣupti for these are differentiations of His infinite Jñāna-Śakti. These are veiled during Laya, that is the kinetic stresses (Śakti Viśvarūpā) become potential (Śakti Cidrūpiṇī). What is potent becomes latent. The world becomes "Memory" which at the next creation is "remembered" just as in the individual the world is lost to him in dreamless sleep, and when waking he sees and recalls the events of a past day. Yet here the world exists during our sleep for others. But when Īśvara goes to sleep things do not remain as they are. Things return to their causal form or seeds. During Laya, Īśvara has a massive experience of the totality of these "seeds," for as Śruti says "I am one, I will now be many."

To the question whether this creative act is instantaneous or successive it may be replied probably neither the one nor the other. That is the category of time is inapplicable to creation as a whole. Creation considered as an instanteneous flash or a successive flow is Vyāvahārika and not Pāramārthika. On this basis however there is a difference of opinion between Dṛṣṭi-sṛṣṭi-vāda and Karma-sṛṣṭi-vāda. According to the first, and to me preferable, view, as Īśvara thought, so at once the whole world appeared in its stages as subtle and gross. At every moment also creation is taking place. It is not something wholly in the past. According to the second or more commonly accepted doctrine, the Tattvas came out gradually, the one after other, in a specified order (Krama) though such Krama is not referable to time as we know it and which appeared at a lower stage. This later time is the Janmakāla of the Kālavādins according to whom all is Kāla. The Supreme Time or Mahākāla is Nirguṇa, Nirviśeṣa, Nirvikāra or Brahman.

As regards the cosmic cycle it is claimed to be proved by (a) induction from observed facts of experience which, all giving sings of periodicity, afford a basis for generalization; and (b) the alleged actual remembrance by Ṛṣis and other super-souls such as Jaigiṣavya of Caturyuga, Manvantara, Kalpa and so forth. Apart therefore from Śruti the proof is inductive and experimental and not deductive.

Creation proceeds from the generic to the specific. When Laya as a state of potential stresses passes into Sṛṣṭi which is a system of kinetic stresses was have first the most genetic condition of the latter, namely Sāmānya-spanda, that is general undifferentiated movement. It is the manifestation of the tendency of Laya to pass into Sṛṣṭi. From the standpoint of Conscisouness it is the first stage of "seeing" (Īkṣaṇa) that is cosmic ideation on the part of Īśvara. In the individual it is the borderland between Suṣupti is breaking and Svapna is drawing to pass into Jāgrat. The inertia of the first has passed but the specialised movements of the second and thrid are not yet in evidence. It is a kind of massive undifferentiated state containing potentially all specialities. The Śabda or acoustic aspect of the tendency of potential stress to pass into kinetic stress is the Praṇava or Mantra "Om."

This tendency realises itself in the first place in Bhūta-sṛṣṭi by Īśvara. Īśvara has consciousness of his Ānandamaya Body and Causal Body. The latter means the experience, "I am all" (Śarvātmakatva). He experiences Himself as all whether as a whole, as generals or particulars. As Knower of all He is Sarvajña, as Knower of its varieties He is Sarvavit. They are to Him, Himself, for the Māyā with which He is associated does not govern Him and therefore His knowledge does not bind Him. The stage of Īśvara though not governed by, is yet associated with, Māyā and is therefore not that of Supreme Mokṣa. Īśvara wills to be many and the Bhūtas issue from him. As Īśvara He does not think Himself to be their creator. The creation of the Bhūtas (Bhūta-sṛṣṭi) according to the Vedantic order means the evolving of (a) the Apañcīkṛta Bhūtas or Tanmātras and (b) their primary compounds which are again (aa) Sūkṣma that is Antaḥkaraṇa, Indriya and Prāṇas and (bb) Sthūla that is the Pañcīkṛta Bhūtas. Broadly speaking these are the elements of creation; the creation of which implies also their natural names or Bījas. Thus, from Om are evolved the Bījas of the Bhūtas Ham, Yam, Ram, Vam, Lam and other Bījas such as Hrīm the Māyā Bīja or Praṇava of the differentiating Śakti. These elements are special (Viśeṣa) in relation to the tendency and general movement (Sāmānya-spanda) above mentioned, but are general (Sāmānya) in relation to the derivatives which follow.

There then follows Bhautika-Sṛṣṭi by Hiraṇyagarba that is the creation of the secondary compounds; that is again the mixing up of the "elements" into diverse forms first the typal and then the variational. This is done by Īśvara in His aspects as Hiraṇyagarbha. These too have their natural names (Śabda). Hiraṇyagarbha who is the Lord of Brahmaloka thinks himself to be a creator. This is a state of duality in which He thinks that all things are His. Hence Hiraṇyagrabha as affected by Māyā is a Jīva.

Lastly coming to the completed Sthiti we have actions and reactions of the Bhūtas and Bhautikas such that the continue as a system of the kinetic stresses. These actions and reactions have their natural names which may be called phenomenal Śabdas. Some of these namely those which fall between our limits of sensibility are sensible to us. So much as to Śabdas clasified with reference to aspects of creation.

Śabdas may be either directly or indirectly apprehended. In the latter case they are received. The ordinary individual does not hear the natural name or sound of Agni or "Ram" directly. He is told that it is so having received it from those who have heard that sound. It is "received" (Āpta) and not directly apprehended (Śākṣātkṛta). For, from the point of view of apprehension, Śabdas are of two kinds, Sākṣātkṛta and Āpta. The Śabda range of Īśvara, Hiraṇyagarbha, and Virāṭa may be thus represented.

Thus, Īśvara has no Āpta or received (indirect) Śabdas; but all Śabdas are directly apprehended (Śākṣātkṛta by Him. Hiraṇyagarbha, as Hiraṇyagarbha, that is a particular aspect of Īśvara, has direct apprehension of Bhautika-sṛṣṭi Śabdas and Sthiti Śabdas and indirect of Bhūta-sṛṣṭi and Laya Śabdas; Virāṭa as Virāṭa has direct apprehension only of Sthiti Śabda and indirect apprehension of the rest. This deals with the Samaṣṭi or collective aspects of Experience.

Coming to the individual or Vyaṣṭi aspects we have the corresponding state of Prājña, Taijasa and Viśva. These unlike the collective states are mutually exclusive, the one of the other, and may thus be figures. Prājña has direct but veiled or partial apprehension of his own Vyaṣṭi causal (Laya) Śabda but not of others. This Śabda is however not sound as language for himself. Taijasa has both direct and indirect experience of Vyaṣṭi *(i.e.* some) subtle Śabda. and Virāṭa has the same of gross Śabdas.

Here in these two cases here is gradation. The gross ear has capacities of varying degree. A scientist may by means of a delicately constructed apparatus hear sounds which are not sensible to the natural ear. A Yogi may hear still more. Thus, if either were to hear the rise of sap in a tree that sound would be the direct approximate natural name of that vegetable function. A Yogi in Ṣaṭcakrabheda or piercing of the six centres by Kuṇḍalinī-Śakti may, it is said, directly apprehend the Bījas Om, Ham, Yam and the rest, as the passage of Śakti gradually vitalises the six centres. A Yogī by mounting to a higher or the highest plane of existence can have direct experience (Sākṣātākāra) of any or all kinds of Śabdas. The Absolute Ear hears the

Śabda Tanmātra in Ākāśa, not through the impact of undulations, but it hears movement as movement.

In Brahmajñāna the Yogi becomes the Brahman Itself when all stress ceases and there is Peace.

## Chapter 6

# ETERNALITY OF ŚABDA

The term "eternal" may mean "always is" (a) without change or (b) with change. The former is existence uncontradicted in the three times. Change again may be either immanent (Svagata) or its reverse (Taditara). Thus, if there be only one circle (A) any change going on within it is Svagata change or distinction (Bheda). But if there be two circles A and B of which the latter added a part of itself to the former with the result that A is changed, this is not Svagata. Thus, Svagata change is Advaita whilst Non-Svagata change presupposes Dvaita.

Applying then these observations to the Brahman and Jīva, the former has three aspects: (a) Brahman as Pure Cit (Brahma svarūpa) (b) Brahman as Cit-Śakti. (c) Brahman as Māyā Śakti or Prakṛti. In the first or transcendent sense Brahman is Pure Cit and this always is as such. From the finite point of view we may their ignore (veil) it or accept it, but it is ever given. It is the changeless background of all change; but Itself has no kind of change. This is the Niṣkala Paramaśiva to whose powers or Śaktis we next proceed.

Cit-śakti is Cit as Śakti, that is Cit immanent in the

world the forms of which as Mind and Matter are productions of Māyā-Śakti. This immanent Brahman (Cit-Śakti) in the sense of the All (which Professor P.N. Mukhopādhyāya aptly calls "Fact" as opposed to "Fact-section") always is as such. For the all (Pūrṇa) never ceases to be all. All is all. Śruti says that Pūrṇa remains Pūrṇa be taken from it. Brahman as Cit-Śakti and has only Svagata change or movement. Brahman as Māyā-Śakti— what the author cited calls Stress as distinguished from the background of Cit— is Brahman as Prakṛti. This is eternal in the sense that it always is, though either as latent or as patent, as a kinetic force or as a tendency. Here eternity does not exclude change of condition. Brahman as Prakṛti has Svagata change. We must not then confound the terms Real and Eternal. According to both real and eternal, for "real" is here used in the sense of that which does not change (Kūṭastha) whereas Māyā with its changes is neither real nor unreal "Eternal" therefore includes "change of condition". Non-eternal or finitized being is, pragmatically considered, marked by three kinds of change and distinction (Bheda), *viz.*, Intrinsic (Svagata) such as the distinction which exists between the leaves and branches of the same tree, and extrinsic which is again of two kinds, *viz.*, Sajātīya such as the distinction which exists between one kind of tree and antoher kind of tree, and Vijātīya such as the distinction which exists between a tree and the earth and rocks which surround it.

The eternal Śabda-Brahman manifests at creation (Sṛṣṭ i) and lapses into its quiescent ground in dissolution (Laya). The Śabda of its first creative movement is the Nāda or Dhvani "Om." From this issue all particular Śabdas both Varṇātmaka and Dhvanyātamaka. A given particular is obviously not the same for ever. But are particulars as such eternal? The creation of particulars is recurrently eternal in the sense that during each Sṛṣṭi particulars appear. But are the particulars themselves eternal? The question may mean either of two things. In the first sense the obvious answer is, as stated, in the negative. Then are particulars as such eternal? In other words are these particulars in all times, in Sṛṣṭi as well as in Laya? This given particular (say the pen with which I am writing) may not be in all times, but will not some particulars (though different from those now given) exist always? There is a genus or type (Jāti) with its particulars (Vyakti). The Jāti never exists without its Vyaktis. Some Vyaktis (though different from those now given) will be associated with the Jātis in all times; though both may be either latent or patent. In Laya for instance the Jātis associated with their Vyaktis become latent. Associated with what Vyaktis? Not the present ones; but the Vyaktis immediately antecedent to the state of Prakṛti equilibrium. A given Vyakti is Vyakti-viśeṣa. Any Vyakti or some Vyakti is Vyakti Sāmānya. The former is not, but the latter is, eternal though it may be either veiled or unveiled. The Jātis are eternal and manifested in every creation and their Śabdas are eternal. The Vyaktis are only eternal in the sense above explained. Each creation is not an exact copy of the previous creation in every particular. Particulars through revolving round certain fixed Jātis (latent or patent) change. Thus a given Jīva may be now a Brāhmaṇa. Through Karma he changes and after death he may change his Jāti and become a Śūdra or a Devatā. And so he may go on until he reaches the antecedent state of Mahāpralaya. Let is be supposed that at that moment he is a Devatā again. He is a Devatāvyakti associated with Jāti. In Pralaya he will be veiled as such together with his Jāti, and together with all his Saṁskāras active (Prārabdha) as well as nascent (Sañcita). It is the resultant of these Saṁskāras that will determine his condition of birth after the expiry of Prakṛti's equilibrium. The end of this journey is reached only in Liberation (Mukti).

Then is the Vyakti Śabda eternal? If by this term is meant a Śabda denoting a given Vyakti (Vyaktiviśeṣa) then this is a proper name (non-connotating) and is not eternal. But with the exception of a few proper names (those which are attached as arbitrary signs to this Vyakti or that) all names or words represent Jātis that is groups or classes of things. A Vyakti-viśeṣa is represented by either a proper name or a specific combination of class names, such as, 'this paper I am writing on'; all these being class names the combination of which makes or denotes a Vyakti-viśeṣa.

Only such Śabdas as are approximate natural names (either simple or in combination) are eternal and the rest are not. The Veda claims to give the names of class things and class functions which are approximately natural. Hence (granting this claim), these Śabdas are eternal (Nitya) By Veda is here meant Vaidika language and by natural name Vaidika-Śabda. Thus, assuming that the word "Gauh" is an approximate natural name, it has existed in every universe and has thee meant the animal cow. If the word "Cow" as a variation of this has originated in some time, in some place and in some persons, then outside this limitation of time, place, and person the word has not existed and has not represented the Artha or animal cow. The ultimate test of a natural name is of course experimental verification. Vaidika language invovles different strata. Natural names are of different kinds and degrees. Whether other Śabdas and their combinations are eternal depends on whether those words and their combinations are or are not approximate natural names.

Apart from tradition the proof is experimental verification of Yoga. If they are variations of natural names (Vaidika-Śabda) the extent to which they vary, and the conditions of time, place, and person to which they are subject, must determine the nature of their bond with their Arthas. No *a priori* answer is possible. Śabda-Brahman thinks creatively, his Pratyaya being cosmic ideation (Śṛṣṭi-kalpanā). The Śabda of this is Om and the Artha is the totality of the univese denoted by, and potentially inhering in, the creative impulse of which Om is the sound-expression. From this Om was derived all the letters (Varṇas) and sounds (Dhvanis). There Vaidiki-Varṇas ae eternal and represent in themselves and their variations all the possiblities of articulate speech in all languages. In Veda the Karma of these Varṇas is eternal and therefore the Vaidiki words are also, it is claimed, eternal. The vowels are continuous sounds formed by varying the size of the mouth cavity. The vowel sounds produced by the voice are due (See Catchpool's "Text-book of Sound", p.290) to the vibrations of two cartilaginous plates, the "vocal chords" placed at the top of the windpipe, edge to edge with a narrow slit between them; air blown through this slit from the lungs keeps the plates vibrating. The apparatus is really a free reed. The vocal chords have muscles attached to them which can vary the frequency of the vibration and the pitch of the sound produced. The different vowel sounds are produced by varying the size and shape of the mouth cavity. The consonants are particular interruptions of those sounds. They cut short the vowel sound but cannot themselves be sounded without vowels. And for this reason the vowels are known as the Śaktis of the consonants.

This subject of the Varṇas occupies an important place in the Tantra-Śāstra in which it is sought to give a practical application to the very ancient doctrine concerning Śabda. The letters are classified according to their place of pronunciation (Uccāraṇa) such as gutturals, labials, dentals and so forth. The lips, mouth, and throat form a pipe or musical instrument which being formed in various ways and by the aid of the circumambient air produces the various sounds which are the letters of the Alphabet. Pāṇini (see part I of Siddhānta Kaumudī) and Patañjali's Mahābhāṣya deal with the effort of Prayatna is speech, dividing it into inner (Āntaraprayatna) and outer effort (Bāhyaprayatna). The former is of four kinds Spṛṣṭa, Iṣat Spṛṣṭa, Vivṛtta, Samvṛtta according as the effort fully or slightly touches the place of origin of the sound and according as the mouth is open or closed Bāhyaprayatna is of eleven kinds namely Vivāra, Saṁvāra, Śvāsa, Nāda, Ghoṣa, Aghoṣa, Alpaprāṇa, Mahāprāṇa, Udātta, Anudātta, Svarita. Vivāra pronunciation is with the mouth open, Saṃvāra when it is closed. In Śvāsa there is a predominant use of the breathing, in Nāda there is a humming sound, in Ghoṣa ringing sound, Aghoṣa being the opposite of this. In Alpaprāṇa the sound is quickly pronounced, little demand being made on the Prāṇa, Mahāprāṇa being the opposite of this. In Udātta the sound is given with a loud voice, in Anudātta with a low voice, and Svarita is a mixture of these two. In Pāṇini various letters are assigned to each of these classes of Prayatna. Thus, the consonants from Ka to Ma belong to Spṛṣṭa Āntara-Prayatna; Ya, Ra, La, Va to Iṣat Spṛṣṭa Āntara-Prayatna and so on.

The Tantra-Śāstra in its doctrine and practice of Ṣaṭ-cakrabheda indicates various parts of the body which are "touched" in the pronunciation of various letters. By this is meant that in the sounding of certain letters various parts of the body take a part. Thus, the letter Va is pronounced from that part of the body wherein is the Mūlādhāra, and the letter Ha from between the eyebrows in Ājñā-Cakra. The sound produced by the body in motion (for the external cause of sound is something in a state of vibration) is propagated by sound-waves in the circumambient air. The rise and fall of pressure which occur as sound-waves arive at the ear, produce by their effect on its structures the sensation of sound and the nature of this sensation depends on the nature of the rise and fall of pressure, in other words, on the character of the sound waves.

According to Indian doctrine, God evolved man after having evolved most (if not all) other species of living beings so that language (as also intelligence, moral sense, and many other things which had been less perfectly devleoped in the lower animals) became more developed in man. The lower animals were "approaches" to man, the difference between man and animal being according to this doctrine a difference of degree and not of kind. It is possible then that there may be an inchoate Varṇātmaka-Śabda in the higher animals, though it is to be noted that the proposition (which is dealt with elsewhere) that "there is no thinking without languge" is true only if by thinking is meant some kinds only of cognitive processes. Apart from these man gets on without language and therefore also the animals. It is only the after construction on perceptive processes which call for language and this we find mainly if not wholly in man alone. Pātañjala-Darśana also discusses the question of transmigration into an animal body. In this case there is a soul which had been in a human body or even in a Devatā body before and has therefore the Saṁskāras (linguistic and others) of those births instinct therefore may be (partly if not wholly) "lapsed intelligence" and its Dhvanyātmaka language a partly veiled Varṇātmaka or human language.

What is eternal then is Śabda in its aspects as Causal Stress or Śabda-Brahman, the letter (Vaidika Varṇa) evolved from the primordial Dhvani the Praṇava or "Om", and the combinations of these letters which constitute approximately natural names. These according to Hinduism are the Vaidika-Śabdas. Whether that claim is well founded is another question which is not here discussed.

## Chapter 7

# ŚABDA AS LANGUAGE

It has been said that there is no thought without language. This proposition requires examination both from the Brahman and Jīva standpoint. If it be assumed that there is no thinking without language this merely establishes the necessary connection of thought and language and not a law that words or names must come to the mind first and then thoughts. They may be inseparably connected as aspects of one and the same concrete, that is actual, process but between aspects there is no sequence. When a gun is fired the explosion of the cartridge is the causal stress. This manifests to the ear as a report, to the eye as a flash and also it may be by the movement of the object hit. But the last three are co-effects of the first that is the explosion. In the same way when there is a centre of Causal stress in Cit we have several lines of effectual manifestation. But it cannot be said that one line of effectual manifestation causes another. Now, Śruti as already mentioned calls creation Śabda-prabhāva and Śabda-pūrva, both terms implying sequence as between a cause and its consequence. When again Śruti says "Brahma created Devatās with the Śabda '*Etc*'," what is meant is that the causal stress of that special creation manifests to His absolute "Ear" as a sound which is the pure form of what we can *approximately* utter and hear as the sound

*"Etc."* We may, as stated, have several lines of effectual manifestation on there arising a centre of causal stress in Cit, one of which is (say) the sound *"Ete"*, and another the appearance of the Devatās. But we cannot say that one line of effectual manifestation causes another. Therefore, when Śruti says that Śabda underlines, precedes and enters Jagat, Śabda is not used in the sense of sound but as the causal stress or initial Spanda which from the subjective aspect is Icchā-śakti. The universe is creative ideation (Sṛṣṭikalpanā). To use the terms of human speech this ideation is intuitive and not inferential and therefore does not involve language which is one of Its products. The proposition that a Vyāvahārika sense and is then true if by "thinking" is meant the formation of concepts of general notions, judgments and drawing inferences. For even in us, intuitive processes, such as perception and ideation, are done without language. To use the apt language of Professor Pramathanātha Mukhopādhyāya, words are an "after-thought or after-construction in relation to the intuitive experiences of life." (See as to the principles from which this statement follows "Approaches to Truth" and "The Patent Wonder"). To begin with experience is had without language (Aparaśabda) both in the Turīyā (Aśabda condition) and the Suṣupti, Svapna and Jāgrat it is to be recognised that there are some ways in which language may be associated with thinking processes. On the other hand some processes may go on without language. In Svapna and Jāgrat Avasthā, Arthas and Pratyayas necessarily imply the *passibility* of sound manifestation, that is, vocal language, but do not always *actually* suggest their acoustic counterparts. In some cases they do go on apparently without language, though thee is always the possibility of their being expressed in language. A child seas, hears and so forth almost without language, so does

the animal and we ourselves in part. Most of the particular objects of perception have during such perception no specific names for us; still we perceive them and may afterwards recall the class names. Absence of language occurs primarily in two cases, namely in intuitive perception and intuitive ideation. Much seeing and hearing is done intuitively and without language. By intuitive ideation is meant the forming of a mental image of an object. Thus I see tree; close my eyes and see it again in mental image. Many such sights and sounds pass through our mental range from time to time which do not always call up their names. But though these intuitive processes may actually go on without language, there is the possibility of their being vehicled in language, and in description, analysis, classification, judgment and other mental elaborations such linguistic vehicle is indispensable. For the movement it is required to describe, analyse, classify perceptions, recourse must be had to language. Looking, I see a thing and very well see it. But this seeing is often done without actually remembering the name "tree" or "mangoe tree." To describe, classify and otherwise to elaborate this seeing I must remember the name. In this sense language is called an "after-construction." Language again is a system of signs either natural or arbitrary, either vocal or non-vocal, by which we describe things and consider the attributes and relations of things. In this definition four marks are employed, namely, natural, arbitrary, vocal and non-vocal. Taking two at a time there are six combinations namely natural vocal natural non-vocal arbitrary, vocal non-vocal. The last two may be at once rejected as the marks in them are contradictory. The first four give us four kinds of signs which exhaust possible language. Of the first the example is Vaidika-Śabda including Bīja Mantras uttered by the vocal organs and of the second we may instance "expressive" sings made to a man (who does not understand the spoken language) by means of the hand or other bodily organ in order to indicate a particular object. The third and foruth classes refer to arbitrary forms of the first two. Arbritrary-vocal is an arbitrary combination of natural vocal sings, each seprately being vocal and natural but their combinations being arbitrary as where two or more natural words are taken and an arbitrary meaning is given to the whole groups, *e.g.* code words. In the same way it may be possible to combine two or more non-vocal natural sings and give the whole thing an arbitrary meaning. A particular name attached to a thought or thing may be arbitrary as in the case of some proper names, but names as such are necessary to higher mental processes directly and also to intuitive processes implicity. All proper names however are not arbitrary Those that are, are attached as signs to obejcts to denote them or mark them off from other objects. They do not connot any attributes or relations of the things to which they may be attached. Our perceptions and ideations often go on without language Many rapid automatic inferences are drawn and habitual actions are performed without language. But sometimes those processes are with their language accompaniment and the moment we want to review, describe, classify, and judge these processes, their language accompaniment apears in consciousness.

Now, Śabda according to previously given definitions is either Para or Apara. The former is Movement of Stress considered in itself, that is, apart from conditions of its manifestation to specialised sense organs or sense capacities. One of these sense capacities is the ear which is subject to degrees, since the capacity of one individual is greater than that of another. The gradation points to a highest or absolute capacity which may be called the Absolute Ear. The appearance or manifestation of Paraśabda or causal Stress to the highest capacity (wherever that be) is Śabda-Tanmātra. This last is still a manifestation and not the Stress itself. It is the Stress in itself appearing to an ideal ear. It is this stress-in-itself regarded from a special standpoint. Just as we conceive an absolute ear, so we may conceive an absolute eye, tongue and so forth. Each means the Ideal limit (a mathematical term) of certain capacities of specialised feeling which are exercised in us in varying degree. Śabda Tanmātra therefore means not sound in general or undifferentiated pure sound *only,* but Sāmānya (general) sounds including the highest, the Praṇava or Mantra "Om," as well as Viśeṣa (special) sounds. In the Tanmātra form they are both of them sounds as apprehended by the highest capacity and therefore not subject to the conditions of *variability.* "Sound in itself" or "sound as such" therefore does not *necessarily* mean "undifferentiated sound." Thus, a dove is cooing in grove of mangoe tree had by. I hear it. You may hear it better. By a Scientific instrument (megaphone, microphone) it may be heard better still and so on. But what is that sound as apprehended by a perfect capacity of hearing? What is this cooing sound in itself or the standard of this cooing sound of which you, I and the Yogi hear so many variations? The answer to this will give us the Tanmātra of a Viśeṣa sound.

Now, Paraśabda is not language. Aparaśabda including Śabda-Tanmātra is. In the individual (Vyaṣṭi) consciousness there is intuitive consciousness (which answers to Pratyaya) of veiled Ānanda. The Artha is the temporarily equilibrated causal body. But this Artha does not manifest itself to the sleeper at that time in language. In Suṣupti the individual is without language though he has an Intuitive experience of his Vyaṣṭi Ānandamaya causal body. But the Artha is Suṣupti, though wanting language, must have its Paraśabda.

The individual is a centre correlated to other centres in a cosmic system. For a while he is in equilibrium in Suṣupti. Dynamically this means that the algebraic sum of the forces of the other centres exerted upon the individual and of the forces of his own causal body exerted upon the other centres in zero. It follows therefore that the whole cosmic system need not be in equilibrium whilst the individual (that is, his causal body) is in equilibrium. His slumber does not mean the slumber of the Universe. The question is not here discussed as to the forces constituting the individual causal stress during Suṣupati. This I deal with elsewhere. To explain equilibrium in Suṣupati we require only to assume that the resultant action of the universe on the individual causal body and the resultant reaction of the individual causal body on the universe annul each other during Suṣupti or dreamless sleep. They (at the former) need not be separately nil. Hence, the going by the individual into slumber means an actual stressing attitude of the cosmic system which is Paraśabda. But for a certain attitude of the external system there would be no equilibrium in the internal system. Nay more: this Paraśabda may manifest itself as sound (*i.e.*, as language) to other centres such as Śabda-Tantra to the Absolute Ear, Sūkṣma-Śabda of varying degree to the Yogika ear, or as the self-produced physical sounds of the sleeper to the gross ear. Just as a Devatā has a Bīja mantra of Primary Natural Name so his each other individual Jīva, corresponding to their respective causal bodies, and these may be heard in varying degree by finer ears and fully by the Absolute Ear. But the individual does the sleeping without language just as he may make sounds in his sleep without being conscious of it whilst a person sitting by him hears them. Laya or Cosmic Suṣupti is the dreamless slumber of Bhagavān or Īśvara. If our own analogy can be pushed up to this, then this cosmic Suṣupti is also without language, though it is an intuitive experience by God of His own causal body. Since there are no *other* centres here and no absolute ear other than that of Īśvara (who is *ex hypothesis* in Suṣupti), this intuitive experience is absolutely without language (Mauna). It is silence itself. But Paraśabda is there still, namely equilibrated Samaṣṭi (Causal Stress) Hence language or no language, the correlation of Śabda and Artha persists. Thus, language is not the *whole* of Śabda.

Śabda, Artha and Pratyaya are the three poles of a polar triangle. In all planes of consciousness below the pure or transcendent plane this polar triangle necessarily holds. In Īśvara experience the three poles meet together at a point so that Śabda= Artha = Pratyaya. In the Individual Suṣupti experience also they are not clearly distinguishable Language can be put for Śabda (causal movement or stress) only when there arises the possibility of its being apprehended as sound by some hearing capacity (either absolute or relative). A name or a word ceases to be such when the apprehension by the appropriate cognitive capacity is not there. A name is a manifestation to such cognitive capacity and when the conditions of manifestations are not there the manifestation disappears. But the causal stress (Paraśabda) of the name remains. Hence in Vyaṣṭi Suṣupti actual names or words (or vocal language) lapse back into their causal stress. The operation is essentially the same is Samaṣṭi Suṣupti or Laya. So, that Śabda is (that is, equals) language, *actual or possible,* in all cases. In the lower planes (Svapna, Jāgrat), however, language may be put for Śabda but subject to this provision that the language-pole may be regarded as being sometimes above and sometimes below the threshold line of normal or pragmatic consciousness. Thus in the case of the intuitive processes afore-mentioned we may save the polar triangle by assuming that the language pole though not apparent is still there below the threshold line ready to be called up whenever occasion should arise. Thus, the development from infancy may be shown by the following diagram in which A = Artha, P = Pratyaya and S = Śabda as language, shown as being above or below the line which is the threshold--

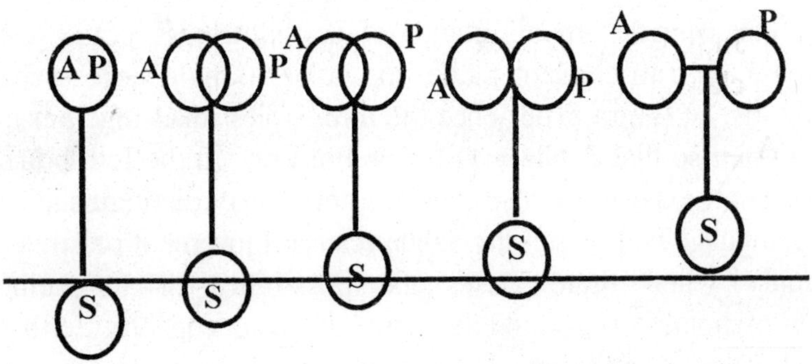


In this diagram, showng the child's development, the five diagrams do not represent definite stage but only the gradual separation of A and P and the rising of S above the line. First no language or more strictly speaking only simple rudimentary sound – Artha and Pratyaya merge into one, there being no discrimination. The Artha and Pratyaya are more and more discriminated and their language correlate is more and more developed and brought above the threshold line. Animals probably remain in the first two stages of the child.

In Jāgrat and Svapna, Artha and Pratyaya are all necessarily associated not merely with Śabda but with that condition of Śabda which we call language. But the association may be either manifest or unmainfest. In the latter case whilst Artha and Pratyaya are above the threshold line of normal consciousness, language is below it, so that in the intuitive processes above described Artha and Pratyaya alone *seem* to appear, though their normal associates are waiting for them below the threshold line. The moment it is desired to review, describe and classify Artha and Pratyaya, then the Śabdas as words appear.

Thus:

Judging, inferring, classifying etc. — Some intuitive Processes

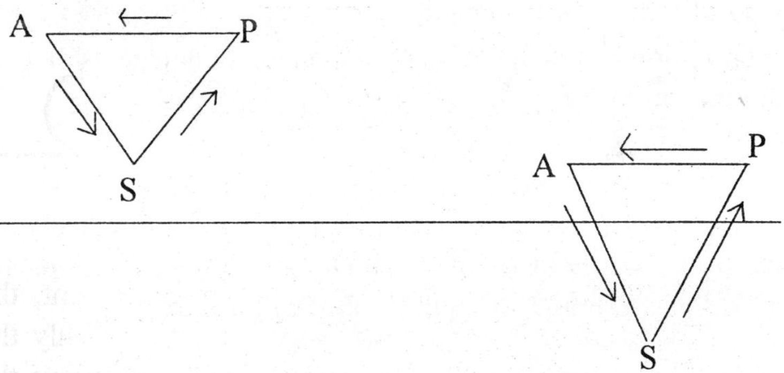


The above account, whilst saving psychology, would imply that Śabda, Artha, Pratyaya being invovled (though as identities) in Īśvara consciosuness must be invovled in all downward experience also. It is however necessary to clearly understand that Śabda is not necessarily language in all cases, and that language may be either consciously or sub-consciously given. According to the scheme suggested the correlation of Artha, Pratyaya and Śabda as language is essential in the planes of Jāgrat and Svapna, but they may be latent as regards the third partner in some intuitive process, but patent in others as well as in conceiving, judging, inferring and so forth. The conclusion therefore is: (1) The Turīya state is undifferentiated. Hence in it there no Artha, Śabda, Pratyaya. A, S and P *severally* vanish. (2) The Suṣupti state (Samaṣṭi or Vyaṣṭi) is temporarily equilibrated Consciousness in which there are A, S and P, but their resultant is ineffectual. In the Vyaṣṭi consciousness there are Artha, Śabda, Pratyaya. But these three seem to blend into one and are not clearly distinguishable. Here Śabda is not language to the subject himself. (3) The Svapna and Jāgrat states in which the temporarily equilibrated consciousness ceases are actually stirring Vyaṣṭi or Samaṣṭi consciosuness. In them there is Śabda, Artha, and Pratyaya, but in some intuitive processes (perceptional and ideational) Śabda as language is below the threshold line of the normal Consciousness.

Thus, the cosmic and individual states must all be ultimately explained (so far as this can be) by the dynamical theory of Stress or Śakti in which an investigation is made as to the conditions of equilibrium and movement.

# Chapter 8

# NATURAL NAME

What is a natural name? Everything is composed of moving material forces. Even what seems stable is in movement, though they are sometimes held together they are disrupted and dissolved. Matter itself is only a relatively stable form of cosmic energy. Because all is in movement, the world is called Jagat or that which moves. Everything is moving which is not the unmoving (Niṣ panda) Brahman. This movement, which is the world, is apprehended by man as sound, touch and feel, form and colour, taste and smell. This is its effect on the sense organs (Indriyas) and mind (Manas), which are again themselves in movement, being ultimately composed of the same Tanmātras which are the components of the mind's objects or matter. All movement is accompanied by sound. In other words, movement presented to a subject is apprehended by the ear and mind as sound, just as it is apprehended by the eye as form and colour, or by the tongue as taste. We say 'ear and mind,' for it is to be remembered that according to Indian notions the Indriya or sense is not the physical organ ear, eye and so forth, but the faculty of mind operating through that organ as its instrument. The physical organs are the usual means whereby on the physical plane the functions of hearing and so forth are accomplished. But as they are mere instruments and their power is derived from the mind, a

Yogī may accomplish by the mind only all that may be done by these physical organs, and indeed more, without the use of the latter. So, also a hypnotised subject can perceive things, even when no use of the special physical organs ordinarily necessary for the purpose is made. The Paramountcy of mind is shown by the fact that an object is not perceived unless the mind gives its attention. So, in the Bṛhadāraṇyaka Upaniṣad it is said, "My mind was elsewhere: I did not hear." Now movement being accompanied by sound, let us suppose we could hear (which we cannot do through the individual natural ear) the sound produced by the generating stress or constituting forces of (say) the household fire; then the sound so head would be the natural name of that fire. Again the sap rises in the trees. Could we hear the forces constituting this rising sap, then the sound heard would be the natural name of that vegetable function, and so on Natural name in its purest sense may therefore be defined as the sound produced by the generating stress (Śakti) or constituting forces of a thing, not as apprehended by this ear or that (which apprehends within limits and subject to conditions) but by what may be called the supreme and Infinite Ear which apprehends unconditionally sound, which is sound as it is. By Supreme Ear is meant the power (Śakti) of apprehending sound in itself or as such, without subjection to the varying conditions of Time, Place (*i.e.*, Plane) and Person. It is that which hears causal stress of a thing as such or unconditionally. Then the natural name of a thing is that sound which the Supreme Ear hears Natural language in its highest sense is a language of natural names only. In this sense no language below the absolute plane can be such. In this sense even the Vedic language and its Mahāmantra "Om" is not natural language.

The relative ear does not hear such stress unconditionally. To it therefore a thing has no natural name. In this connection we must distinguish between the sound accompanying causal stress and the sound which a thing gives forth under the action of stimuli. The latter may be heard, but the former not. Fire or heat acting upon various things may produce various sounds which the ordinary relative ear, hears, but its causal stress is experienced as a sound which a Yogī alone hears.

Nevertheless there may be according to the Śāstra what is called an approximate natural name, that is the sound of the causal stress heard by a Yogi and transmitted imperfectly by him. We say 'imperfectly', because it is transmitted by an imperfect agent as a sound which can be heard by the gross ear. Prajāpati hears the causal sound by his Supreme Ear (not gross or physical) and utters it by His Supreme Tongue to His Sādhaka who, not yet himself possessing the Supreme Ear, hears it a little imperfectly. In him the primordial sound is somewhat veiled. By Sādhanā he either attains the Supreme Ear or stops short of it. In the former case he is like Prajāpati hmself. In the latter case he communicates by his relative "tongue" the imperfectly heard primaeval sound to his disciple (Śiṣya) who can by Yoga either verify the archetypal sound, or falls short of it. In this way the primordial sounds descend down to our relative planes, where the natural sounds, that is, causal sounds of many objects, are not represented at all, and those that are represented are so, suitable to conditions of relative ears and relative tongues. According to the Mantra-Śāstra the Bīja Mantras represent approximately natural names. Thus, the causal stress of fire is a sound heard by the Yogi which is said to be represented for the ordinary relative ear as the sound or

Bīja "Ram" (रँ). Vital function under different stimuli produces various sounds, some of which the ordinary ear hears, but the causal sound of vital function as breathing is represented by the Prāṇa-Bīja "Haṁsa" and so on. If attention is paid to breathing it will be found that the outward breath is in the form of the letter Ha and the indraw breath of Sa. It is not possible to indraw the breath and say the letter Ha, but it is pushed forth by the outward breath. And so, with "Om." The creative energising out of which this world evolves is Śabda and it is an immense sound (Nāda) to the Supreme Ear as uttered by the Supreme Tongue which is also Nāda. But no finite ear can hear it perfectly and no finite tongue can utter it perfectly. The sound which has descended to us as "Om" cannot therefore be a natural name of the creative process in the full sense; but having descended through the Mānasaputras and a line of Gurus each of whom more or less closely approximated to the pure sound in his personal experience, it is practical taken as an *approximate* natural name of the initial creative action. It is an open continuous sound, uninterrupted by any consonant which clips it, vanishing as it were upward in the Nādabindu which is placed on the vowel. The same observations apply to Ham (हँ), Yam (यँ), Ram (रँ), Hamsaḥ (हँसः), and other Bījas.

So much for "natural name" in the pure sense and approximate sense of the term.

The term "natural" in this connection can however be interpreted in five different senses:

(1) Sound as produced by causal stress. Śabda is stress which may or may not reach the normal of consciousness. If two things are affecting one another, then the name for

the total mutual action is stress, of which the respective actions of each of those things are the elements or partials or components. Thus, we have stress for three things, for four things, and so on. Ultimately we reach universal stress which is an infinite system of correlated forces. A particular thing may be defined as a partial experience of this infinite system which has been well called by Professor P.N. Mukhopādhyāya (to whom I am indebted in the matter here discussed) "fact section". This experience is Jīva. The infinite system is however never really finitized by these partials. When the stress between one such partial and another touches the normal of consciousness in either or both, we may have under circumstances and within certain limits sensation of sound in either or both. The stress is Śabda and the sound is Dhvani. It is stress or Śabda which constitutes a thing. Whether this Śabda is followed or accompanied by a certain Dhvani or not will depend upon *(a)* the magnitude of its action in relation to a percipient subject, and *(b)* upon the condition of the percipient's perceptive organs. Hence, in order that the sound of a thing's constituent stress may be heard, the rates of vibration of the air must be such and such, the ears and brain must be such and such and so forth. Thus, most objects of experience, though influencing the individual, do not express themselves in sound *to him* such as the earth, rocks, sun, moon, and stars. Sound as produced by causal stress and apprehended by the Supreme Ear and uttered by the Supreme Tongue is natural name in its pure sense and in this sense none of our sounds ae natural. If by this approximate 'natural name' of a thing we mean its sound (that is, the sound produced in us by its causal stress) as apprehended by the relative ear to which it is revealed, then most things have no natural names to us, though they may have to other beings with different perceptive conditions. A being who has an experience of the causal stress itself and whose ears (gross or subtle) can respond to it in any form (*i.e.,* whatever be the rates of vibration of air and ether) knows the natural names of all things. Such a Being is Prajāpati Himself and Souls that resemble Him. Hence, the natural names of such things are revealed through Vākya which, though the Jīva a not completely verify now, he may progressively verify by peronal experience, and ultimately completely verify by personal experience too. In this sense only do Śruti and Āgama, that is the Tantra Śāstras, give the natural names of Artha, sensuous or super-sensuous. The test of a natural name is this – If "Supreme or Absolute Ear" be defined as that which hears causal stress of a thing as such unconditionally, then the natural name of a thing is that sound the Supreme Ear hears. The relative ear does not hear this and therefore to it this has no natural name.

(2) Sound as produced by causal stress is projected on to our planes, with necessary limitations, through Mānasaputras and others. This is *approximate* natural language, such as the Mantras Om, Ham, Ram, and the like; it constitutes one stratum of the Vedic language. In this case the pure sound is represented by a sound capable of being heard by the relative ear. The Yogī who hears the Mantra "Om" does not hear it as the sound "Om", but as a sound which the relative ear can hear as "Om". "Om" is thus only gross sound which approximtes to the real sound only so far as the gross relative ear permits. The pure sound is thus represented by its nearet gross equivalent.

(3) A thing, such as a conch shell or an animal, may under the action of external forces give/ forth variable sounds of certain kinds. This may be perceived by us and

we ordinarily call it its natural sound, and sometimes name it after it as "cuckoo" or "crow." But it is not the sound produced be the "causal stress" (which may be reduced to the motions of electrons and therefore unperceived except by the Yogi). Hence, we must distinguish between the sound produced by causal stress, and the sound which a thing gives forth under the action of stimuli such as the crackle (another onomatopoeic name) of fire when wood is thrown on it. The latter may be heard but the former not. These names, "cuckoo" and so forth, are practically regarded as natural names, though according to the definition they are not. Such names enter into all language, Vaidika and others. Fire or heat acting upon various things may produce various sound which the relative gross ear hears. But its causal stress produces, it is said, the sound Ram (रं), which Bīja Mantra a Yogi alone hears. Vital function under different stimuli is producing various sounds in the body, some of which may be heard, but the causal stress in the form of vital function is represented by the Mantra "Haṁsa" and so on. Prajāpati (as above stated) hears the causal sound or Pure Natural Name by His Supreme Ear (not gross or physical) and utters it by His Supreme Tongue to His Sādhaka, who, not yet possessing the absolute ear, heas it only imperfectly. This, as pointed out before, is the approximate natural name. The Primordial Sound is thus somewhat veiled in him. By Sādhanā he either attains the Absolute Ear or stops short of it. In the former case he is like Prajāpati Himself. In the latter case he communicates by his relative tongue the imperfectly heard Primaeval sound to his Śiṣya, who can either by Yoga himself verify the archetypal sound, or fall short of it. In this way the Primordial Sounds descend down to our relative palnes where *(a)* the natural or causal sounds of many objects are not represented at all, and *(b)* those that are represented are so represented suitably to conditions of relative ears and relative tongues. But these approximate natural names must be distinguished from what are popularly called natural names (in the third class), which are not sounds of the causal stress but are due to the action of external forces on a particular object which is constituted of the causal stress, the sound of which is the true natural name, pure or approximate.

(4) There is then a class of secondary natural names, that is, those which are not, in the primary sense, purely or approximately natural, as sound of causal stress, not natural in the onomatopoeic sense, but which are secondarily natural in that they are out of elements of sounds which are primarily (though approximately) natural.

The Causal Stress when striking the ear produces sound, when striking the eye produces light and colour; and when striking other sense organs produces other kinds of sensation. The stress or constituting force is one and this is Śabda; but it manifests itself differently to the different sense organs. If then, instead of calling a thing in terms of its sound, it is desired to express it in terms of its other manifestation (sensations) to us, we want to state its relations to other perceptive faculties, how in such cases can this be expressed? The "natural sound" in its primary sense cannot do this; the things *as a whole* may be best represented by the natural sound, but not its touch, colour, taste and smell specifically; yet this latter representation is also important and useful. The sound of Bija Ram (रं), for example, may be the approximate natural name of Agni, but unless we can grip the casual stress of Agni itslef, it tells nothing about the attributes and relations of the thing with which we are practically concerned. Ordinarily Ram (रं), Hrim (ह्रीं), Aiṃ (ऐं) Ôm (ओं) are unmeaning. For this reason we hear talk of Mantra being "Jabber" as if any body of men in the world's history deliberately occupied themselves with what was in fact meaningless jabber. That is not necessarily to say that the theory is correct, but that is not absurd and without sense as supposed. Now-a-days when the Śāstra is nearly lost, it may be so in those cases where the Mantras are said without understanding. These Bījas may be made to *denote* things or processes, but ordinarily unless it is possible to penetrate into the kernel itself) they do not *connote* qualities or attributes of things; and hence are what J.S. Mill calls non-connotative terms. They are however according to Śāstra realy connotative. Hence in the average plane man requires other terms besides Ram (रं) to represent Agni. Suppose we take the quality "burning" (Dāhikā-Śakti). Then in order to express Agni it terms of this quality we may do (or it might have been done for us by linguistic tradition). either of two things: *(a)* Taking the letters (Varṇas) and remembering that each represents the natural sound of a certain thing or process, it is possible to make such a permutation and combination of them (taken two or more at a time) that "burning" a be represented by the combination thus formed. Here a compound term is formed (either by ourselves or by tradition) by the collection in due order or elementary approximate natural sounds (*viz.*, the letters). To express the same attribute more than one such combination may be possible. *(b)* Or there may exist already simple roots (Dhātu) formed in their turn either by the combination of elementary natural sounds or in the onomatopoeic fashion *(see 3 ante)*, which with proper prefixes and suffixes can be made to connote "burning" and thus evolve the term Agni. Here again, to express the same quality or relation, different words may be evolved by ourselves or by tradition. Thus there are synonyms or Paryāya. These secondary names may be arranged in grades in accordance with the degree of their closeness to primary names. Hindu philologists distinguish between Śaktyārtha and Lakṣyārtha, that is, Abhidhāśakti and Lakṣaṇāśakti and classify each.

This in itself is a vast subject. It is sufficient to say here that words have two Vṛttis, namely, Abhidhā and Lakṣaṇā. The first is Śakti in the sense that it compels the understanding of the thing denoted by a word. The object "cow" is described by and is the Vākyārtha of the word of Śabda "cow". The second only approximately denotes the object (Artha). It, so to speak, leads the hearer to the door but does not enter. Lakṣya is that denoted by Lakṣaṇā, which means a sign, that is, object denoted by a sign. Thus, the world Brahman is not Vākyārtha of the Supreme Brahman (Nirguṇa-Parabrahman), but it is Vākyārtha of the Saguṇa-Brahman. The word Brahman is only Lakṣyārtha of the Supreme Brahman.

We may say that these secondary names ae not indifferent as to their expressiveness of the qualities and relations of things. Some do it better and more closely than othes Agni, Vahni, Hutāśana, and other names of Five are connected with the Bīja Mantra Ram (रं) in this sense, that while the latter approximately represents the natural name of the things *as a whole,* the former express the attributes and relations of the thing specifically regarded. Hence, whilst "Ram" (रं) is apparently non-connotative, the former are connotative.

(5) Primary and secondary names may be combined in such order (Krama) and metre or harmony (Chandaḥ) that by vitalizing one another, these in combination may appear as an approximate name of a thing or process. In this manner a Vaidika or Tāntrika Mantra (consisting of several words) may, it is said, naturally denote a Devatā or a function.

Beside these five sense of natural sound of which pure and absolute sense is that first given, there is non-natural or artificial sound or name, which means an arbitrary name taken at random to denote a thing such as some proper names.

The test of natural name is it is said, twofold and capable of experimental verification: (1) Whether the causal stress of a thing makes a sound (say the Bīja Yam) may be verified by Yoga. The thing being given, a sound evolves. (2) This sound repeatedly and harmonically uttered, that is in Japa of Mantra, must create or project into perception the corresponding thing. This too is capable of experimental verification. In this case the sound being given, a thing evolves.

## Chapter 9

# VAIDIKA ŚABDA

The Vedas communicate the natural names of some things, subject to the necessary limitations involved in their representation suitably to conditions of relative ears and tongues. No Vedic word is an absolute natural name. This cannot be. Just as in the Tantra Śāstra we find Bīja mantras, which are said to represent approximately natural names, scattered here and there in a varied mass of ordinary Sanskrit which *remotely* represent natural sounds, so is the case in Śruti. There are, it is said, closely approximate natural names, combined according to natural laws of harmony (Chandaḥ), forming Mantras which are irresistibly connected with their esoteric Arthas (Devatās); but these are commented upon, explained, applied and so forth in passages which do not express natural names in this sense. On analyzing these Mantras themselves, both Vaidika and Tāntrika, there are found some sounds which are not and other which are in natural use. Here each word in the Mantra does not necessarily stand for an approximate natural sound (that is produced by causal stress). These tendencies to the archetypal forms may be varying. But in the Mantra it is their order of combination and rhythm that mainly counts. Thus, *as a whole* the Mantra may be the approximate natural name of a Devatā or function. Its creative and projecting power lies in the two things: *(a)* The mutual aiding and inhibiting of the sounds in the Chandaḥ; the veils of the individual sounds are removed by the order of their collocation. Here the "Curves" of sound are constructive and not destructive. *(b)* The cumulative effect of the repetition of sounds and strings of sounds also may produce the aforesaid result. By repetition is there summation of stimuli.

So that by analyzing the Vaidika language we get this:

(1) Certain approximate natural names, standing alone or in groups, such as Om, Ham, Haṁsaḥ, Svāhā and so on. These are fundamental sounds or primaries.

(2) Certain combinations of sounds which, though not natural distributively, naturalize each other in and by the order and harmony of the combinations. Thus, arise Mantras which become approximate natural names of objects and processes. These may gather creative momentum by repetition.

(3) A large mass of sounds or names used to explain the meanings and applications and results of the above which need not be natural names in the above sense.

Hence, it follows that the Veda which is heard by the gross ear and spoken by the gross tongue is not a system of natural names. It is however claimed to be a system of approximate natural names in varying degree. The Veda of the Absolute Ear and Tongue is a system of absolute natural names.

Then is the relative and approximate Veda the

primordial, universal, unitary language? The answer must be in the negative, but in the case of the first class of names it is amongst all languages most nearly so upon the basis of the theory here dealt with. In the second class of names it is less so and in the third it is least so.

There are four different strata in Vaidika experience. First there is the nameless Supreme Experience; then the three above described. Śabda, Artha and Pratyaya are absolutely connected in the absolute plane but progressively less so in the lower strata. The natural connection of Śabda and Artha means that the latter being given, the former is there whether audible by us or not; the former being given, the latter is created or projected. But we must distinguish between what is here called natural name and what often receives that term. Thus, a conch-shell is blown. What is the natural name here? Not the sound which we may make it give forth, for these are produced by our effort and vary, but the sound of the causal stress which generates and keeps together the shell. The blowing sound is only practically natural. What is the basis of the Vaidika theory? In the final resort experimental verification is the test as in Āyurveda.

Besides the division of name into natural and arbitrary, of the former into absolute and relative and of the latter into primary and secondary, name may be classified according as it is *(a)* typal or *(b)* variational, as for example of the first the Sanskrit word "Gauḥ" and of the second the English word "Cow". Language according to Indian notions is not something arbitrary and invented. No man ever invented a language. Volapuk, Esperanto and the like are mere combinations of the sounds of pre-existing language. The Vaidika Language was revealed by Īśvara to the Mānasaputras and others and through them to men. This itself as ordinary world (Laukika) speech became corrupted and when rectified was called Sanskrit, that which has been purified. A distinction must therefore be made between the original Vaidika language and current Sanskrit in which however there are words which also occur in the Vedas. Now, the ordinary orthodox view in that there is a typal or standard language and that this is the universal language of which all other are variations.

Whenever a typal standard name has a variation, the following questions arises: *(a)* When does that variation appear and for how long does it last? *(b)* In what places or planes does that variation arise? *(c)* In what persons or groups or persons does that variation appear or for whom does it arise?

Briefly stated a variation is always subject to conditions of time, place and person. Then a variation may be *(a)* common (Sāmānya), or *(b)* special (Viśeṣa). The former is what comprises a whole class of objects. Thus, "Cow" is a sound variation appearing in a whole class of persons; Gāi or Gābhī with another class of persons namely Bengalis. The special variation is one appearing in an individual object. Thus, one individual pronounces the word "Cow" slightly differently from what another does. Every person in fact has his own way of pronunciation.

Again a variation may be *(c)* voluntary, or *(d)* involuntary. The former is due to the free will of a peron or a group of persons; the latter is not so.

The typal sounds are eternal. They are latent however during cosmic sleep (Suṣupti). The Sāmānya variations of the typal sounds are not eternal in the sense and to the extent that the types are; they appear when the conditions of their expressions appear, and disappear when these go.

If we take these four divisions two at a time we get six possible combinations – (1) Common and special variation, (2) Common and voluntary variation, (3) Common and involuntary variation, (4) Special and voluntary variation, (5) Special and involuntary variation, (6) Voluntary and involuntary variation. Of these, the first and last are impossible being self-contradictory. Of the remaining for the second is not eternal. In so far as a common variation is due to the free will of a person of persons it has an absolute beginning; for if it be simply the repetition of a previous cosmic order, then it is not a free act but predetermined. The third class are eternal but not to the extent the types are. Comparing them with the latter we can say that they are passing, though recurrently. Types too are recurrently passing during creation (Sṛṣṭi) and dissolution (Laya), but their cycles of recurrence are larger. They are eternal in the full sense in so far as they approximte to their type. For the same reasons given as regards the second class, the fourth class is not eternal. The fifth class is not eternal in so far as it is brought about by the part volitions of persons. The whole questions is however of so great difficulty, that it is difficult to fully unravel the tangle in which we find it. How and where are we to draw the line between voluntary and non-voluntary, between absolute will and finite will? Is again the cosmic cycle exactly recurrent or not? From a practical point of view we may perhaps not greatly err if we say: (1) that the general plan and the types are recurrent and eternal; (2) that the common variations are recurrent and eternal subject to more conditons; and (3) that the special variations are practically not eternal.

It is claimed for the Veda that it is a system of standard and typal and therefore natural names. But natural name has, as already explained, various meanings. There are therefore different strata of natural names in Veda. Name may be either *(a)* natural or *(b)* conventional, that is arbitrary. With the latter we are not here concerned. Natural name may be *(c)* Absolute, that is, as apprehended unconditionally or *(d)* Relative, that is, as apprehended subjected to varying conditions. Veda as a manifestation is not the first. Absolute name is only heard on the unconditioned plane. We are therefore concerned with the relative natural name. This may be either *(e)* primary, or *(f)* secondary. The first is the causal stress, thing or functioning as a whole, as represented approximately to the relative ear and is again twofold as *(g)* the elementary sounds of letters (Varṇa), and *(h)* as compound sounds, such as are found in Bījas and roots (Dhātu). In the Yoga Bhāṣya, that is Vyāsa's commentary on the Pātañjala-Darśana (3, 17), it is said: *Tatra vagvarṇeṣvarthavatīti.* According to this, each letter is intrinsically *Sarvābhīdhāna-śakti-prachita,* that is, possessing the power (Śakti) to denote and connote all object (Artha). For, as the Viśvasāra Tantra says: "What is not here is nowhere" *(Yannehāsti na tat kvacit).* A letter (Varṇa) is the whole cosmos in miniature. One Varṇa differs from another in the relative latency of the univese of Artha invovled in it, the universe being the same in both. The come to denote special Arthas by virtue of the order (Krama) of their collocation *(Kramānuro'vhinorthasaṅketenāvacchinnaḥ).* Their particular meanings of Saṅketa are thus due not to intrinisic difference but to the order (Karma) in grouping.

In the relative secondary natural name, functioning is specifically represented.The specific attributes and relations ae given. These again may *(i)* appeal directly to the ear, and be either *(j)* self-produced, or *(k)* induced or excited; or *(l)* they may appeal to other senses and either *(m)* consist of single words which are combinations of Varṇas themselves, or Dhātus, or *(n)* of combination of words which may be either harmonic, or *(p)* non-harmonic but Kramika.

The first and main division of this scheme is into natural and arbitrary. As to this it is to be observed that all names are made up of elements of sounds or letters (Varṇa). But to naturally connote an Artha, the Varṇas cannot be arbitrarily selected and arranged. To naturally represent a given Artha, certain Varṇas which are in some way connected with that Artha must be chosen and arranged according to a certain order (Krama). A word in which such selection and order are not in evidence is a conventional name, *e.g.*, a telegraphic code (though even in this there is a designed Krama), many proper names, and algebraical symbols. The Krama of the Vaidika Śabdas is said to be eternal. To explain this further; let it be supposed that it is desired to evolve a certain Artha, say an atom of hydrogen. A certain number of moving electrons arranged in a certain order must be chosen. The number and order being different we have a different kind of atom. Suppose again it is desired to evolve water. Two atoms of hydrogen and one atom of oxygen must be taken and so arranged by electric or other influence that a molecule $H_2O$ is evolved. So, also is the case of any compound material substance. The Varṇas are in relation to ordinary sounds, what the atoms are in relation to material substances. The atoms can be aggregated into molecules and things only in certain definite proportions and not arbitrarily; so with the Varṇas and natural words.

Further as radio-activity and other facts prove, an atom is a system of moving electrons. It is not therefore absolutely simple and elementary. Similarly, what we recognise as the Varṇas may not be absolutely simple or elementary sounds; they are however so for all practical purposes, as the atoms are for all chemical purposes. There are about 75 different atoms but the electrons which make them up are of the same kind; their number and arrangement account for the differences of Oxygen, Hydrogen, Carbon and other atoms. In the same way the garland or rosary of letters (Varṇamālā) may be evolved out of the same kind of elementary sound by differential aggregation. It may be that the basic elementary sound is the uninterrupted Anāhata Dhvani finitised into various points (Śabdabindu) or atoms (Śabdaparamāṇu) of sound.

So again taking any curve, say a circle-- its circumference may be regarded as the sum of an infinite number of small bits of straight lines: these are the elements. Any ritualistic diagram, such as, say, the Sarvatobhadramaṇḍala, or a Yajña or Homa a be similarly regarded. Hence a natural word may be compared to, and in the case of a Bīja Mantra can be represented by, a diagram (Yantra) which in that case, becomes the graph of the Bīja in question, or of causal stress of which that Bīja is the acoustic manifestation and counterpart. Lastly an electron is an unit charge of electricity, which after all may be only an element of ether in stress. This element of ether in stress is Paraśabda Paramāṇu according to the definition given; and as heard by the relative ear it is Śabda Paramāṇu. So that this last and the electron are naturally connected. Hence, Śabdas (aggregates or Śabda Paramāṇus) and Arthas (aggregates of electrons) are connected. But as electrons aggregated at random will not make a natural Artha, so Śabda-Paramāṇus aggregated at random do not make a natural name.

Physically the vibrations represented by a Varṇa can be resolved into component vibrations which are harmonic motions. As Fourier's theorem gives it, a complex harmonic motion may be analysed into simple harmonic motions. All the ordinary letters are complex harmonic motions; and physically speaking a simple harmonic motion is Śabdaparamāṇu. Physiologically each single vibration acting on the ear, nerves and brain centres, produces a single pulse of cerebral agitation, a single, "nerve-shock," admits of "more or less," so that the primary group gives approximate natural names *par excellence,* and the secondary group gives in varying degree approximate natural names. Within the secondary group the class *(h),* that is Mantras, represent the closest approximation to natural names.

The test of a natural name is ultimately expertimental, that is the sound (Śabda) being given, the object (Artha) is evolved: the object being given the sound is evolved. In absolute natural names these relations are at once established. In relative names they are established in varying measure through Krama and Japa. Ultimately the question whether Veda is a system of approximate natural names is thus a question of fact.

This leads to a consideration of the claim made by Veda that it is the standard language, an eternal system of natural means of which all others are variations. Hitherto we have dealt with the matter philosophically. We now approach the historical and philological question. The two must be kept apart. Much may be said in favour of the philosophical theory, namely, that the relation between Śabda and Artha is eternal, that there is some Śabda which is the natural name of the Artha, that this natural language is the standard language, that all others are a staying away from and variation of the true norms and so on. But the point now arises as a question of fact, *viz.*, assuming all that is said in theory, is the Vaidika language, that is the language in which the Vedas are as they exist to-day, the eternal standard langauge? The orthodox affirm that it is, and that the sound "Gauḥ" is the natural name and standard representation in speech of the object "Cow" for all eternity. That the relation of Śabda and Artha is eternal and that some Śabda may be natural names of objects are philosophically probable. It is however an entirely different matter when it is affirmed that the Vaidika speech, as existing today is that language. Philologists and historians will deny this for they will point out changes in that speech and make claim as regards priority in age for the language of other peoples. Assuming that there was, as the Biblical tradition runs, once, a universal language, it will be denied that the Vaidika language as known to us today its that. It will moreover be shown that even in Veda itself there is evidence to the contrary. Thus, it has been argued that according to the Śatapatha Brāhmaṇa the original language was monosyllabic. With this question of philology and history I am not here concerned. But the ultimate philosophical question is, "Who if any one, first said that *this* sound meant *that* thing?" The Indian answer is that the relation of the word and the object denoted are eternal and not a conventional thing, that there is a system of Natural Names, whatever in fact that may be. This stands clear of the claim made for the Vedic language, as it exists to-day, that it is that system.

# Chapter 10

# THE TATTVAS

A Knowledge of the Mantra Śāstra involves an understanding of the thirty-six Śaiva-Śakta-Tattvas. Thus, it is said that Śakti is in Śākti-tattva, Nāda in Sadākhya Tattva, Bindu in Īśvara-Tattva. What then are these Tattvas to which reference is made both in the Śaiva and Śākta-Tantras? Unless these be fully understood, no progress in knowledge of the Mantra Science as here described may be expected.

The Śaiva-Śākta Śāstras call experience as Śakti by the term Vimarśa. Experience has two elements-- the "I" (Aham) and the "This" (Idam), the subjective-knowing aspect (Grāhaka) of the Self and the objective or known (Grāhya) aspect of the Self. For it must be remembered that an object is nothing but the one Self appearing through Māyā as non-Self to Itself as subject. At base the experienced is nothing but the experiencer: though this is not realised until the bonds of Māyā which make subject and object appear to be different are loosened. The "I" side of experience is that in which the Self rests in the light of one's own Self without looking towards another *(Ananyonmukhaḥ ahaṁ-pratyayaḥ);* just as the experience (Vimarśa) which looks towards another is called – *Idaṁ*

*(Yastu anyonmukhaḥ so idaṁ iti pratyaya)*. But this "Other" can only be the Self, for there is in reality nothing but the one Self. It is experienced, however, differently. In the Supreme state it exists with the 'Ahaṁ' in a mingled union; in the Pure experience between this state and Māyā the "Other" is recognised to be an aspect of the self; in impure experience governed by Māyā the object appears to be different from the limited self.

Experience again is, at its two poles, Perfect Experience of the Perfect Universe and the Limited experience of the three worlds of reincarnation. Between these two extremes there are intermediate experiences marking the stages whereby the one pure Spirit or Consciousness involves itself in matter.

The Hermetic maxim says: "As above so below". Similarly, the Viśvasāra Tantra says: "What is here is there, what is not here is nowhere." *(Yad ihāsti tadanyatra, yan nehāsti na tat kvacit)*. Śaiva doctrine says: "That which appears without, only so appears because it exists within." *(Vartamānāvabhāsānāṁ bhāvānāṁ avabhāṣaṇaṁ antahsthitavatāṁ eva ghatage bahirātmānā)*. "The manifestation of those things which presently appear, happen in the form of external things because they exist within." Therefore what exists in our experience, evolved from the supreme also exists in the Supreme experience though in another way." The Supreme experience called Parāsaṁvit is not a mere abstract objectless knowing (Jñāna). It is the coalescence into one undivided unity of the "I" and the "This," that is, of Śiva and the supreme unmainfested Śakti. The former is the illuminating (Prakāśā) knowing aspect and the latter that Vimarśa aspect which is "the known." But here the two are undistinguishably one. This supreme experience has the immediacy of feedling. It is Bliss (Ānanda) which is defined as "Resting in the Self" (Svarūpaviśrānti). In the Māyika world the Self concerns itself with what it takes to be the non-Self. Here, the Universe which is the object of Śiva's experience is the Perfect Universe, that is Surpeme Śakti which is but another aspect of Himself as consciousness. She is beautifully called in the Parāprāveśikā: "The Heart of the Supreme Lord" *(Hṛdayaṁ parameśituḥ)*. For the Māyika experiencer *(Māyā pramātṛ)* the universe is the manifested world of objects seen as different from himself. Supreme Śiva and Śakti exist in mutual embrace and love. "Bliss is supreme love" *(Niratiśayapremāspadatvaṁ ānandatvaṁ)*. The Supreme state is described by the Bṛhadāraṇyaka-Upaniṣad in the words: "He indeed was just as man and woman in embrace" *(Sā ha etāvān āsa yathā stripuṁāmsau samparivaktau);* when there is neither within nor without, when all thought of lover, loving and loved are forgotten in the joy of blissful unity. The experience is spaceless, timeless, full, all-knowing, almighty. This is the state of Śiva without Kalā (Niṣkalā) or Paramaśiva. This is Parāsaṁvit which is beyond all Tattvas (Tattvātitā). As the Perfect Universe it is called Parānāda (Supreme "Sound") and Parā-vāk (Supreme "Speech"). Paramaśiva is an experience of the Perfect Universe, that is, of Parānāda *(Amarṣa parānādagarbhaḥ)*. Such universe is pure Śakti (Śakti-svarūpa).

Our worldly experience is as it were an inverted reflection of all this seen in the causal waters of Māyā. Māyā-Śakti is the sense of difference (Bhedabuddhi) which makes the Puruṣa, who is subject to is, see the Universe in the form of an observing self with a multitude of objects conceived of as being outside of and separate from it. In the Māyika world each self excludes the other selves. In the Supreme experience there is one Self experiencing Itself. The Puruṣa is Conscious, subject to Māyā and the five Kañcukas which are limiting forces contracting the natural perfections of the Self. Thus, the Perfect state is formless, the world state is with form: the first is spaceless, timeless, all-pervading, the latter is the reverse and so forth. Kāla produces limitations of time. Niyati destroys independence (Svatantratā), regulating the Puruṣa as to what he should or should not do at any given moment of time. The Supreme experience is full and in want of nothing (Pūrṇa). Rāga Kañcuka creates interest in objects as something other than the self and therefore desire for them. The all-knowingness (Sarvajñatā) and all-mightiness (Sarvakartṛtā) of the Surpeme Śiva are circumscribed through the action of Vidyā and Kalā, and the Puruṣa becomes a "little knower" and a "little doer."

The intermediate Tattvas next described explain the process how from the creative aspect of the Perfect Experienced the imperfect World-experience comes into being. Śiva has two aspects in one of which he is Transcendent and in the other creative and Immanent. The creative (Sakala) aspect of the Supreme Śiva (Niṣkala-Paramaśiva) is called Śiva-tattva, wherein is the Śakti called Unmanī. Through operation in His creative aspect Śiva becomes His own object as the Manifested Universe. For in truth there is nothing else than Paramaśiva. Śivatattva is the first creative movement (Prathama spanda) of the Unmoving Paramaśiva. Śakti-tattva is only the negative aspect of, or in, the Śiva-tattva. The function of Śakti is to negate *(Niṣedhavyāpārūpā śaktiḥ)*. She who is Consciousness negates Herself, that is, deprives experience of the element of objectivity which is Itself as Parā-Śakti. There is thus left only the other side of experience which is Prakāśamātra, that is, what we should call the "I" (Aham) side of experience when regarded as consisting of an "I" and "This" (Idam). Because in this experience there is not trace of objectivity whatsoever either of such objectivity latent or expressed as exists in the Supreme or other lower and derived form of experience, the Śiva Tattva is called "the very void" *(Śūnyātiśūnya)*. It is the experience in which the self is not looking towards any other *(Ananyonmukhaḥ ahamprtayayaḥ)*. The objective content, so to speak, of Consciousness is a mere negation. It is Śūnya because it is empty of obejctive content. Śakti-tattva is also spoken of as the Will (Icchā) of Śiva as yet Unmanifest and inseparable from him *(Santatasamavāyinī)*.

This account of Śakti's operation is extraordinarily subtle, explaining as it does how the supreme unitary experience is also the first source of dual experience. Such latter experience and the stages whereby the latter is fully developed can only be produced by positing an aspect in which there is a breaking up of the unitary experience. This is done by first blotting out from the Perfect experience its object or the Perfect Universe (Parā Śakti, Paranāda) thus leaving a mere subjectivity. To the subjectivity thus disengaged there is again gradually unveiled the universe at first as unmanifested and then (through Māyā) as manifested Śakti. In Para Samvit the "I" and the "This" existed as one undistinguishable unity. In Śiva Tattva through the operation of the associated Śakti Tattva, the "This" *(Idam)* is withdrawn from experience so that the "I– experience" *(Aham-vimarśa)* alone remains. To this the 'Idam' or Universe is again by degrees presented, when there is no longer an undistinguishable unity of "I" and "This" but an "I– This" in which both, though distinguishable, are yet part of the Self which eventually through Māyā-Śakti becomes an "I" *and* "This" in which the two are severed one from the other. How this occurs, the description of the remaining Tattvas explains. The Śiva-Śakti Tattva is not an emanation, because it ever remains the same whether in Creation or Dissolution. It is the seed and womb of the whole universe.

The first emanation or manifestation (Ābhāsa) of and by Consciousness is called the Sadākhya or Sadāśiva Tattva. Here, it is to be observed that the cause ever remains the same and what it was, though appearing differently in the effect. The Supreme Experience changelessly endures even though in its creative aspect it gives birth to the Universe. This Ābhāsa is like the Vivartta or Māyā-vāda, the difference between the two lying in the fact that according to the former the effect is real, and according to Śaṁkara, unreal. This difference again depends on the definition given of "reality".

Real evolution (Pariṇāma), in which when one thing is evolved into another it ceases to be what it was, exists only in the compounded products of the material world.

In Sadāśiva-Tattva there is the commencement of the first subjective formation of ideas. It is called Nimeṣa (closing of the eyes) as contrasted with Unmeṣa (opening of the eyes) of the next stage of experience. In the former the Universe as Śakti is seen only faintly. The Self hazily experiences Itself as object. It is the first step in evolution and the last in involution. Unmeṣa is the distinct blossoming (Sphuṭatvam) and externalization (Bāhyatvam) of the Universe. The "This" (Idam) is faintly perceived by the "I" (Aham) as part of the one Self, the emphasis being therefore on the "I" side of experience. Sadāśiva is He whom the Vaiṣṇavas call Mahāviṣṇu, and the Buddhists, Avalokiteśvara who sheds compassion on all. According to tradition, this is the source whence the Avatāras come. It is in this Tattva that there is what the Mantra-Śāstra calls Nāda-Śakti.

The third stage of the developing consciousness is Īśvara Tattva, externalization of the last. The Universe (Idam) is experienced by the "I" (Aham) distinctly and yet as part of, and not separate from, the one Self. As in the last experience the emphasis was on the "Aham," here it is on the "Idam." This Tattva is called Bindu in Mantra-Śāstra, and is so called because Consciousness here completely identifies itself with the Universe as unmanifested Idam, and thus subjectifies it and becomes with it a Point (Bindu) of Consciousness. Thus by way of example the mind is completely subjectified and exists for each of us as a mathematical point, though the body, to the extent to which it is not subjectified, appears as an object or extending thing.

The fourth Tattva is known as Vidyā, Sadvidyā, or Śuddhavidyā. In the experience of this stage, emphasis is equal on the "I" and the "This" *(Sāmānādhikaraṇya)*. In Śiva-Tattva there is the I-experience (Aham Vimarśa); in Sadāśiva the I-This experience (Aham idam Vimarśa); in Īśvara-Tattva the This- I experience (Idamaham Vimarśa). In each case the stress is laid on the first term. In Vidyā-Tattva there is an equality of either term in an experience which is that of the true relation of the Aham and the Idam, consisting of a synthesis (Saṁgamana) of the two on a single "basis" (Adhikaraṇa) and not on two different 'bases' according to the experience of those under the influence of Māyā (Māyāpramātṛ), thus eliminating the duality which exists in the latter experience.

By equality of the "I" and the "This", experience is in the state of readiness for the next stage in which the two are to be severed. Sadvidyā as being the intermediate stage between the pure (Śuddha) and impure (Aśuddha) Creation is called Parāparadasā. It is also spoken of an experience of difference in the form of Mantra *(Bhedābhedavimarśanātmaka-mantrarūpa)*. It is experience of difference because the Idam is separated from the Aham. It is the experience of non-difference because they are still regarded as part of one Self. The experience is compared to that of the Īśvara of the Dvaitavādins, who sees the Universe as different from Himself and yet as part of and in connection therewith. "All this is my manifestation" *(Sarvo mamāyaṁ vibhavaḥ)*. The experience is said to be in the nature of Mantra, because here we are in the region of pure spiritual ideation. As yet, there is no objective manifestation such as exists in our world. Below this Tattva it is said that there were created eight Pudgalas, that is, Jīvas in the form of knowledge (Vijñāna-rūpa) and then seven crores of Mantras and their Maṇḍalas.

At this point Māyā-Śakti intervenes and divides the Aham and Idam, and the Kañcukas or limitations of the natural perfections of Consciousness make. It subject to time and space, birth and death, limitation, and desire for object, which It now conceives of as persons and things other than Itself. This is the Puruṣa-Prakṛti-Tattva. Puruṣa in Śaiva-Śākta philosophy is the Ātma or Jīva subject to Māyā and the Kañcukas which are limiting forces whereby the Self as Pure Consciousness loses Its natural perfections.

Prakṛti is the Śāntā Śakti of Śiva in contracted form existing as the equilibrium of the Guṇas which are themselves a gross form of the Śaktis of Will (Icchā), Action (Kriyā) and Knowledge (Jñāna). All things exist in Her who is of the nature of feeling in a homogeneous mass. Puruṣa is enjoyer (Bhoktā) and Prakṛti the enjoyed (Bhogyā). The latter is at first the barest objectivity seen as different from the experiencing Self as Puruṣa. Prakṛti then differentiates into the Tattvas of Mind (Anataḥkaraṇa), Senses (Indriya), and Matter (Bhūta) which constitute our universe.

Puruṣa does not merely mean man not indeed any animal. Every single thing in the Universe is Puruṣa. Thus, an atom of sand is a Puruṣa or consciousness, indentifying itself with solidity (Pṛthivī), manifesting its limited Consciousness as atomic memory and other ways. What Consciousness thinks, that is, identifies itself with, that it becomes.

To sum up, the Supreme Experience (Parāsaṁvit) has a creative aspect (Śiva-Śakti-Tattva), which is a Consciousness of "I" (Aham-vimarśa) which gradually experiences the Universe (Idam) as part of Itself, at first faintly with predominant "I", then clearly with predominant "This", and then as equal "I and this", ready for severance by Māyā. The latter then cleaves consciousness in twain, thus setting up a dichotomy of Subject and object, though in truth the object is nothing but the Self as its own object. Lastly Śakti, as Prakṛti differentiates into the multitudinous beings which make the universe. But throughout it is the one and only Śiva whether as the Supreme Experience or as the Consciousness embodied in solid matter. Śakti, Nāda, Bindu mentioned in previous articles are Śakti Tattva, Sadākhya-Tattva and Īśvara-Tattva (here described), considered from the standpoint of the Mantra Śāstra which treats of the origin of Śabda or Sound.

With the Tattvas, the Kalās are associated. These are the forms of activity (Kriyā) of the Tattvas as Śakti. Thus Sṛṣṭi (Creation) is a Kalā of Brahmā, Pālana (Protection) is a Kalā of Viṣṇu and Mṛtyu (Death) is a Kalā of Rudra. It is, however, not always as easy to see the appropriateness of the Kalā as in the simple examples given. The Śākta Tantras speak of 94 Kalās, namely, 19 Kalās of Sadāśiva, 6 of Īśvara, 11 of Rudra, 10 of Viṣṇu, 10 of Brahmā, 10 of Fire, 12 of Sun, and 16 of Moon.

According to Saubhāgya-ratnākara the 19 Kalās of Sadāśiva are Nivṛtti, Pratiṣthā, Vidyā, Śānti, Indhikā, Dīpikā, Recikā, Mocikā, Parā, Sūkṣmāmṛtā, Jñānāmṛta, Amṛtā, Āpyāyanī, Vyāpīnī, Vyomarūpā, Mūlavidyā, Mantrakalā Mahāmantrakalā, Jyotiṣakalā.

The 6 of Īśvara are Pitā, Śvetā, Nityā, Aruṇā, Asitā, Anantā.

The 11 Rudra Kalās are Tīkṣṇā, Raudrī, Bhayā, Nidrā, Tandrā, Kṣudhā, Krodhinī, Kriyā, Utkārī, Amāyā, Mṛtyu.

The 10 of Viṣṇu are Jadā, Pālini, Śānti, Īśvarī, Rati, Kāmikā, Varadā, Halādinī, Prīṭi, Dikṣā.

The 10 of Brahmā are Sṛṣṭi, Ṛddhi, Smṛti, Medhā, Kānti, Lakṣmī, Dyuti, Sthirā, Sthiti, Siddhi.

The 10 of Fire are Dhūmrārci, Ūṣmā, Jvalini, Jvālini, Visphuliṅginī, Suṣrī, Surūpā, Kapilā, Havyavahā, Kavyavahā.

The 12 of Sun are Tāpini, Tāpini, Dhūmrā, Marīci, Jvālinī, Rucī, Suṣumnā, Bhogadā, Viśvā, Bodhinī, Dhāriṇī, Kṣamā.

The 16 of Moon are Amṛtā, Mānadā, Pūṣā, Tuṣṭi, Puṣṭi, Rati, Dhṛti, Śaśini, Candrikā, Kānti, Jyotsnā, Śrīḥ, Prīti, Aṅgadā, Pūrṇā, Pūṇāmṛtā.

Out of these 50 are Mātṛkā-Kalās which manifest through the Paśyanti, Madhyamā, and Vaikharī stages (Bhāva) as the gross letters (Varṇa). The 50 Mātṛkā-Kalās are given in the same account as follows: Nivṛtti, Pratiṣtha, Vidyā, Śāntī, Indhikā, Dīpikā, Mocikā, Parā, Sūkṣmā, Sūkṣmāmṛtā, Jñānāmṛtā, Āpyāyani, Vyāpini, Vyomarūpā, Anantā, Sṛṣṭi, Ṛddhi, Smṛti, Medhā, Kānti, Lakṣmī, Dyuti, Sthirā, Siddhi, Jadā, Pālini, Śānti, Aiśvaryā, Rati, Kāmikā, Varadā, Āhlādini, Prītiḥ, Dīrghā, Tikṣṇā, Raudrī, Bhayā, Nidrā, Tandrā, Kṣudhā, Krodhinī, Kriyā, Utkārī, Mṛtyurūpā, Pītā, Śveta, Asitā, Anantā. These 94 Kalās are worshipped in the Wine Jar which holds Tārā dravamayī, or the Saviour=Mother in liquid form. She Herself, is called Saṁvit-Kalā and so the Yoginīhṛdaya-Tantra says—

*Deśakālapadārthātma yad yad vastu yathā yathā,*
*Tattadrūpeṇa yā bhāti taṁ śraye saṁvidaṁ kalām.*

# Chapter 11

# ŚAKTI – POTENCY TO CREATE

In the previous chapter I have referred to Śakti, Nāda, Bindu. In this and the two next I will deal in greater detail with each of these three concepts of Śakti. One of the clearest accounts known to me of the evolution of Śakti is that given in the authoritative Tāntrika=Prakaraṇa called Śāradā (also spelt Sāradā) Tilaka by Lakṣmaṇācārya. This work was formerly of great authority in Bengal. Its value is much increased by the commentary of Rāghava Bhatta. As this work with its commentary is of prime importance, and is cited throughout the following chapters, I may here note the following account which Lakṣmaṇācārya gives of himself at its close. Mahābala a great sage was succeeded by his son Ācāryapaṇḍita, a Deśika (Tāntrika-Guru). His son Śrīkṛṣna-Deśika had a son Lakṣmaṇa-Deśika who wrote the Śāradā-Tilaka. Rāghava, in his commentary called Padārthādarśa, says that Lakṣmaṇa was the disciple of Utpalācārya, who was the disciple of Somānanda, who was the disciple of Vasugupta, who was the disciple of Śrīkaṇṭha. This is the Gurupaṅgkti of Lakṣmaṇa. His disciple was the great *Kāśmirian* Abhinava-Gupta, the author of Paramārthasāra. The latter's disciple was Kṣemarāja, the author of the Śivasūtra Vimarśini. The date generally assigned to Abhinava-Gupta is the eleventh century. Therefore. Akṣaya Kumāra Maitra, Director of the Varendra Anusaṁdhāna Samiti, who has supplied me with these details of the Gurus and Śiṣyas of the author, concludes that the Śāradā was written at the end of the tenth or beginning of the eleventh century. Rāghava mentions 1510 A.D. as the age of his commentary. Taking this to be the Vikrama Saṁvat we get 1454 A.D. as its date. These details serve another purpose. There are persons who insist on a total disconnection between the Śaiva and Śākta-Tantras. Lakṣmaṇācārya was a member of the Kāśmirian Śaiva School, and his work was, as I have started, of great authority among the Bengal Śāktas.

The Śāradā (Chapter, I, verse 7) says: "From Sakala-Parameśvara vested with the wealth of Sat, Cit, Ānanda issued Śakti; from Śakti came Nāda; and from Nāda issued Bindu."

*Saccidānandavibhavāt sakalāt parameśvarāt,*
*Asicchaktis tato ṅādo nādād bindu saṁudbhavāḥ.*

Parameśvara is here Śiva-Tattva. He is Sakala, because He is with the creative Kalā or Śakti. As already explained Śakti, when Vyaṣṭirūpā, that is individualised, is called Kalā. Śiva is always with Śakti. But in the supreme state, Śakti is unmanifest and exists in Her own (Svarūpa) form as Being-Consciousness-Bliss (Saccidānandamayī, Cidrūpiṇī), undistinguishable from Śiva. Sakala-Śiva is thus Saguṇa-Brahman. He is said to be vested with the wealth of Sat, Cit, Ānanda or Being, Consciousness and Bilss to show that His association with Avidyā does not deprive Him of, or affect, His own true nature (Svarūpa). Śiva has two aspects. In one of these He is the Supreme Changeless One who is Saccidānanda and Saccidānandamayā. This is Parāsaṁvit. In other He changes as the Universe; change being the experience of the Jīva so created. The cause of such change is Śiva-Tattva inseparably associated with Śakti-Tattva.

"There issued Śakti." This is Śakti Tattva of the Thirty-six Tattvas. Śakti evolves Nāda, and Nāda, Bindu. These are aspects of Śakti preparing to create the Universe and are dealt with in future chapters. Here I am concerned with Śakti-Tattva only: that is, with that form of Śakti which is specifically so called; since Nāda, Bindu and the rest are all but names for different aspects of Śakti.

It may be asked how Śakti can be said to issue from that which was already with Śakti. Rāghava Bhatta explains that the author here follows the Sāṁkhya principle of the appearance of realities from realities (Sadutpattivāda) and speaks of the condition of readiness (Ucchūnāvasthā) of Her who being without beginning or end existed in a subtle state identified with Caitanya in Dissolution *(Yā anādirūpā caitanyādhyāsena mahāpralaye sūkṣmā sthitā)*. Adhyāsa is the attribution of the nature of one thing to another according to which something is considered to be what it is not. In other words during Dissolution there is some potential principle in the Brahman which, as manifest, appears not to be Consciousness (Cit), but which owing to the absence of operation during the dissolved (Laya) state is identified with Cit. The distinction is very subtly marked by the Sanskrit word Cit for Śiva and Cidrūpiṇī for Śakti. Cit is there in either case, for ultimately there is nothing but Consciousness. But that principle which in creation manifest as seeming Acit is in itself Cidrūpiṇī. One is Consciousness and the other is a principle in the form of Consciousness. I prefer to look at Śakti from the Consciousness aspects which is Her own form (Svarūpā) and to say that Śakti in Dissolution is what She really is, namely, Cit. In creation Consciousness, as Śakti, has power to veil Its own true nature, and when we are ourselves subject to this power we attribute unconsciousness to It. The substance in either case in this: in Dissolution, Consciousness and Bliss alone is. Then without derogation to the changelessness of Consciousness there is an apparent dichotomy into subject and object, that is, Consciousness and Unconsciousness. Śakti is conceived as ready to create the Universe composed of Guṇas as its effect (Kārya). In other words, pure Consciousness becomes the world-experience. The Prayogasāra says: "She, who is eternal and all-pervading, the Genetrix of the Universe, issues from Him." Vāyavīya-Saṁhitā says: "By the will of Śiva, Parā-Śakti is united with Śiva-tattva and at the beginning of Creation appears from It just as oil from sesamum seed when pressed." The Pañcarātra is also cited by Rāghava Bhatta as saying, "The Parama Puruṣa at the beginning of creation, seeing that She who is Saccidānandarūpiṇī is the source (Adhiṣṭhāna) of the manifestation of all Tattvas makes manifest eternal Prakṛti." These statements, like all our accounts in such matters, are pictorial thinking, being necessarily imperfect attempts to explain the manifestation of activity of Consciousness.

Cause and effect are really one, but appear different. The first aspect of Śakti is its causal (Kāraṇa) aspect. But this again may be analysed into the various stages of its capacity and preparedness to create. These stages are marked by certain names which again are mere labels denoting states of Śakti. Thus, Nāda and Bindu are names for those aspects of Śakti which are more and more prone to Creation (Ucchūnāvasthā). Nāda and Bindu are but two states of Her Creation *(Sṛṣṭyūpayagyavasthārūpau)*. Śakti-Tattva is the first kinetic aspect of Brahman. Śakti then becomes more and more kinetic until, as Bindu, Śakti is Īśvara-Tattva. This Bindu differentiates into the Triangle of Divine Desire called the Kāmakalā upon which there is that Brahman Sound (Śabda-brahman), which bifurcating into Śabda and Artha, is Śakti in its aspect as effect (Kārya) or the manifested Universe of Mind and Matter. This "Tāntrika" account gives firstly an apparent "development" in the causal body of Śakti being in the nature of a resolution of like to like; and then a real development (Pariṇāma) of the effects (Kārya) produced from the causal body. The whole is necessarily described after the manner of a gradual process stated in terms of our own psychological experience. But such a process exists only in time which first appeares with the Sun and Moon. Bhāskarācārya in his commentary on the Lalita Sahasranāma (Verse 117) cites Gorakṣanātha as saying in his Mahārthamañjarī, "In a moment the world is created and in a moment it is destroyed."

Śakti-Tattva and Śiva-Tattva are inseparable (Santata-Samavāyinī), the former being only the negative aspect of the latter. Both exist even in Dissolution, the first emanation proper being Sadākhya which corresponds with Nāda in the above-mentioned verse. Śiva-Tattva is defined in the Tattva-Sandoha 1, as follows: "That, beyond which there is none other, moved of His own will in order to create the whole world. The first movement (Spanda prathama) is called the Śiva-Tattva by those who know".

*Yad ayaṁ anuttaramūrtir.*
*ṇijecchyākhilaṁ idaṁ jagat sraṣṭuṃ,*
*Paspande saḥ spandaḥ*
*prathamaḥ Śiva-tattvaṁ ucyate tajjñaiḥ.*

As the Vimarśini on the Pratyabhījñā says-- It is the "I-experience not looking towards another" *(Ananyonmukhau ahaṁpratyayaḥ)*. It is the self-side of experience, Prakāśa or Jñānamātra, which is such because of the negation of all objectivity or not-self by Śakti-Tattva. For this Jñānamātra, She, as Vimarśa-Śakti, provides through gradual stages the objects of its experience. Her function is negation *(Niṣedha-vyāpārarūpā Śaktiḥ)* of all objectivity so as produce the mere subjective knowing (Prakāśamātra) which is the Śūnyātiśūnya. She then evolves from Herself the objective world in order that it may be the content of the Śiva consciousness. She is pure Will ever associated with Śiva. She is the seed of the whole Univese of moving and unmoving things then absorbed in Herself.

*Icchā Śaiva svacchā*
*santatasamavāyini satī śaktiḥ,*
*Sacarācarasya jagato,*
*bījaṁ nikhilasya nijanilīnasya.*
(Tattva-Sandoha, 2).

She is thus called the Womb (Yoni), or Seed-state (Bījāvasthā), and by the Parapraveśikā, "Heart of the Supreme Lord" (Hṛdayam Paramaśituḥ). The Yoginīhṛdaya-Tantra says that men speak of the heart of Yoginī; She is Yoginī because She is connected with all things both as Cause and Effect. This Yoginī is knower of Herself (Yoginī svavid). She is called the Heart: for from the Heart all issues. She is the Heart of the Universe: the pulsing movement of which are Herself as Śakti. What more can be said than the words of the Yoginīhṛdaya, "What man knows the heart of a woman; only Śiva knows the heart of Yoginī"?

In the Pratyabhījñā-hṛdaya (S.4) it is said "The auspicious supreme Śiva desiring to make manifest the Universe which is one with Himself first of all shines forth as the one Cit, as the Very Void detached from Māyā (that is, there is no objectivity) and as undifferentiated Illumination (that is, Prakāśa or Jñāna). He next appears in the form of diverse experiencers consisting of an infinite, endless number of Tattva, words and being which are in the nature of a blooming forth of Consciousness and Bliss." *(Śrīparamaśivaḥ svātmaikyena sthitaṁ viśvaṁ avabibhāsayiṣuḥ pūrvaṁ cidaikyākhyāti māyānāśṛta-śiva-paryāyaśūnyātiśūnyātmatayā prakāśyāl-hedena prakāśamānalayā sphurati; tataḥ cid-rasāśyānatarūpaśeṣa-tattva-bhuvana-bhāva-tattat-pramātrādyātmatayāpi, prathate.*

The substance of the matter may be stated thus: whilst from the static transcendental aspect (Para-śiva, Parāśakti) Consciousness changelessly endures, there is from the kinetic creative aspects (Śiva-Śakti) a polarisation in consciousness, the poles of which are Śiva and Śakti representing the Aham and Idam aspects of experience. Owing to this polarisation there is in lieu of the unitary experience a division into the knower, knowing and known, Mātṛ, Māna, Meya, as it is called. Consciousness then identifies itself with the products of its own kinetic Śakti, that is, with mind as the subject of experience and with matter as its object. This polarisation is explained in the Śākta-Tantras by the illustration of the grain of gram (Canaka). Under the sheath of the grain of gram two seeds are found in such close union that they appear when held together as one. With, however, the tearing of the outer sheath the two halves of the seeds fall apart. These two seeds are said to be Śiva and Śakti and the encircling sheath is Māyā. Like all attempts to explain the unexplainable, the illustration is to some extent defective, for in the gram there are two separate seeds-- but Śiva-Śakti are an undistinguishable unity. Commentator on the Ṣatcakranirūpaṇa *(The Serpent Power)* cites the following; (v.49); "In the Satyaloka is the formless and lustrous One. She is like a grain of gram devoid of hands, feet or the life. She has surrounded Herself by Māyā. She is Sun, Moon and Fire. When casting off (Utsṛjya) the covering She divides in two (Dvidhā bhittvā) and becomes intent (Unmukhī) on creation, then by differentiation of Śiva and Śakti arises creative ideation (Sṛṣṭikalpanā)." By "differentiation" is meant the polarisation of Consciousness into subjective (Prakāśa) and objective (Vimarśa) aspects. The Self sees another. The same commentator cites the Prapañcasāra Tantra as saying that the Parabindu divides into two parts of which the right is Bindu, the male, Puruṣa or Ham, and the left is Visargaḥ, the female Prakṛti or Saḥ. Haṁsaḥ is the Union of Prakṛti and Puruṣa and the Universe is Haṁsa. In however, the MSS, on which my edition of this Tantra is based it is said the Parabindu divided by Kāla becomes threefold– Bindu, Nāda, Bīja. The difference is of no moment for this Bindu (Kārya) is Śiva and Bīja is Śakti, and Nāda is merely the relation (Mithaḥ-saṁvāyaḥ) of the two. The combined Haṁsaḥ indicates the same relation as is expressed by Nāda. In the Kulacūḍāmaṇi Nigama (Chap. I, vv. 16-24), the Devī says of the first stage: "I, though in the form of Prakṛti lie hidden in Being-consciousness-bliss *(Ahaṁ prakṛtirūpa cet saccidānandaparāyaṇā)*. Then in the initial creative stage when Karma ripens the Devī in the words of the Nigama "becomes desirous of creation and covers Herself with her own Māyā." This is the appearance of the kinetic Śakti. The same doctrine is stated with greater or less detail in various ways. Unitary experience, without ceasing to be such, is yet, as Jīva polarised into the dual experience of the Māyika world. Consciousness as Cit-Śakti and Māyā-Śakti projects from itself, in a manner conformable with our own psychological experience, the object of its experience. The Māyika experiencer (Māyā-pramātrī) takes what is one to be dual or many. This is the division of Śiva and Śakti which are yet eternally one. All action implies duality, Duality is manifestation. Manifestation is nothing but an appearance to consciousness. As there is ultimately but one Self, the Self appears to itself; that is, consciousness is polarised. These two poles are the continuity of the "I" (Aham) and its ever-changing content which is "This" (Idam).

Just as there is absolute rest and a world movement, so Śakti or Creative Consciousness is itself of twofold aspect, static and dynamic. Cosmic energy in its physical aspect is potential or kinetic, the first being that state in which the equlibrated elements of power hold each other in check. It is not possible to have one without the other. In any sphere of activity, according to those views, there must be a static background. If one Spiritual Reality be assumed it cannot be actually divided into two. It is possible, however, that there should be a *polarisation* in your experience whereby what is indivisibly one and the self, appears as many and the not-self. How? The answer is Māyā, that Power of Hers whereby what is impossible to us becomes possible. Māyā is Śakti, but Śakti is not to be identified only with this form of it. In the thirtysix Tattvas, Māyā is a particular and comparatively gross form of Śakti which appears after the evolution of the Sadvidyā-Tattva. It is defined as that Śakti which is the sense of difference (Bhedabuddhi); that is, the power whereby the individual consciousness, distinguishing itself from others, considers itself separate from them. Śakti is understood differently in the Śākta Tantra and in Śaṁkara's Māyāvāda; a matter of primary importance from the point of view of Sādhanā and with which I will deal on some future occasion. Whetever be the description given, all accounts must end in the inconceivable Śakti (Acintyā). She the One, the Primordial Śakti (Ādyā-Śakti) appears as many; and so the Śākta Sādhaka saying, *"Aham Devī no cānyosmi"* (I am the Devī and none other), thinks to himself "Sā'ham" (She am I).

# Chapter 12

# NĀDA – THE FIRST PRODUCED MOVEMENT

Śakti-Tattva dealt with in the preceding Chapter is really the negative aspect of the Śiva-tattva. Though spoken of separately the two are indissolubly one. Śakti-tattva, as the Tattva-sandoha says, is the Will of Śiva as yet unmanifest:

*Icchā saiva svacchā santatasamavāyinī satī śaktiḥ.*
*Sacarācarasya jagato bījam nikhilasya nijanilīnasya.*

These two principles (Śiva-Śakti-Tattva) are the ultimate potency of creation, and as and when they (considered as one Tattva) commence to act, the first movement towards manifestation takes place. After the previous restful state of Śiva-Śakti there follows the union for the purpose of creation of the two principles which are Śiva-tattva and Śakti-tattva. So, it is said in the Śākta-Tantra, *"Śiva-Śakti-samāyogāt jāyate sṛṣṭi-kalpanā"* (From the union of Śiva and Śakti arises creative ideation). This union and mutual relation is called Nāda. As the relation is not some substantial thing apart from Śiva or Śakti, Nāda is really Śiva-Śakti; passing from the state of mere potency into that of the first ideating movement, from which at length, when finally perfected, the whole universe is evolved. The Śākta Tantras frequently employ erotic symbolism to explain the creative process. This has led a missionary author to the conclusion that "throughout its symbolism and pesudo-philosophisings there lies at the basis of the whole system... the conception of the sexual relationship as the ultimate explanation of the universe." An American author reviewing one of my works has called it "a doctrine for suffragette monists" – "religious feminism run mad." Both statements are examples of those depreciative misunderstanding which are so common in Western descriptions of Eastern belief and which seem so absurd to anyone who has understood the subject. How can "sexual relationship" which exists on the gross plane of matter be the ultimate explanation of That which has manifested not only this but all other relations and subjects. As for "feminism" and the supposed priority of the feminism principle, the doctrine has no more to do with either than with old age pensions or any other social question. We are not dealing with the biological question whether the female antedates the male principles, of the social question of the rights of Woman, but with those ultimate dual principle, aspects of the one active Consciousness, which projects from Itself both man and woman and all other dualities on the universe. Śiva and Śakti are one and neither is higher than the other. But how are European writers to be blamed when we find a distinguished Indian Sanskritist affirming that according to Śākta doctrine "God *is* a woman" (the italics are mine).

Śakti is spoken of as female, that is, as Mother, because that is the aspect of the Supreme in which It is thought of as the Genetrix and Nourisher of the universe. But God is neither male nor female. As the Yāmala says for the benefit of all such ignorants, *"Neyam yoṣit na ca pumān na ṣaṇdo no jadaḥ smṛtaḥ."* These are all symbolisms borrowed from the only world which we ordinarily know– that around us. As for the charge of pseudo-philosophy, if it be that, then the same criticism must apply to the Advaitavāda Vedānta. For the Śākta-Tantra is the Sādhana-śāstra of Advaitavāda presenting the teaching of Vedānta in its own manner and in terms of its own ritual symbolism. Thus, it is said that Nāda is the Maithuna of Śiva and Śakti and that when Mahākāla was in Viparīta Maithuna with Mahākālī ( a form of Maithuna again which is symbolical of the fact that Śiva is Niṣkṛya and Śakti Sākṛya) there issued Bindu. For Maithuna, others substitute the logical term Mithasamavāyaḥ as a description of Nāda, which is Kriyāśakti. Before the appearance of Śabda there must be two. Unity is necessarily actionless. Two involves a third– which is relation of both; a Trinity of Power which is reflected in the Trimūrti of the Māyika world as Brahmā, Viṣnu, Rudra.

From Nāda came Mahābindu and this latter differentiated into the Tribindu which is Kāmakalā, the Mūla of all Mantras. In Pralaya, Śiva and Śakti, exist as the "to in one"; Śiva as Cit, Śakti as Cidrūpiṇī: the Parā Śakti– not being different or separated from Śiva *(Avinābhāvasambandha)* and being undivided supreme Cit-Śakti *(Akhaṇḍa-paracicchakti)*.

The Śāradā-Tilaka (1-7) then says: From the Sakala-Parameśvara vested with the wealth of Saccidānanda *(Saccidānandavibhavāt)* appeared Śakti (Śakti-Tattva); from Śakti Nāda and from Nāda, Bindu (Mahābindu). Sakala means with Kalā; that is, the Brahman with what the Sāṁkhya calls Mūlaprakṛti, that which the Vedānta calls Avidyā and the Śākta-Tantras or Āgamas call Śakti. On the other hand Niṣkala Śiva is Nirguṇa Śiva or that aspect of the Brahman which is unconnected with the creative Śakti; just as Sakala-Śiva is the Brahman so associated. Śiva in either aspects is always with Śakti; for Śakti is but Himself; whereas the Śakti associated with Paramaśiva is Cidrūpiṇī and Viśvottīrṇā or beyond the Universe, the Śakti which is associated with the creative Śiva is that which appears as Universe (Viśvātmikā). The Parāśakti is one with Caitanya at rest. The other aspect which ripens into Nāda and Bindu denotes the "swollen" condition of readiness *(Ucchūnāvasthā)* of Her who existed in a subtle state in the great dissolution (Mahāpralaya). These two Śaktis (Nāda, Bindu) are stages in the movement towards the manifestation of the Self as object, that is, as the Universe.

In these, the mere readiness or potency of Śakti-tattva to act develops into action. In Nāda-Śakti therefore Kriyā predominates. When we speak of stages, development and so forth, we are using language borrowed from the manifested world which, in the sense there understood, is not appropriate to a state prior to manifestation; for such manifestation does not take place until after the appearance of the Puruṣa-Prakṛti-Tattva and the development from the latter of the impure Tattvas from Buddhi to Pṛthivī. But a Sādhanā Śāstra, even if it had the power to do otherwise, could not usefully use terms and symbols other than those borrowed from the world of the Sādhaka. The Prayogasāra says that the Śakti who is "turned towards" the state of Liberation *(Nirāmaya padonmukhī)* awakes as Nāda and is turned to Śiva *(Śivonmukhī)* as which time She is said to be male *(Pumrūpā)*. For then She becomes Ham in Haṁsaḥ.

She who was one with Paraśiva in Pralaya as the coalesced "I" (Aham) and "Thus" (Idam), now in Her creative aspect as Śakti-tattva transforms Herself into Nāda. Nāda is action (Kriyāśaktirūpa). In simple language, potency and readiness to create, (Śaktitattva) so as Bindu, which is a further development of Kriyā Śakti dealt with in the next chapter.

According to Rāghava Bhatta in his Commentary on the Śāradā some writers do not speak of Nāda, though the author of the Śāradā does so in order to indicate the sevenfold character of Tārā. The Nāda state is however indicated by those Ācāryas who speak of Kāla. So, it is said, "in the Kālatattva which is Sound" *(Ravātmanikālatattve)*. In the Hymn to Bhuvaneśī also it is said, "Obeisance to Thee who art called Tattva in the character of sound" *(Namaste ravatvena tattvābhidhā me)*.

Nāda occupies the same place in the Mantra scheme as the Sadākhya-Tattva of the 36 Tattvas, for Bindu is Īśvara Tattva. They are each transcendent aspects of Śabda in the respective Tattvas. As Consciousness reaches forth to enjoyment and the "I" is separated from the "This" what was mere diffusive consciousness as Sadākhya-Tattva is objectified into the all-embracing Ākāśa, the Guṇa of which is gross Śabda; that is something experienced as an object apparently different from and other than ourselves.

Nāda which etymologically means "Sound" is a technical term of the Mantraśāstra. The latter Śastra is concerned with Mantravidyā, and Mantra is manifested Śabda which also literally means "Sound". By "Sound" of course is not meant gross sound which is heard by the ear and which is the property of the Kāryākāśa developed as

Vikṛti from the Prakṛti-Tattva which, with the Puruṣa-Tattva, occupies the place (though without its dualities) of the Puruṣa and Prakṛti of the Sāṁkhya. Gross sound belongs to the impure creation as Guṇa of Ākāśa or the ether which fills space. To avoid misconception, it is better to use the word Śabda which with Artha is manifeted in the "Garland (or Rosary) of Letters" (Varṇamālā) with which I will later deal.

Nāda is the most subtle aspect of Śabda, as the first putting forth of Kriyāśakti Paranāda and Parā Vāk are Parāśakti. Nāda into which it evolves is the unmanifested (Avyaktāmā) seed or essence (Nādamātra) of that which is later manifested as Śabda, devoid of particularities such as letters and the like *(Varṇādiviśeṣa-rahitaḥ).* It develops into Bindu which is of the same character. From the Mantra aspect, as the source of Śabda, this Mahābindu as it differentiates to "create" is called the Śabda-brahman. Bindu when differentiated is also the source of the Vikṛtis or Tattvas and of their Lords (Tattveśa). In its character as Śabda-brahman it is the source of the manifested Śabda and Artha *(Śabdaśabdārthakāraṇaṁ)* Śabda-brahman is thus a name of Brahman as the immediate creative source of the manifold Śabda and Artha.

What Śabda-brahman is, has been the subject of contention, as Rāghava Bhatta's commentary shows. It is sufficient to say here (where we are only concerned with Śabda-brahmātmaka) Bindu so far as it is necessary to explain Nāda that Rāghava Bhatta says the Śabda-brahman is the Caitanya in all being *(Caitanyaṁ sarvabhūtānaṁ).* This cosmic Śakti exists in the individual bodies of all breathing creatures (Prāṇī) in the form of Kuṇḍalinī (Kuṇḍalīrūpa). Nāda therefore which assumes the aspect of

Bindu is also Caitanya and Śakti. Nāda is thus the first emanative stage in the production of Mantra. The second is Bindu, or Śabda-brahman; the third is Tribindu (Bindu, Nāda, and Bīja) or Kāmakalā; the fourth is the production of Śabda as the Mātṛkās which are the subtle state of the subsequently manifested gross letters (Varṇa) and the last is these gross letters (Sthūlaśabda), which compose the manifested Śabda or Mantra composed of letters (Varṇa), syllables (Pada) and sentences (Vākya). Thus, Mantra ultimately derives from Nāda which is itself the Kriyā-śaktirūpa aspects of Śiva-Śakti who are the Supreme Nāda (Paranāda) and Supreme Speech (Parā-vāk). The Prayogasāra says: "Oh Devī ! that Antarātmā in the form of Nādātmā itself makes sound *(Nādate svayaṁ),*" that is, displays activity. "Urged on by Vāyu (that is, the Prāṇa-vāyu in Jīvas) it assumes the form of letters." Nāda again is itself divided into several stages, namely, Mahānāda, or Nādānta, the first movement forth of Śabda-Brahman; Nāda, when Śakti fills up the whole Universe with Nādānta, in other words, the complete movement of which Nādānta is the commencement; and Nirodhinī, which is that aspect of Nāda in which its universal operation having been completed, it operates in a particular manner and is transformed into Bindu, which is the completion of the first movement of Śakti, in which She assumes the character of the Creative Lord of the Universe (Īśvara-Tattva). Nādānta considered as the end and not the commencement of the series is that in which there is dissolution of Nāda *(Nādasya antaḥ layaḥ).* Above Bindu, the Śaktis which have been already given in previous articles becomes more and more subtle until Niṣkala Unmanī is reached which as the Yoginīhṛdaya says, is uncreate motionless speech *(Anutpannaniṣpandāvāk),* the twin aspects of which are Saṁvit or the Void (Śūnya-Saṁvit) and Saṁvit as tendency to manifestation in a subtle state *(Utpatsuḥ samvid utpattyavasthā sūkṣmā)*. Unmanī is beyond Kāraṇarūpā-Śakti; where there is no experience *(Bhānam)* or Kāla or Kalā nor of Devatā or Tattva, in the sense of category, as that which distinguishes one thing from another. It is *Svanirvāṇam param padam,* the Nirvikalpa-nirañjana-śiva śakti which is Guruvaktra.

Nāda and Bindu exist in all Bīja Mantras which are generally written with the Bindu above and the Nāda below, for this is the form of the written Candrabindu. In however some of the old pictorial representations of Oṁkāra the real position of Nāda is shown as being over Bindu as an inverted crescent. Thus, the great Bīja. Hrīm is composed of Ha, Ra, Ī and Ma. Of these Ha–Ākāśa, Ra– Agni, Ī– Ardhanārīśvara and M-- Nādabindu. The five Bhūtas are divided into two groups Amūrtta (formless) and Mūrtta (with form). Both Ākāśa and Vāyu belong to the first group, because until the appearance of Agni as Rūpa, there is no colour and form. Agni therefore heads the second division. When Ākāśa is with Agni there is form; for Ra is the first manifestation of Rūpa. This form is in Arddhanārīśvara, the combined Śiva-Śakti, who hold all in themselves. The first three letters represent the Ākāra or form aspect. The Mantra receives its complete form by the addition of the Māhātmya which is Nāda-Bindu which are Nirākāra (formless) and the Kāraṇa (cause) of the other three in which they are implicitly and potentially contained; being in technical phrase Antargata of, or held within Bindu, which again is Antargata of all the previously evolving Śaktis mentioned. The meaning of the Bīja-Mantra then is that the Cidākāśa is associated (Yukta) with Rūpa. It is thus the Śabda statement of the birth of General Form; that is, Form as such of which all particular forms are derivations. Hrīm is, as pronounced, the gross-body as sound of the ideation of Form as such in the Cosmic mind.

The degree of subtlety of the Śaktis preceding and following Nāda is in the Mantra-Śāstra indicated by what is called "the utterance time" (Uccāraṇakāla). Thus, taking Bindu as the unit, Unmanī is Nirākāra and Niruccāra, formless and without utterance, undefined by any adjective: being beyond mind and speech and the universe (Viśottīrṇā). The Uccāraṇakāla of Samanī (so named *Manaḥsahitatvat,* on account of its association with mind; the preceding Śakti Unmanī being *Tadrahitā* or devoid of that), is 1/256, or Vyāpikā 1/128 and so on to Nādānta 1/32, Nāda 1/16, to Arddhacandra which is 1/2 of Bindu and to Bindu itself.

Nāda is thus, in the Mantra-Śāstra, that aspect of Śakti which evolves into Bindu, which latter as differentiating into the Tribindu is called the Śabda-brahman, who is the creative source of Śabda and Artha and thus of the revealed Śabda which Mantra is.

I would in conclusion meet an objection, which I have heard urged, namely that the Mantra-Śāstra treats its subject with unnecessary complexity of detail. It is undoubtedly difficult and requires careful study. Simple minds may be satisfied with the statement that God created the world. Veda too gives an explanation of the cosmic problem in two words "He saw" *(sa aikṣata)*. But who saw, and what, and how did He see? How also if there be only One came there to be anything to see? And what is "to see" (īkṣaṇa)? For the process is not like looking out of a window and seeing a man passing. "He" is Consciousness which is in Itself (Svarūpa) actionless. How then did "It" see and thus become active?

Because It has two aspects, one (Niṣkala-śiva) in which It is actionless and the other (Sakala-śiva) in which It is actionless and the other (Sakala-śiva) in which It is Activity as the embodiment of all the Saṁskāras. In this last aspect It is called Śakti. The latter term denotes Active Consciousness. How can one and the same thing have two contradictory aspects, we cannot say, otherwise than by affirming Svabhāva. By way of analogy we can refer to what psychology calls dual and multiple personalities. The ultimate Reality is alogical and unexplainable (Anirvacaniya) That it is one and not two is, it is said, proved by Veda and the actual experience (Svānubhava) had in Yoga. What is "seeing"? It is not the observing of something outside which was there before it was observed. "Seeing" is the rising into consciousness (void of objects) of the memory of past universes existing in the form of the Saṁskāras. Before this can occur, Consciousness must obscure to Itself Its nature and (though in truth an unity) must experience itself as an "I" observing a "This" which it has through Māyā Śakti projected outside Itself. There is no answer again to the question how this is possible except inscrutable Śakti (Acintya Śakti). But just as a man rising from deep sleep has first a more or less bare awareness which is gradually filled out with the thought of self and particular objects; consciousness coming to itself, so that in the waking state it again recognises the world which had vanished utterly in dreamless slumber; so it is with the Cosmic Consciousness. Just as man does not pass at once from dreamless slumber to the fullest waking perception, so neither does the Cosmic Consciousness. It passes gradually from its dreamless slumber (Suṣupti) state which is the general dissolution (Mahāpralaya) to the waking state (Jāgrat) which is consciousness of the gross universe. The degrees in this emanative process are the Tattvas described earlier Manifestation, which is nothing but presentation of apparently external objects to the inner consciousness, is, as experienced by the limited consciousness, gradual. The seeds of the "I" and "This" are first formed and then grown. The first principal stage is that before and in Īśvara Tattva of Bindu and which therefore includes Nāda. The second is that of the World-consciousness arising through the agency of Māyā-śakti. These two stages are marked by two principal differences. In the first the "This" (Idam) is seen as part of the self, the two not being differentiated in the sense of inner and outer. In the second the object is externalised and seen as different from the self. In the first, when the Self experiences itself as object, the latter is held as a vague undefined generality. There is, as it were an awareness of self-scission in which the self as subject knows itself as object and nothing more. The degrees in this process have been already explained. In the second not only is the object defined as something which appears to be not the self, but there are a multiplicity of objects each marked by its own differences; for Māyā has intervened. The whole world-process is thus a re-awakening of the Cosmic Consciousness from sleep to the world, into which at Dissolution it had fallen; and the Tattvas mark the gradual stages of re-awakening, that is re-awakening to the world, but a falling into sleep so far as true Consciousness is concerned. So in Kuṇḍalīyoga when Kuṇḍalinī sleeps in the Mūlādhāra, man is awake to the world; and when she awake, the world vanishes from Consciousness which then regains in own state (Svarūpa). There is no reason to suppose that judged in terms of our present experience, the change is other than gradual. But how, it may be asked, is this known or what the stages are; for were we there. As individuals we were not; for we speak of that which preceded the formation of the Sakala Jīva Consciousness. But Jīva was there as the plant is in the seed. It is the one Jīva who displays himself in all the Tattvas. Those who fall back into the seed have experience of it. There are, however, two bases on which these affirmations rest. In the first place there is correspondence between all planes. "What is without, is so manifested because it is within"; not of course in the exact form in which it exists without but in the corresponding form of its own plane. We may therefore look for instruction to our daily life and its psychological states to discover both the elements and the working of the cosmic process. These also disclose a gradual unfolding of consciousness from something in the nature of mere awareness to the definite perception of a variety of multiple objects. But the normal experience is by its nature limited. That normal experience is, however, transcended in Yoga-states, when consciousness becomes Nirālambapuri, that is, detached from worldly objects: the experience wherein it is (in part at leat) available for the instruction of others. Secondly the Śāstras are records of truth beyond the senses (Atīndriya-Tattva). The Tattvas are not put forth as mere speculative guesses or imaginings of which might have been. When however, supersensual truth is described in language it is necessarily expressed in terms, and with the use of symbols, of present experience. That experience is had under conditions of time and space and others. We know and speak of mere potency ripening into actuality, of potential energy becoming more and more kinetic, of shifting states of consciousness and so forth. These are matters the knowledge of which is drawn from the world around us. But this does not necessarily make them wholly untrue of unreal as applied to higher planes. One of the commonest errors is to raise false partitions between things. The experience is real for it is Śiva's and His experience is never unreal. It is according to its degree (that is on its plane) real; an expression (limited though it be) of the ultimate Reality Itself. We can think in no other terms. But it is also true that these terms and symbols, having only complete validity on our plane, are no longer wholly true for Consciousness as it rises from it. But other forms of Consciousness must take their place until the Formless is reached. The Tattvas explain (limited though such explanation be by the bounds of our thought and language) the modes through which the returning Consciousness passes until it rests in Itself (Svarūpaviśrānti) and has Peace. And so the Buddhist Mantrayāna aptly defines Yoga (which in Tibetan is called rNal-rByor) in the sense of result, as the "Finding rest or peace." This final state, as also those intermediate ones which lie between it and the normal individual world-consciousness, are only actually realised in Jñāna-Yoga (by whatsoever method Jñāna is attained) when the mind has been wholly withdrawn from without and faces the operative power of Consciousness behind it (Nirāmaya-padonmukhī).

But here we are dealing with Mantra-yoga when the mind is thinking the states which Jñāna, in whatever degree, realises as Consciousness. The Mantra-Śāstra looks at the matter, of which we write, from the standpoint of Mantra that is of manifested Śabda its object. Kuṇḍalinī is both Jyotirmayī, Her Sūkṣmarūpa and Mantramayī, Her Sthūlarūpa. We beginning with the latter. All things are then defined in terms of Śabdārtha and of the various causal forms which precede it. The first of such produced forms is Nāda which becomes Bindu and then on the differentiation of the Tattvas the "hidden sound" (Avyakta-rava), the Logos of Cosmic Word utters "the Garland of Letters" (Varṇamālā) of which all Mantras are formed. It traces the degrees in which the ideating Cosmic Consciousness becomes, as Supreme Speech (Parāvāk), the Genetrix of the subtle and gross Śabda which are the Mātṛkās and Varṇas respectively. That Supreme Speech (Parāvāk) is without idea of language, but is represented as gradually assuming the state in which it utters both and projects from Itself into the sensual world the obejcts (Artha) which they denote. The actual manifestation of these from Para-śabda through Paśyantī, Madhyamā and Vaikharī, will be described in another Chapter.

The practice of Mantra-Yoga not only gives, from a merely intellectual standpoint, an understanding of Vedānta which cannot ordinarily be had by the mere reading of philosophical texts; but also produces a pure Bhāva ripening into Mahābhāva through the purification of mind (Cittaśuddhi) which such practice (according to the rules of Sādhanā laid down in the Tantras or Mantra-śāstra) gives, as one of its Siddhis. What a Western, and sometimes the English educated Indian, does not understand or recognise, is the fact that the mere reading of Vedāntic texts without Citta-śuddhis will neither bring true understanding nor other fruitful result. The experienced will find that this apparent complexity and wealth of detail is not useless and is, from an extra-ritual standpoint, to a considerable extent, and from that of Sādhana wholly, necessary. A friend of mine was once asked by a man in a somewhat testy manner "to give him a plain exposition of the Vedānta in five minutes." It takes years to understand perfectly any science or profession. How can that, which claims, to explain all, be mastered in a short talk? But more than this; however prolonged the intellectual study may be, it must be, to be fruitful, accompanied by some form of Sādhanā. The Tantra-Śāstras contain this for the Hindu, thought it is open to him or any other to devise a better if he can. Forms ever change with the ages, while the Truth which they express, remains.

# Chapter 13

# BINDU OR ŚAKTI – READY TO CREATE

From Nāda, previously described, evolved Bindu *(Nādād bindu-samudbhavaḥ)*. What, then is Bindu? Literally the term means a "Drop" or a "point" such as the Anusvāra breathing. But in the Mantra-Śāstra it has a technical meaning. It is not, as a distinguished Indian Sankritist called it, merely a "Drop". It is not that "red drops" mix with "white drops" and so forth, a description of his, which reminds one more of the pharmacy or sweet shop than the Śāstra. This and other statements betray an ignorance of Indian tradition and a mental attitude alien to Indian thinking which distinguishes so many of those whose should have been captured in the net of an English education. Those who speak another's language and think another's thought must see to it that their own Indian self is not, through the dangers to which it is thus exposed, lost. But even an educated Western, ignorant of the Śāstra, but with a knowledge of the history of religious thought would have perceived the significance of the term Bindu when he had learnt that one of its literal meanings was a "Point".

In an anonymous Mystical Work published in the

eighteenth century by one of the "French Protestants of the Desert" called Le Mystere de la Croixe, it is said (p.9), "Ante omina Punctum exstitit; non to atomon, aut mathematicium sed diffusivum. Monas erat explicite; implicite Myrias. Lux erat, erant et Tenebrae; Principium et Finis Principii, Omnia et nihil: Est et non".

"Before all things were, there was a Point (Punctum: Bindu) not the Atom or mathematical point (which thought it is without magnitude has position) but the diffusive (neither with magnitude nor position). In the one (Monas) there was implicity contained the many (Myrias). There was Light and Darkness: Beginning and End: Everything and Nothing: Being and Non-being (that is the state was neither Sat nor Asat)." The author says that the All is engendered from the central indivisible Point of the double triangle (that is, what is called in the Tantras, Ṣaṭkoṇa-Yantra) regarded as the symbol of creation. "Le Tout est engennré du point central indivisible du double triangle." This "Point" is one of the world's religious symbols and is set in the centre of a Ṣaṭkoṇa or in a circular Maṇḍala or sphere. On this symbol St. Clement of Alexandria in the secondary century A.D. says that if abstraction be made from a body of its properties, its depth, breadth, and then length, "the point which remains is a unit, so to speak, having position; from which if we abstract position there is the notion of unity" (Stromata V.2., Ante Nicene Library, Vol.IV). Again Shelley in his "Prometheus" says: "plunge into eternity where recorded time seems but a point."

Where does the Extended universe go at the Great Dissolution (Mahāpralaya)? It collapses so to speak into a Point. This point may be regarded as a mathematical point in so far as it is without any magnitude whatever, but as distinguished from it, in that it has in fact no position. For there is then no notion of space. It need hardly be said that this is a symbol, and a symbol borrowed from our present experience cannot adequately represent any state beyond it. We only conceive of it as a point, as something infinitesimally subtle, which is in contrast with the extended manifested universe which is withdrawn into it. This point is Bindu. But this again is to make use of material images borrowed from the world of objective form. Bindu is an aspect of Śakti or Consciousness; therefore it is interpreted also in terms of our present consciousness. As so interpreted and as Īśvara-Tattva, in which it is, Śakti is called Bindu; because here consciousness completely identifies itself with the universe as unmanifested *Idam* and thus subjectifies it and becomes with it a point of consciousness. Thus by way of example the individual mind is completely subjectified and exists for each of us as a mathematical point (and so it is spoken of by some as being of atomic dimension) though the body to the extent to which it is not subjectified appears as an object or extended thing. We do not conceive of our own minds as extended because of this complete subjectification. In the same way the consciousness of Īśvara completely subjectifies the universe. He does not of course see the universe as a multiplicity of objects outside and different from himself; for if He did, He would be Jīva and not Īśvara. He sees it as an object which is a whole and which whole in Himself. In Sadākhya-Tattva "Otherness" (Idam) is presented to Consciousness by Śakti. This *Idam* is then faintly perceived (to use the language of the Vimarśinī on Īśvara-Pratyabhījñā III. 1, 2) "in a hazy fasion *Dhyāmalaprāyaṁ)* like a picture just forming itself *(Unmīlita-mātra-citra-kalpaṁ);* seen by the mind only and not as something seen outside by the senses (*Antaḥkaraṇaikavedyaṁ)*. The object thus vaguely surges up into the field of consciousness in which the emphasis is on the congnitive aspects of "I" (Aham). This however is not the "I" or "This" of our experience, for it is had in the realms beyond Māyā. The "This" is then experienced as part of the Self. In Īśvara Tattva all haziness gives place to clarity of the "This" which is thus seen completely as part of the Self; the emphasis being on the "This". After equal emphasis on the "I" and "This", the two are in Śuddhavidyā-Tattva wholly separated by Māyā. When therefore the Yogī passes beyond the Māyik world his first higher experience is in this Tattva.

Nāda and Bindu are states of Śakti in which the germ of action (Kriyā-śakti) so to speak increasingly sprouts with a view to manifestation producing a state of compactness of energy and readiness to create. Rāghava Bhaṭṭa (Com. Śāradā 1.7) speaks of them as two states of Śakti which are the proper conditions *(Upayogyāvasthā)* for creation. They are, like all else, aspects of Śakti, but are names of those aspects which are prone to and ready for creation *(Uccūnāvasthā)*. Bindu is said to be the massive or *Ghanāvasthā* state of Śakti. The Prapañcasāra Tantra says that Śakti is seized with the desire to create and becomes Ghanībhūtā *(Vicikirṣur ghanibhūtā)*. Thus, milk becomes *Ghanībhūtā* when it turns into cream or curd. In other words, Śakti is conceived as passing gradually from its subtle state through Śakti-tattva and Nāda (in its three-stages ) and becomes what is relatively gross or massive as Power which is fully equipped to pass from the stage of potency into that of active manifestation. That stage is Bindu which is called Mahābindu or Parabindu to distinguish it from the other Binduṣ into which it subsequently differentiates.

The commentary of Kālīcaraṇa on the Ṣaṭ-Cakranirūpaṇa (see *The Serpent Power,* V.4) citing Toḍala-Tantra (Ch. VI) says that the Supreme Light is formless; but Bindu implies both the Void (Śūnya) and Guṇa also. Bindu is the Void in so far as it is the Supreme Brahman. It implies Guṇa as being the creative of Śakti aspect of the Brahman which subsequently evolves into the Puruṣa and Prakṛti-Tattvas of which the latter is with Guṇa. The commentary to V.49 states that this Bindu is the Lord (Īśvara) whom some Paurāṇikas call Mahāviṣṇu and others the Brahmapuruṣa: and (V.37) that Para-bindu is the state of "Ma" before manifestation; being; Śiva-Śakti enveloped by Māyā. As to this it may be observed that the letter M is male, and Bindu which is the nasal breathing, sounded as M, is the unmanifested Śakti or Ma which is revealed upon its subsequent differentiation into the three Śaktis from which the universe proceeds. Bindu as the Cause is *Cidghana* or massive Consciousness and Power in which lie potentially in a mass (Ghana), though undistinguishable the one from other, all the worlds and beings about to be created. This is Parama-Śiva and in him are all the Devatās. It is thus this Bindu which is worshipped in secret by all Devas (V.41) and which is indicated in its different phases in the Candrabindu (Nāda-Bindu), Śakti and Śānta of the Om and other Bīja mantras.

The Bindu is in Satyaloka which, within the human body, exists in the pericarp of the thousand-petalled Lotus (Sahasrāra) in the highest cerebral centre. It is, as I have already said, compared to a grain of gram (Caṇaka) which under its outer sheath (which is Māyā) contains the two seeds (Śiva and Śakti) in close and undivided union.

Kālīcaraṇa (V. 49) thus cites the following: In the

Satyaloka is the formless and lustrous one. She is like a grain of gram devoid of hands, feet and the like. She has surrounded Herself by Māyā (that is She is about to create by the agency of this Power of Hers). She is Sun, Fire and Moon, She being intent on creation *(Unmukhī)* becomes twofold *(Dvidhā bhitvā)* and then, by differentiation of Śiva and Śakti, arises creative ideation *(Sṛṣṭikalpanā)*. Śiva and Śakti are of course not actually divided for they are not like a *chapatti* or some other material thing. It might seem unnecessary to make such obvious remarks, did not experience tell me of the absurd misunderstandings which exist of the Scripture. When we read that God "*is* a woman," that the Śākta Tantra is "Feminism" with a doctrine similar to that of Prof. Lester Ward's primacy of the female sex, that "the conception of the sexual relationship is the ultimate explanation of the universe" and so forth, no caveats, however obvious, are unnecessary. What of course is meant is that, whereas in Pralaya, Śiva and Śakti existed as one unity of consciousness, They in creation, whilst still remaining in themsleves what They always were, project the universe which is Śakti; and then we have the Paramātmā and Jīvātmā consciousness which seem to the latter to be different.

Although Parabindu and all which evolves from It are nothing but aspects of Śakti and in no wise different from it, yet as representing that state of Śakti which immediately precedes creation, it is this state of Śakti which is said to be the cause of the universe of name and form (Nāmarūpa); concepts and concepts objectivefied; or Śabda the word and Artha is meaning. The states of Śakti preceding Bindu are those in which the Bindu state is in process of being "evolved" according to what we may call an Avikṛta-Pariṇāma and when evolved it is the cause of the universe.

Really they are merely aspects of one and the same pure Śakti. This is not an evolution in time. As Plotinus says, the universe "was formed according to intellect (here the Cosmic Power of Prapañca-Śakti which manifests as Mahat) and intellect not preceding in time but prior" (in the sense that cause precedes effect). This again, as all descriptions, (in so far as they are applicable to the transcendent Śakti) is imperfect, for sequence of cause and effect involves to our minds the notion of time. This Supreme Bindu as containing in Himself all Devatās is the ultimate object of adoration by all classes of worshippers (V.44) under the name of Śiva, or Mahāviṣṇu or the Devī as those call it "who are filled with a passion for Her Lotus Feet." The sectarianism of the lower mind, still existent in both East and West, is here shown to be a matter of words (the fight for which is of such interest to many) and is reduced to its real common denominator. As the Lord says in the Gītā, Whomever men may worship, all such worship comes eventually to Him.

Para-bindu is thus the Head of every line of creation; of the Tattvas from Buddhi to Pṛthivī and their Lords (Tattveśa) and of the Śabda or Mantra creations; all belonging to the Vikāra-Sṛṣṭi or Pariṇāma-ṣṛṣṭi. The development after the manifestation of Prakṛti is a real evolution (Pariṇāma), for Consciousness has then been divided into subject and object in time and space. What is spoken of in terms of a development in the Īśvara body is not that. There Śakti assumes various aspects with a view to create but without manifestation. Śakti-tattva, whilst remaining such, assumes the aspects of Nāda and Bindu.

The next stage is thus described in the Śāradā-Tilaka (Ch . 1-8, 9) as follows:

*Paraśaktimayaḥ sākṣāt tridhā, sau bhidyate punaḥ.*
*Bindur nāda bijamiti tasya bhedāḥ samīritāḥ.*
*Binduḥ śivātmako bījaṁ śaktir nādas tayor mithaḥ.*
*Samavāyaḥ samākhyātaḥ sarvāgamaviśāradaiḥ.*

That which is supreme Śakti again divides Itself into three, such divisions being known as Bindu, Nāda, Bīja. Bindu is said to be of the nature of Śiva and Bīja of Śakti, and Nāda as the mutual relation between these two, by those who are learned in the Āgamas.

One Mss. I have seen has 'Bindur nādātmako', but the commentary of the Ṣaṭcakra (V.40) explains this as Śivātmaka. These form the three Bindus (Tribindu). Nāda here again is Trait d'Union, the Yoga of the other two Bindus as the Prayogasāra calls it, (See Rāghava's Comm. to V.8 of Ch. I Śāradā). These are Śiva, Śiva-Śakti, Śakti. By this it is not to be understood that Śiva or Śakti are ever altogether dissociated but the aspects may be regarded as Śiva or Śakti-pradhāna respectively. Bhāskarācārya in his valuable commentary on the Lalitā-Sahasranāma says "From the causal (Kāraṇa) Bindu proceeds the effect (Kārya) Bindu, Nāda, and Bīja. Thus, these three which are known as supreme, subtle and gross arose". *(Asaccakāraṇabindoḥ sākṣāt krameṇa kāryabindustato nādastato bījaṁ iti trayaṁ utpannaṁ tadidaṁ parasūkṣmasthūlāpadair apy ucyate.* V.132.).

One text of the Prapañcasāra-Tantra says that the Parabindu divides into two parts, of which the right is Bindu, the Male, Puruṣa or Ham, and the left Visarga the

Female, Prakṛti or Saḥ making the combined Haṁsaḥ. Haṁsaḥ is the union of Prakṛti and Puruṣa and the universe is Haṁsaḥ. In however the Mss. on which my edition of that Tantra is based it is said that the Bindu (Para) divided by Kāla becomes threefold as Bindu, Nāda, Bīja. Substantially the matter seems one of nomenclature, for the two Bindus which make Visarga become three by the addition of the Śiva-Bindu. Moreover as Ham is Śiva and Saḥ is Śakti, the combined Haṁsaḥ implies the relation which in the Śāradā account is called Nāda. So, it is also said from the first vowel issued "Hrīṁ," from the second Haṁsaḥ, and from the third the Mantra "Hrīṁ, Śrīṁ, Klīṁ", the first indicative of general form; the second being a more Sthūla form of Ākāśa and Agni (Sa=Ākāśa; Ra= Agni) held as it were within the "skin" (Carma) of the enveloping Arddhanārīśvara; the third commencing with the first and last letters including all the 24 Tattvas and all the fifty letters into which the general Form particularises itself.

Para-bindu is Śiva-Śakti considered as undivided, undifferentiated principle. On the "bursting" of the seed which is the Parabindu the latter assumes a threefold aspect as Śiva or Bindu, Śakti or Bīja and Nāda the Śiva-Śakti aspect which, considered as the result, is the combination, and from the point of view of cause, the inter-relation of the two (Śāradā I.9) the one acting as excitant (Kṣobhaka) and the other being the excited (Kṣobhya). The commentary on V.40 of the Ṣaṭcakranirūpaṇa speaks of Nāda as the union of Śiva and Śakti; as the connection between the two and as being in the nature of the Śakti of action (Kriyā-śakti-svarūpa). It is also said to be that, the substance of which is Kuṇḍalī (Kuṇḍalinīmaya). All three are but different phases of Śakti in creation (Comm. I. 39) being different aspects of Parabindu which is itself the Ghanāvasthā aspect of Śakti.

Thus in the first division of Śakti, Nāda, Bīndu, Nāda is the Maithuna or Yoga of Śiva and Śakti to produce the Parabindu which again differentiates into the threefold aspects as the Śaktis, though in grosser form, which produced it. Though the Guṇas are factors of the gross Śakti Prakṛti, they are in subtle form contained within the higher Śaktis. This Śakti as the first potentially kinetic aspects about to display itself is the Cit aspect of Śakti and Cit Śakti is, when seen from the lower level of the Guṇas, Sāttvika: Nāda is in the same sense Rājasika, for Śakti becomes more and more kinetic gathering together Its powers, as it were from the previous state of barely stirring potency, for the state of complete readiness to create which is Bindu, and which in the aforesaid sense as Ghanībhūta foreshadows that Tamas Guṇa which at a lower stage is the chief factor which creates the world, for the latter is largely the product of Tamas. Each aspect of Tribindu again is associated with one or other of the Guṇas. These divisions of aspects from the Guṇa stand-point are not to be understood as though they were separate and exclusively concerned with only one of the Guṇas. The Guṇas themselves never exist separately. Where there is Sattva there is also Rajas and Tamas. In the Kriyā, from which the Guṇas develop, one never stands by itself, though it may be predominant. Where there is Icchā there is Jñāna and so forth. And so again Śakti, Nāda and Bindu are not to be severed like different objects in the Māyika world. In each there is implicitly or explicitly contained the other. Parameśvara assumes (for the Jīva) successively the triple aspects of Śakti, Nāda Bindu, Kārya Bindu, Bīja Nāda, thus completing by this differentiation of Śakti the sevenfold causal sound-forms of the Praṇava or Oṁkāra; namely, Sakala Parameśvara (which is Saccidānanda, for even when the Brahman is associated with Avidyā, its own true nature (Svarūpa is not affected), Śakti (Śakti-Tattva), Nāda (Sādākhya-Tattva), Parabindu (Īśvara-Tattva), Bindu (Kārya), Nāda and Bīja. It is not clear to me where (if at all) the Śuddha-vidyā-Tattva comes in according to this scheme, unless it be involved in Nāda, the Mithaḥ-samāvāya; but the Puruṣa-Prakṛti-Tattvas appear to take birth on the division of the Para-bindu into Śiva and Śakti or Ham and Saḥ, Haṁsaḥ being the Puruṣa-Prakṛti Mantra.

The first impulse to creation comes from the ripening of the Adṛṣṭa of Jīvas, on which Sakala Parameśvara puts forth His Śakti (which means Himself as Śakti) to produce the Universe wherein the fruits of Karma may be suffered and enjoyed. All the above seven stages are included in, and constitute, the first stage of *Īkṣaṇa* or "Seeing" and is that stage in which Śabda exists in its supreme or Para form (Para-śabda-sṛṣṭi). She who is eternal (Anādirūpā) existing subtly as Cidrūpiṇī in Mahāpralaya becomes on the ripening of Adṛṣṭa, inclined (Utsuka) towards the life of form and enjoyment, and reveals Herself on the disturbance of the equilibrium of the Guṇas. As the Vāyavīyasaṁhitā says "Parā-Śakti through the will of Śiva is revealed with Śiva-Tattva (for the purpose of creation). Then She manifests as the oil which is latent in, and exudes from, the sesamum seed." Parameśvara is Saguṇa-Śiva or the Īśvara of Vedānta Philosophy with Māyā as His Upādhi. He is Sat, Cit, Ānanda in Māyā body and endowed with all Śaktis *(Sarva-vedānta-siddhānta-sārasaṅgraha* 312, 313, 315). There is, as the Pañcadaśī says, (3-38) a Śakti of Śiva which is in and controls all things which have their origin in Ānanda or Īśvara. When Īśvara is moved to create, this Īśvaraśakti or Māyā which is the aggregate of, and which yet transcends, all individual Śaktis issues from Him and from this Māyā issue all the particular Śaktis by which the universe is evolved and is maintained. The same substance is, to a large extent, to be found in all accounts under a variety of presentment of Symbols; even where there are real differences due to the diversity of doctrine of different Vedāntic schools. This is not the case here: for the account given is a Sādhanā presentment of Advaitavāda. The Śākta-Tantra teaches the unity of Paramātmā and Jīva, though its presentation of some subjects as Śakti, Māyā, Cidābhāsa is different (owing to its practical view-point) from Śaṅkara's Māyāvāda. On this matter I may refer my readers to the article which I recently wrote on Śakti and Māyā in the second number of the *Indian Philosophical Review* (Baroda) since incorporate in my *Śakti and Śākta*.

The three Bindus constitute the great Triangle of World-Desire which is the Kāmakalā; an intricate subject which I must leave for a future chapter. The three Bindus are Sun, Moon and Fire and three Śaktis Icchā, Jñāna, Kriyā associated with the three Guṇas: Sattva, Rajas, Tamas. I do not deal here with the order or correspondence which requires discussion. From them issued the Devīs Raudri, Jyeṣṭhā, Vāmā and the Trimūrtis Rudra, Brahmā, Viṣṇu.

The three Bindus are also known as the white Bindu (Sīta-bindu), the red Bindu (Śoṇa-bindu) and the mixed Bindu (Miśra-bindu). These represent the Prakāśa, Vimarśa and Prakāśa-Vimarśa aspects of the Brahman which are called in the ritual Caraṇa-tṛtīya (The Three Feet). The Gurupādukā-Mantra in which initiation is given in the last or Ṣadāmnāya

Dīkṣā represents a state beyond the Śukla, Rakta and Miśra-Caraṇas. So, it is said in Śruti that there are four Brahmapadās, three here and one the Supreme which is beyond.

As is the case in many other systems the One for the purpose of creation is presented in twofold aspects, for Unity is actionless, and their relation involves a third aspect which makes the Trinity. But this apparent differentiation does not derogate from the substantial unity of the Brahman. As the ancient Rudrayāmala (II. 22) says: "The three Devas Brahmā, Viṣṇu, Maheśvara are but one and formed out of My body."

*Ekā mūrtis trayo devā brahmaviṣṇumaheśvarāḥ.*
*Mama vigrahasaṅkliptāḥ sṛjati avati hanti ca.*

From the differentating Bindu are evolved the Tattvas from Buddha to Pṛthivī in and the six Lords of the Tattvas (preceding Paraśiva the seventh) who are the presiding Devatās of mind and of the five forms of matter. Here on the diremption or dichotomy of Consciousness, Mind and Matter are produced. That is, Consciousness functions in and through the Self-created limitations of mind and matter. It was on this division also that there arose the Cosmic Sound (Śabda-brahman) which manifests as Śabda and Artha. This is the Śabda-brahman: so called by those who ķnow the Āgamas.

*Bhidyamānāt parād bindor avyaktātmā ravo'bhavat.*
*Śabdabrahmeti taṁ prāhuḥ sarvāgamaviśāradāḥ.*
(*Śaradā-Tilaka* I-II)

It will be observed that in this verse the first Bindu is called Para and to make this clear the author of the

Prāṇatoṣiṇī adds the following note: "By Para-bindu is meant the first Bindu which is a state of Śakti *(Parādbindorityanena śaktyavastārūpa yaḥ prathama-bindus tasmāt)*. Śabda-brahman is the Brahman in its aspect as the immediate undifferentiated Cause of the manifested and differentiated Śabda, or language in prose or verse; and of Artha or the subtle or gross obejcts which thought and language dentoe. It is thus the causal state of the manifested Śabda or Mantra.

# Chapter 14

# MĀYĀ TATTVA

What Matter is in itself the sense do not tell us. All that can be predicated of its is its effect upon these senses. The experiencer is affected in five different ways giving rise in him to the sensations of hearing (Śabda); feel by which is experienced the thermal quality of things (Sparśa); colour and form (Rūpa); taste (Rasa); and smell (Gandha). The cause of these are the five Bhūtas which in the general cosmic evolution, are derived from the Tanmātras or general elements of the particulars of sense perception. These again together with the senses (Indriyas) or faculties of mind operating through a particular physical organ as their instruments and Manas the mental faculty of attention, selection and synthesis of the discrete manifold, derive from the still more general aspects of the Cosmic Mind or Antaḥkaraṇa which are the personal forms of limited experience respectively called Ahaṅkāra and Buddhi. These again are evolutes from that form of Śakti which is Prakṛti-Tattva and which in the 36 Tattvas scheme comes into being through the instrumentality of Māyā-Śakti from the preceding Tattvas of the pure creation extending from Śuddha-vidyā to Śiva-Śakti-Tattva, the Svarūpa of the last being Saccidānanda of Pure Spirit. Matter is thus a manifestation or aspect of Spirit. The two are ultimately one. They seem to be two because the fundamental Feeling (Cit) is able, as Śakti, to experience itself as object. As Professor Haeckel says, in conformity with Śākta Monism, Spirit and Matter are not two distinct entites but two forms or aspects of one single fundamental Substance (which is here the Brahman). The one entity with dual aspects is the sole Reality which presents itself to view as the infinitely varied picture of the universe. The two are inseparably combined in every atom which, itself and its forces, possess the elements not only of vitality but of further development in all degrees of Consciousness and Will. The ultimate substance is Śakti, which is of dual aspect as Cit-Śakti which represents the spiritual, and Māyā-Śakti which represents the material aspect. These are not separable. In the universe the former is the Spirit-matter and the latter Matter-spirit. The two exist in inseparable connection (Avinābhāva-sambandha) as inseparable (to use a simile of the Śaiva-Śāstra) as the winds of the heaven from the ether in which they blow. Manifested Śakti or Māyā is the universe. Unmanifest Śakti is feeling consciousness (Cidrūpa). Māyā-Śakti appears as subtle mind and as gross matter and as the life-force and is in Herself (Svarūpā) consciousness. There is and can be nothing absolutely lifeless or unconscious because Śakti is in itself Being– Feeling– Consciousness Bliss (Cid-rūpiṇi), – Ānandamayī) beyond all worlds (Viśvottīrṇā); and appears as apparently unconscious, or partly conscious and partly unconscious, material forms in the universe (Viśvātmaka). The universe is Śakti. Therefore, it is commingled Spirit-Matter. Śakti beyond all worlds is Consciousness. The one Consciousness exists throughout; when changeless it receives the name of Śiva; when the source of, and as all moving object, it is called Śakti.

The universe arises through a negation of veiling of true Consciousness. As the Spandarārikā says "By veiling the own true form its Śaktis ever arises" *Svarūpāvaraṇe cāsya śaklayaḥ satalotthitāḥ)*. This is a common doctrine of the three schools here discussed. The difference lies in this, that in Sāṅkhya it is a second independent principle (Prakṛti) which veils; in Māyāvāda Vedānta it is the non-Brahman unexplainable mystery (Māyā) which veils, and in Śākta-Advaita-vāda it is consciousness which, without ceasing to be such, yet veils itself. This statement shortly describes the difference in the three concepts which may however be more fully elaborated.

The Mahānirvāṇa-Tantra says that the vākya. "All this verily is Brahman" *(Sarvaṁ khalvidaṁ Brahma)* is the basis of Kulācāra. But Brahman is Consciousness; and it cannot be denied that there is an element of apparent unconsciousness in things. Śāṅkhya says that this is due to another Principle independent of the Puruṣa-consciousness, namely, the unconscious Prakṛti, which is real, notwithstanding its changes. But according to Advaitavāda Vedānta there is only one Reality. It therefore denies the existence of any second independent principle. Śaṅkara attributes unconsciousness to the unexplainable (Anirvacanīyā), wonder (Māyā), which is neither real (Sat), nor unreal (Asat) nor partly real and partly unreal (Sadāsat), and which though not forming part of Brahman, and therefore not Brahman, is yet, though not a second reality inseparately associated and sheltering with Brahman (Māyā Brahmāsritā) in one of its aspects (Īśvara); owing what false appearance of reality it has to the Brahman with which it is so associated. It is an eternal falsity *(Mithyābhūtā sanātanī)*, unthinkable, alogical, unexplainable *(Anirvacanīyā)*. The reflection of Puruṣa on

Prakṛti gives the appearance of consciousness to the latter. So, also the reflection (Cidābhāsa) of Brahman on unconscious Māyā is Īśvara and on unconscious Avidyā is Jīva. Though Māyā is thus not a second reality, the fact of positing it at all gives to Śaṅkara's doctrine a tinge of dualism from which the Śākta doctrine (which has yet a weakness of its own) is free. The Śākta doctrine has no need of Cidābhāsa. It says that Māyā is a Śakti of Brahman and being Śakti, which is not different from the possessor of Śakti, (Śaktimān), it is, in its *Svarūpa,* consciousness. It is then consciousness which veils itself; not unconscious Māyā which veils consciousness. According to Śaṅkara, man is the Spirit (Ātmā) vestured in the Māyika falsities of mind and matter. He accordingly can only establish the unity of Jīva and Īśvara by eliminating from the first Avidyā and from the second Māyā, both being essentially-- and from the transcendent standpoint – nothing. Brahman is thus left as a common denominator. The Śākta has need to eliminate nothing. Man's spirit or Ātmā is Śiva. His mind and body are Śakti. Śiva and Śakti are one. The Jīvātmā is Śaiva-Śakti, the latter being understood as its world-aspect. So is the Paramātmā; though here Śakti, being uncreating, is in the form of Consciousness (Cidrūpiṇī). The supreme Śiva-Śakti exists as one. Śiva-Śakti as the world is the Manifold. Man is thus not the Spirit covered by a non-Brahman falsity but Spirit covering itself with its own Power of Śakti. As the Kaulācārya Satyānanda says in his Commentary (which I have published) on the 4th Mantra of the Īśopaniṣad– "The changeless Brahman which is consciousness appears in creation as Māyā *which is Brahman* (Brahmamayī), Consciousness (Cidrūpiṇī), holding in Herself unbeginning (Anādi), Kārmika tendencies (Karma-saṁskāra), in the form of the three Guṇas. Hence, She is Guṇamayī (Her substance is Guṇa) despite being Cinmayī (Consciousness). *As there is no second principle,* these Guṇas are Cit-Śakti." Hence, in the words of the Yoginī-hṛdaya-Tantra, the Devī is *Prakāśavimarśa-sāmarasyarūpiṇi.* There is thus truly no unconscious Māyā and no Cidābhāsa. All which exists is Consciousness as Śakti. *"Ahaṁ strī"* as the Advaitabhāva Upaniṣad exclaims. And so the grand doctrine "All is Consciousness" is boldly and vigorously affirmed. Those who worship the Mother, worship nothing unconscious but a Supreme Consciousness which is Love, the body of which Love is all forms of consciousness-unconsciousness produced by and which is, Her as Śiva's Power. In short, Śaṅkara says that there is unconsciousness which appears to be conscious through Cidābhāsa. Śākta doctrine says Consciousness appears to be unconsciousness or more truly to have an elements of unconsciousness itn it (for nothing even empirically is absolutely unconscious) owning to the veiling play of Consciousness itself as Māyā-Śakti. The result is in the end the same-- "All is Consciousness"– but the method by which this conclusion is attained and the presentement of the matter is reversed.

This presentment again is in conformity with scientific research which has shown that even so-called "brute matter" exhibits the elements of that sentiency which, when evolved in man, is the full self-consciousness. It has been well said that sentiency is an integrant constituent of all existence, physical as well as metaphysical, and its manifestation can be traced throughout the mineral and chemical as well as the vegetable and animal worlds. It essentially comprises the functions of relation to environment, response to stimuli and atomic memory in the lower or inorganic plane, whilst in the higher in the organic plane it includes all the psychic functions such as consciousness, perception, thought, reasons, volition and individual memory. Throughout it is the one Mother who works, now veiling Her Bliss in inorganic matter, now more fully revealing Herself by gradual stages as the vitivity (which She is) displays itself in the evolving forms of worldly life. As Haeckel says, sentiency, is like movement, found in all matter. To reach this conclusion we must assume (as the Śaiva-Śākta schools do) that Kriyā and Icchā, its preliminary, are functions of Consciousness. Abhinava-Gupta in his Commentary on the Pratyabhījñā-Kārikā says, "The characteristic of action is the manifestation of all objects. These objects again characterised by consciousness-unconsciousness are in the nature of a shining forth (Ābhāsa). The universe is thus described as a "going forth" (Prasara) of Śiva".

The ultimate reality is Saccidānanda which, as the source of appearances, is called Śakti. The latter in its Sat (Being) aspect is omnipresent, indestructible (eternal) source and basis, both of the Cosmic Breath or Prāṇa as also of all vital phenomena displayed as the individual Prāṇa in separate and concrete bodies. Śakti is Life which in its phenomenal sense as manifested in individual bodies, issues form, and rests upon, and at basis is, Sat. In this aspect manifested Śakti is vitality which is the one fixed unalterable potential in the universe of which all other forms of energy are particular effects. Life is the phenomenal aspects of spirit in which, as its Cause, it is at the great dissolution merged. There is no absolute end of life but only to certain structures of life. As it had no end it has no absolute beginning. It appears only in creation from the depths of Being which is its unmanifested ground. The search for the "origin of life" is futile; for it issues from Brahman who, in a supreme sense, is Infinite Life. Life is throughout the Universe. Every atom of dust is quivering with it, as are the most sensitive organic structure. In the latter case it is obvious, in the former it is not so, but is yet traced. The existence and functions of life cannot be explained on exclusively mechanical principles. What is called mechanical energy is the effect and not the cause of vitality or Śakti as the Mother of all. The purpose of evolution is to take up the living potential from some lower grade, develop it and hand it over to a higher grade of forms.

Śakti as Cidānanda is, Icchā-Śakti, the source of all forms of will-power and, in matter, of mechanical energy; and as Jñāna-Śakti, of all forms of mentality and feeling, and as Kriyā, of all forms of activity (Kartṛtva), being in itself all-mighty.

The ultimate changeless Reality, in its aspect as Śakti, veils and contracts in various degrees its power of will, knowledge and action. This veiling, negation, limitation or contraction is seen at its fullest in so-called "dead inert brute" matter. This allegation of lifeless inertia is however the result of superficial observation. It is true that in gross matter (Bhūta) the light of consciousness is turned down to its utmost. it is no where however even empirically extinguished. Cit is faintly manifested by scientific experiment in gross matter; more clearly in the micro-organisms between such matter and the vegetable world, in which, as in the animal world evolved from it, vitality is so obvious that we have been wont to call these alone "alive." Śākta doctrine starts with the Full (Pūrṇa) and deals with the creation of things as a cutting down thereof. From a scientific point of view we may commence with the world as it is, taking inorganic matter as the starting point. From such a stand-point we may speak (See "Veda's vital molecule" and "Notes on the radical Vitality of all concrete matter" by G. Dubern) of a Radical Vital Potential in all matter, universal, omnipresent, indestructible, all-powerful; the source as will-power of mechanical energy, and as rudimentary sentiency of all mentality. From the Śāstrika standpoint the process is one of veiling and unveiling. Śakti veils itself down to and in Pṛthivī-Tattva of gross matter (Bhūta); and thereafter gradually unveils Herself up to and in man who in Samādhi realises his *Svarūpa* as pure, unveiled, Consciousness.

This veiling by Śakti takes place first in Śiva-Śakti-Tattva by the complete negation of the "*Idam*" of experience; and then through action of the *Idam* on the subjective aspect of the consciousness of the pure creation, in which subject and object exist as part of the One Self; and then through that form of Śakti which is Māyā which effects a severance of subject and object which are then experienced no longer as part of the one Self but as separate. The point of junction between Pure and Impure experience is the Tattva variously called Vidyā, Sadvidyā or Śuddha-vidyā, the first truly realistic stage of the Yogi. Because it is in the intermediate state, it is called Parāpara-daśa (Īś. Prat. III, 1-5) and, as the Svacchanda-Tantra (IV, 95) says, the "Experience in the form of Mantra of both difference and non-difference". After this Tattva, Māyā intervenes.

In the Tattva-Sandoha (v.5) it is said, "*Māyā* is the sense of difference (Bheda-buddhi) in all Jīvas which are parts of Her. Just as the shore hodls in the sea, so She ever obstructs the manifestation (Vibhava) of Ātmā which but for Her is otherwise unobstructed."

*Māyā vibheda-buddhir*
*nijāṁśa-jāteṣu nikhilajīveṣu.*
*Nityaṁ tasya niraṅkuśa–*
*vibhavaṁ veleve vāridhe rundhe.*

So also in the Īśvara-Pratyabhījñā it is said, "That which is nothing but the notion of difference (Bhedadhī) in things entertained by the Doer (Kartā) through in Himself of the nature of consciousness, is Māyā-Śakti, whom others, as in the case of Vidyeśvaras, call Vidyā".

*Bhedadhīr eva bhāveṣu kartur bodhātmano'pi yā.*
*Māya śaktyeva sā vidyetyanye vidyeśvarā yathā.*
(III, ii, 6)

She is Vidyā-Śakti when She reveals in the Paśu state of the Ātmā whose true nature is Lordship (Aiśvarya), but when She veils (Tirodhānakarī) then She is called Māyā.

*Tasyaiṣvaryasvabhāvasya paśu-bhāve prakāśīkā.*
*Vidyā-śaktis tirodhānakari māyābhidhā punaḥ.*
(*ibid.*, 7)

Śiva has two functions namely Tirodhāna, that by which he veils Himself to His worshipper, and Anugraha whereby He, through His grace, reveals Himself by the "descent of Śakti" or grace (Śakti-pāta). She is both Madhumati "Honey" and Māyā (Lalitāsahasranāma, v. 139). She is that saving (Tāraka) knowledge by which the ocean of the Saṁsāra is crossed. The Citkalā or Aṁśā of the great Consciousness enveloped by mind and matter is the Śakti which, as the Padma-Purāṇa says resides as the core of the "inner working" of all Jīvas and the Ānandakalikā or Gem of Bliss therein; She again as the Lalitāsahasranāma says (v. 142) is basis of the false (in the sense of impermanent) universe *(Mithyā jagadadhiṣṭhānā)* created by, and which is Her Māyā, the power of the Lord (Śāṇḍilya-Sūtra, 86) which obscures and which, as the Śākta Devī-Purāṇa says, is called Māyā, because it is the marvellous instrument whereby unheard of results are produced like those of dreams of Magic. She is in all systems, wheher as Prakṛti, Māyā or Māyāśakti, the *finitising* principle whereby forms are created in the formless Consciousness. This She effects by causing that duality of feeling of the self and not-self in the grand experience which is Mahāsattā. Under Her influence the Self experiences Itself as object in all the forms of the universe, which when completed is objectively seen as an evolution from Prakṛti-Tattva, that state of Śakti which is evolved by the action of Māyā and the five Kañcukas develoepd from Her. These are specific aspects of the great general limiting Power (Śakti) which Māyā is. With this Prakṛti is associated Puruṣa-Tattva, the two combined being Haṁsa. Puruṣa-Tattva is Ātmā enveloped by the Kañcukas, derived from Māyā and specific of its operation Śakti as Prakṛti, subject to the influence of the Kañcukas, develops on the dis-equilibrium of Her Guṇas from Herself, as Vikṛtis, the impure Tattvas (Aśuddha-Tattva) extending to Pṛthivī. At this point conscious vital energy materialises, forming, what has been called by the author cited "the crust of the vital molecule" of all forms of solid matter. Subjectively therefore the Māyā process is the establishment of a dichotomy of subject and object in which would otherwise be in unitary experience; and objectively it is the creation of the various psychical and physical forms into which the Universal Substance projects becoming in the course of such emanation more and more gross. Bindu as the Mantra designation of Īśvara-Tattva and its evolutes which are more and more gross (Sthūla); until passing the first four states of descreasing subtelty of matter. Substance emerges as the solid atoms of matter of which the physical universe is composed. These compounds being the subject of the senses are the materials of physical science which seeks to work the process backwards. At a point, search on the path of objectivity is closed. If it would know more, the mind must turn in one itself and release itself from all objectivity which Māyā is and fall back into that group of Consciousness (Māyātīta) whence it has emerged. From the Mantra aspect dealing with the origin of language, the undifferentiated Śabda which arises on the differentiation of the Bindu into Puruṣa-Prakṛti or Haṁsa develops, with the creation of mind and matter, into the manifested Śabda and Artha which are the Varṇas or letters (springing from the subtle Mātṛkas) expressed in Vaikharī speech made up of letters (Varṇa), syllables (Pada), and sentences (Vākya or the uttered Mantra). Mantra again is the thought *(Man)* which saves *(Trā, Trāyate)*: Saves from what? From firstly the evil which man, subject to Māyā, commits; and then, by the thorough purification of the mind (Citta-śuddhi), from Māyā Herself who is transformed in the Sādhaka into Vidyā-Śakti. Mantra is thus here a pure thought-form; a pure Vṛtti or modification of the Antaḥkaraṇa which is Devatā. The senses and mind are also Devatās being operations of the one Divine Śakti. Through Mantra the mind is divinely transformed. Contemplating, filled by, and identified with, Divinity in mantra form, which is a Sthūla (gross) aspects of Devī, it passes into Her subtle (Sūkṣma) Light form (Jyotirmayī Devī) which is the consciousness beyond the world of māyika form; the Īśvara and Īśvarī who as Śabda-Brahman are the source of, and appear as, that Māyā which is the Creatrix both of the objective world of Mind and Matter and of the manifested Śabda and Artha; the Word and its Meaning derived from the Mother in Her aspect as Supreme Nāda (Parā-nāda) and Supreme Speech (Parā-vāk).

## Chapter 15

# THE KAÑCUKAS

The six Kañcukas including Māyā which may be regarded as the root of the other five are Kāla, Niyati, Rāga, Vidyā, Kalā. The term Kañcuka means sheath or envelope. The same Tattvas are also called contractions (Saṅkoca), for creation is the contracted (Saṅkucadrūpā) form of infinite Śakti. It is to be observed that Māyā, Niyati and Kāla, occupy in the philosophy of Pāñcarātra-Āgama the very place which is held in the Śaiva-Śākta system by the Kañcukas (See as to this Dr. Otto Schrader's Ahirbudhnya-Saṁhitā 63, 64, 90). The author cited opines that the six Kañcukas are only an elaboration of the older doctrine of the three powers of limitation (Saṅkoca) of the Pāñcarātra which are Māyā, Kāla, Niyati. The same idea is expressed by these two terms, namely limitations by which the Ātma, in its form as the finite experiencer, is deprived of the specific attributes which It, as the Perfect Experience, possesed. Consciousness reaching forth to the World of enjoyment becomes subject to the Kañcukas and thus becomes the impure, finite, worldly experience where subject and object are completely different; which experience is, as it were, the *inversion* by the contraction and negation of Śakti of the perfect Experience from whose Śiva-Śakti-Tattva aspect proceeds. Infinite Consciousness whilst still transcendentally retaining its Svarūpa is, as Śakti narrowed to the degree which constitutes our experience on the material plane. The process may be represented in Diagram by an inverted triangle representing the Yoni or Śakti, in the form of the Pure Tattvas, resting on the point of an upright triangle. The point of intersection is Māyā from which proceeds the second triangle representing the impure Tattvas, which constitute worldy experience. Seen in the waters of Māyā all is reversed. Through the operation of Māyā and Kañcukas, Śakti assumes the gross contracted form of Prakṛti-Tattva which in association with Puruṣa-Tattva is Haṁsa. Śiva and Śakti are the Bird Haṁsa. Haṁsa is both male (Pūṁ or Puruṣa) and female (Prakṛtī). Haṁ is Śiva and Saḥ is Śakti. This Haṁsa-dvandva are in their gross form the universe *(Puṁ-prakṛtyātmaka haṁsas tadātmakaṁ idaṁ jagat)*. Puruṣa is the Ātmā enveloped by the Kañcukas which are the contractions of Consciousness and Its Powers. Māyā is the root and cause of all limitations of the powers (Vibhava) of consciousness (Ātma) for Māyā is the sense of difference (Bhedabuddhi) between all persons and things. Each Puruṣa (and they are innumerable) being as the Svacchanda-Tantra says, an universe of his own. Each Puruṣa creates under Māyā his or its own universe. The Kañcukas are thus the delimitations of the Supreme in Its form as Śakti. It was Eternity (Nityatā) but is now orderly and delimination (Pariccheda) productive of apprearance and disappearance (that is life and death). This is the operation of the Time-power of Kāla which is defined as follows in the Tattva-Sandoha (V.11) "That Śakti of His which is Eternity (Nityatā) descending and producing appearance and disappearance (birth and death); and which ever in regulated manner performs the function of division or delimitation (paricchẹda) should be regarded as in the form of *Kāla*-Tattva."

*Sā nityatāsya śakti nikṛṣya nidhanodaya-pradānena nityataparicchedukariklṛptā syāt kāla-tattva-rūpeṇa.* Kāla is the power which urges on and matures things. It is not in itself subjective or empirical time, though it gives rise to it. It is transcendental Time without sections (Akhaṇḍa-Kāla) giving birth to time as effect (Kārya-Kāla). This gross time with parts (Sakala-Kāla) only comes in with the creation of the gross Tattvas. So, it is said "Time leads me in time" (See Ahirbudhnya 64-67. See also the same Author's Ueber den stand der Indischen Philosophiẹ zur zeit Mahāvīras und Buddhas 17-30). Consciousness as Śakti is contracted into the mode of temporal thinking. It was freedom and indepẹndence (Svatantratā).. This is now contracted and the Puruṣa is forcibly subjected to guidance and regulation in what he must or must not do in any moment of time. This is Niyati, which is defined in the Tattva-Sandoha (v.12) as follows: "That which constitutes that Śakti of His which is called Independence or Freedom (Svatantratā); this same Śakti, and none other, becoming contracted and subjecting Him perforce to guidance and regulation (Niyamayatī) in a definitely ordered and restricted manner (Niyataṁ) as regards what is to be done or not done (that is, what he must not do at any given movment of time) is Niyati."

*Yāsya svatantratākhyā*
*śaktiḥ saṅkocaśālinī śaiva.*
*Kṛtyākṛtyeṣvāsaṁ*
*niyataṁ amuṁ niyamayan-tyabhun niyatiḥ.*

Niyati is spoken of in Pāñcarātra Āgama as the subtle regulator of everything (Sūkṣma-sarva-niyāmakaḥ. Ahirbudhnya VI. 46); and is said by Dr. Schrader to include in that system the functions of the three Śaiva-Śākta Kañcukas, Vidyā, Rāga and Kalā (Ahirbudhnya 64-65). It was completely satisfied with Itself for there was then no other. It was the Full (Pūrṇa) and thee was nothing else for it to interest Itself in and thus want. This Śakti becoming limited, makes the Puruṣa interested in objects and thus attaches them to enjoyment. This is Rāga which is defined in the Tattva-Sandoha (v. 10) as follows:

"There is another Śakti of his which is eternal complete satisfaction; the same becoming limited and attaching him ever to enjoyment, this Śakti is reduced to the condition of Rāga-tattva."

*Nitya-paripūrṇatṛptiḥ*
*śaktis-tasyaiva parimitā nu satī.*
*Bhogeṣu rañjayantī*
*satataṃ amuṁ rāga-tattvatāṁ yātā.*

The Brahman is as the Īśa-Upaniṣad says Pūrṇa the Full, the All which wants nothing; for there is nothing to the All which It can want. But when the one Experience becomes dual, and, subject and object are separate, then the self as subject becomes interested in objects that is in things other than itself. Icchā in the sense of desire implies a want of the fullness which is that of the Supreme perfect experience. In the supreme creative sense Icchā is the direction of Consciousness towards activity. The term Rāga is commonly translated desire. It is however properly that interest in object which precedes desire. Rāga is thus that interest in objects, seen as other than the self, which ripens into desire (Icchā) for them. Such Icchā is thus a limitation of the all-satisfied fullnes of the Supreme.

The power of the Surpeme was to know or experience all things and so its is Sarvajñata. This is limited and the Puruṣa thereby becomes a "little knower." This Kañcuka is called Vidyā which is defined in the Tattva-Sandoha (v.9) as follows: "His power of all-knowingness becoming limited and capable of knowing only a few things and producing knowledge (of a limited character) is called Vidyā by the wise of old."

*Sarvajñatasya śaktiḥ*
*parimitatanur alpa-vedya-mātraparā.*
*Jñānaṁ utpādayanti*
*vidyeti nigadyate hudhair ādyaiḥ.*

The supreme is all powerful, mighty to do all things (Sarvakartṛtā). This power is contracted so that the Puruṣa can accomplish a few things and becomes a "little doer." This is Kalā which is defined in the Tattva-Sandoha (v.8) as follows --

That which was His power of all-doing-ness the same being contracted and capable of accomplishing but a few things and reducing him to the state of a little doer is called Kalā.

*Tat-sarvakartṛtā sā*
*saṅkucitā katipayārtha-mātraparā*
*Kiñcit-kartāraṁ amuṁ*
*kalayañti kirtyate kalā nāmā.*

Kalā is thus nothing but Kartṛttva or infinite activity,

agency, and mightiness cut down to the limits of the Jīva's power; that is lowered to the possibilities of finite action.

Thus, the Śaktis of the supreme which are many become contracted. Consciousness thus limited in six-fold manner by its own Śakti is the Puruṣa associated with Prakṛti. Kalā (in its more generic sense) is said in the Śaiva-Tantrasāra (Āhnika 8) to be "the cause of the manifestation of Vidyā and the root when She is operating on that Kartṛttva which is qualified by the qualifiying conditions of littleness; this limited power of agency having been itself the work of Māyā. Now, the moment that Kalā separates from herself what constitutes this qualifying aspect spoken of above as Kiñcit (little) at that very movement there is the creation of the Prakṛti Tattva which is in the nature of a generality (Sāmānya-mātra) unmarked by any specific form of object of enjoyment, such as happiness, sorrow and delusion; and of which another name is the equalisation of the Guṇas. Thus the creation under the influence of the Kalā-tattva of the limited expriencer (Bhoktṛ, that is, of the Puruṣa and of the experienced (Bogya) or Prakṛti, is quite simultaneous, that is without any succession whatever in the process Thus, being simultaneous they are ever associated."

The eighth Āhnika of the Tantrasāra (the Śaiva and not the Śākta ritual work of Kṛṣṇānanda-Āmavāgīśa) says: Thus, it has been already shown that Kalā is the cause of manifestation of Vidyā and the rest (*i.e.*, the other four Kañcukas leaving out Māya) when she (Kalā) is operating on that agency of doer-ness (Kartṛttva) which is qualified (Viśeṣya) by the qualifying (Viśeṣaṇa) condition of littleness; this limited power of agency (Kiñcitkartṛttva as opposed to Sarva-kartṛttva) having been itself the work of

Māyā. Now, the moment that Kalā separates from Herself that which constitutes this qualifying aspect (Viśeṣaṇa-bhāga) spoken of above as Kiñcit and is an object of knowledge and action, that very movement there is the creation) (Sarga) of the Prakṛti-Tattva which is of the nature of a generality only (Sāmānya-mātra) unmarked by any specific forms of the enjoyable (Bhogya) such as happiness, sorrow, and delusion (which are therefore as yet undifferentiated) and of which another name is the equalisation of their Guṇas (*i.e.,* of Sukha, Duḥkha and Moha or of the Guṇas of Her). Thus, the creation under the influence of the Kalā-Tattva of the Enjoyer (Bhoktṛ or limited experiencer) and Enjoyable (Bhogya or experienced) is quite simultaneous, that is without any succession whatever in the process and being simultaneous they are conjoined.

*(Evaṁ kiñcit-kartṛttvaṁ yan māyākāryaṁ, tatra kiñcittva-viśiṣtaṁ yat kartṛttvaṁ, viśeṣyaṁ tatra vyāpriyamāṇā kalā vidyādi-prasavahetur iti nirūpitam. Idānīṁ viśeṣaṇabhāge yaḥ kiñcit ityukto jñeyaḥ kāryaśca taṁ yāvat sā kalā svātmanaḥ pṛthak kurute tāvad eṣa eva sukha-duḥkha-mohātmaka-bhogya-viśeṣānusyūtasya sāmānya mātrosya tad-guṇa-sāmyā-para-nāmnaḥ prakṛti-tattvasya sargaḥ-iti bhoktṛbhogya-yugalasya samam eva kalā-tattvayattā sṛṣṭiḥ).*

Again in the Tantrāloka (Āhnika 9) it is said "So far it has been shown how Agency (Kartṛttva) which is always accompanied by the power to enjoy (Bhoktṛttva) is (to be found) in that qualified aspect (that is Kartṛttva) of the Tattva called Kalā which (aspect) is characterised by a limited agency (little-doerness)."

Here may be interposed a note of explanation: Kartṛttva is creative activity, ideation and formation as contrasted with a merely induced and passively accepted experience which is Jñātṛttva. Kartṛttva is the power of modifying the *Idaṁ*. The Sāṁkhyas say that the Puruṣa is Bhoktā but not Kartā. But the Śaiva-Śāktas hold that there is no Kartṛttva without Bhoktṛttva. In Parā-saṁvit there is the potential germ of (1) Jñātṛttva, (2) Bhoktṛttva and (3) Kartṛttva held in undistinguishable unity. In Śiva-Śakti Tattva the first exists and the second and third are, through Śakti, suppressed. In Sadākhya there are the first and the incipiency of the second and the third; and in Īśvara-Tattva all three are developed but as yet undifferentiated. The Íśvara consciousness directed to the "Idam" produces equality of attention on "Aham" and "Idam" which is Sadvidyā-Tattva whence arise Māyā and the Kañcukas evolving Puruṣa-Prakṛti. Para-Saṁvit is the pure changeless aspect of Cit. Īśvara is the fully risen creative consciousness wherein is the undifferentiated Śakti which functions as Icchā, Jñāna, Kriyā, Jñātṛttva or Jñāna. Śakti in Īśvara does not invove limited modification; for the whole universe as the Self is present to Self. But in Puruṣa there is such a modification; the Jñātṛttva functioning through Buddhi, the Vṛttas of which are expressions of the changing, limited, and partial characteristics of the knowledge had through this instrument and its derivatives.

The citation continues, "But in what constitutes therein the part "Kiñcit" as a qualifying aspect, Kalā gives birth to teh Pradhāna which arises from that (Kiñcit aspects) as a clear but general objectivity which is separate or distinct from (the Puruṣa)."

*Evaṁ kalākhya-tattvasya kiñcit-kartṛttva-lakṣaṇe.*
*Viśeṣyabhāge kartṛttvaṁ carcitaṁ bhoktṛ-pūrvakaṃ*
*Viśeṣanatayā yo'tra kiñcit bhāgas-tadūbitaṃ*
*Vedyomātraṁ sphuṭaṁ bhinnaṁ pradhānaṁ sūyate kalā.*

That is Kartṛttva is that aspect of Kalā which is characterised by Kiñcit-Kartṛttva. From the qualifying (Viśeṣaṇa, that is, Kiñcit) aspect Kalā produces Prakṛti which is distinct from Kalā as Puruṣa, which Prakṛti exists as a mere general obejctivity which becomes particular when owing to disequilibirum in the Guṇas the Vikṛtis are produced.

Again it is said *(ibid.):* "Kalā reduces the Bhogyā (Prakṛti) and the Bhoktā (Puruṣa) simultaneously by the notion of, or by seeking to establish a difference between the two aspects in herself, namely, Kartṛttva and Kiñcit; by working on Kartṛttva alone), (yet), the Bhoktā and Bhogyā are inseparate from one another. And because what is thus the barest objectivity (Samvedya-mātra) is known (or experienced) later as (or in the form of) happiness (Sukha) sorrow (Duḥkha) and delusion (Vimoha) it is therefore called the equalisation of these (three) in the beginning."

*Samāmeva hi bhogyaṁ ca bhoktāraṁ ca prasūyate,*
*kalā bhedābhisañdhānād aviyuktaṁ parasparaṃ.*
*Evaṁ samvedyamātraṁ yat sukhaduḥkhya-vimohataḥ,*
*bhoktsyate yet tataḥ proktaṁ tatsāmyātmakaṁ āditoḥ.*

When Māyā-Śakti first severs the "Aham" and "Idam" this latter is still experienced as an unlimited whole. The next step is that in which the whole is limited and broken up into parts, for our experience is not of an all-pervading homogeneous whole but of a heterogeneous universe. Kalā, as a development of Māyā-Śakti, belittles the Puruṣa's hitherto unlimited Agency which thus becomes Kiñcit-Kartṛttva. Agency which exists both as to the Knowable (Jñeya) and object of action (Kārya) has two aspects, namely the qualified power of action (Viśeṣya-Kartṛttva) on the part of the Puruṣa and the object or "little" in respect of which Kartṛttva operates, namely the "little" or universe (Kiñcit or Viśeṣaṇa) which is the "Idam" as viewed by Puruṣa after the operation of Kalā Śakti. Kalā operates on agency (Kartṛttva) and not on the "this" which is by such operation necessarily Kiñcit. For if the power and experience of the Self is limited, the obejct is experienced as limited; for the object is nothing but the Self as object. In other words the production of Puruṣa is a positive operation of Kalā whereas the production of Prakṛti is a negative oepration due to the limitation of the Puruṣa which as so limited, experiences the universe as Kiñcit. Prakṛti is thus nothing but the object of Kartṛttva, as it exists when the latter has been whittled down by Kalā. Puruṣa and Prakṛti thus both emerge as the result of the action by Kalā on the Puruṣa. For this reason Puruṣa and Prakṛti are simultaneously produced and are also inseparable.

The following chapters deal with Puruṣa and Prakṛti or Haṁsa; the Kāmakalā or three Bindus arising on the differentiation of the Para-bindu which differentiation witnesses the birth of Haṁsa; and then with the creation of the impure Tattvas (Aśuddha-Tattva) from Prakṛti and the Varṇamālā or the Garland or Rosary of Letters the evolution of which denotes the origin of speech and of Mantra.

# Chapter 16

# HAṀSA

*Haṁsa* is Puruṣa-Prakṛti-Tattva. *Ham* is "Male" or Śiva; *Saḥ* is "Female" and Śakti. Śiva-Śakti are therefore Haṁsa which combined mean the "Bird" Haṁsa, the material shape of which is variously said to be that of the goose, flamingo, brāhminī duck and rightly by others to be legendary. The universe is made of, and informed by this Haṁsa Pair (Hamsa-dvandva) who are Puruṣa and Prakṛti and in all the latter's varied forms *(Pumprakṛtyātmako haṁsas tadātmakaṁ idaṁ jagat)*. Of these the Ānandalaharī says (39) "In Thy Anāhata Lotus I salute the Wondrous Pair who are Ham and Saḥ, swimming in the mind of the Great who ever delight in the honey of the blooming lotus of knowledge." That is, they manifest in the mind of the Great delighting in the honey of Consciousness. This Haṁsaḥ reversed is the Vedantic "So'ham" of which the Sammohana-Tantra (Ch. VIII) says "Hakāra is one wing. Sakāra is the other. When stripped of both wings then Tārā is Kāmakalā." Jīva is Haṁsa. The same Tantra says that the Sādhaka of Tārā is the Lord of both Kādi and Hādi Mata. The Haṁsatārā-Mahāvidyā is the sovereign mistress of Yoga whom the Kādis call Kalī, the Hādis Śrīsundarī and the Ka-Hādis Haṁsaḥ.

The Jñānārṇava-Tantra (xxi-22) speaking of the Citkuṇḍa as the Maṇḍala in the Mūlādhāra where Homa is done, defines as follows the four Ātmās, *viz.*, Paramātmā, Antarātmā, Jñānātmā and Ātmā which form the Cit-kuṇḍa and by the knowledge whereof there is no rebirth. Ātmā is Prāṇarūpī, that is the Ātmā which is in all beings as their Prāṇa. It is Haṁsa-Svarūpī or Jīvātmā manifested by outer and inner breathing (Śvāsa, Ucchvāsa). It is compared to the ether in a pot, which the potter's wheel separates from the surrounding Ākāśa but from which there is no distinction when the pot is broken. The individual breath is the Cosmic Breath from which it seems to be different by the forms which the latter vitalises. Jñānātmā is Sākṣāt-sākṣīrūpaka. It is that which witnesses all and by which the unity of all is known. It is reflected in Buddhi and the rest and is yet in its own form distinguishable therefrom, just as the rays of the moon are reflected on water and seem to be, and are yet, not one with it. It is thus the substratum of Buddhi and of all the subjective or mental Tattvas derivable therefrom. By "Antar" in the term Antarātmā is meant the subtle (Rahasya-sūkṣmarūpaka) Ātmā which pervades all things; the spark of Paramātmā which indwells all bodies (Antargata). It is the Haṁsa known only by Yogis. Its beak is Tāra (Praṇava or "Om" Mantra), Nigama and Āgama are its two wings. Śiva and Śakti its two feet. The three Bindus are its three eyes. This is the Paramahaṁsa; that is Haṁsa in its supreme aspects as the Consciousness ground of the manifested Haṁsa or Jīva. When this Paramahaṁsa is spread (Vyāpta), this is, displayed, then all forms of matter (Bhūta) *viz.*, Ākāśa, Pavana and the rest spirng up in their order. Of these five the root is Citta. This Haṁsa disports itself in the World-lotus sprung from the Mud of Delusion (Mohapaṅka) in the Lake of Ignorance (Avidyā). When this Haṁsa becomes unworldly (Niṣprapañca) and in dissolving form (Saṁhārarūpī) then it makes visible the Ātmā or Self *(Ātmānaṁ pradarśayet)*. Then its "Birdness" (Pakṣitva) disappears and the So'ham Ātmā is established. "Know this" says the Jñānārṇava "to be the Paramātmā."

Puruṣa is Ātmā subject to Māyā-Śakti and the other limiting Śaktis called the Kañcukas. Prakṛti is that state of Śakti which arises as the result of the collective operation of Māyā and the Kañcukas; a transformation of Śakti existing as a homogeneity and general objectivity which develops of its own power, which is the summation of the Śaktis producing it, into the heterogeneous universe. The Puruṣa-Prakṛti-Tattvas arise as a bifurcation in Consciousness on the differentiation of the Para-bindu into the three Bindus which form the Kāmakalā which again may be pictured as the triangular base of the pyramidal (Śṛṅgātaka) figure in the Śrī-Yantra at whose apex is the Baindava-Cakra and Parabindu. The first two Bindus represent the Śiva aspects and the Śakti aspects of the one Consciousness, and the third the mutual relation of Śiva-Śakti aspect of the two. From this differentiation arises in the Mantra line of creation, Paraśabda and manifested Śabda and Artha; in the Tattva line, Buddhi and the rest; and in the line of the Lords of the Tattvas (Tattveśa), Śambhu and the rest. In its most general and philosophical sense Puruṣa-Prakṛti represent that stage in the evolving Consciousness (Śakti) in which, after passing from the mere I-experience *(Aham-pratyaya-vimārśā)*, and the "I-this" or "Aham-Idam," experience, in which the object or Idam is still experienced as part of the self (the completed type of such experiencer being Īśvara). Consciousness emerges as the experience of duality in which the object is seen as outside of, and separate from, the self. This however is a state of mere general objectivity. The final state has yet to be described when undifferentiated objectivity and supreme Sound (Paraśabda) evolve, the first into the differentiated objects of the universe (Aśuddha-Tattva) and the second into the differentiated word (Śabda) and its meaning (Artha) which is the birth of Mantra consisting of letters (Varṇa), syllables (Pada) and sentences (Vākya). With the differentiation of Prakṛti appear multitudinous Puruṣas of varying experience, each living in a universe of its own.

Puruṣa is not merely confined to man but is applicable to every Jīva who is the Enjoyer (Bhoktā) or Puruṣa of the enjoyable (Bhogya) or Prakṛti. Puruṣa again is not limited to the organic life of animals and plants or the micro-organisms which hover between organic and inorganic matter. The term includes the latter also. For whatever may be the popular signification of the term Jīva as living organic bodies, in its philosophical sense all is Jīvātmā which is not Paramātmā. And in this, modern science bears out the notions here described. The former arbitrary partitions made between the living and non-living are being broken down. We may for practical purposes call that "living" which obviously displays certain characteristics which we call "life" such as the so-called vital phenomena manifested by plants, animals and men. But the life and consciousness displayed in organic bodies is not something wholly new which had no place in the inorganic material of which they are composed. All such vital phenomena exist in subdued or potential form in every kind of matter which contains the potentiality of all life. Life as we know it is the phenomenal aspect of Bieng-Itself (Sat). Feeling-Consciousness as we know it is the limited manifestation (manifestation being limitation) of the undifferentiated Feeling-Consciousness which is Cit, Sat and Ānanda. All which is manifested exists potentially in its ground. Each of such manifestations is such ground (Bhūmi) veiled in varying degrees; now more, now less, fully displaying the nature of Spirit, the source of all life, feeling, will and consciousness. Superficial notions based on appearances have given rise to the notion of "dead" matter. But science has given new instruments for and extended the range of our observation and has shown that life and consciousness, though in a subdued or veiled form, exist throughout the universe. Vedānta it its Śākta version says that all forms are the operation of Consciousness as Māyā-Śakti. As the ancient Upaniṣad says and modern so-called "New Thought" repeats "What one thinks that one becomes." All recognise this principle to a certain point. If man thinks inhuman thoughts he dehumanises himself. Vedānta carries the application of this principle to its logical conclusion and affirms that not only does thought operate modifications in and within the limits of particular types of species, but actually evolves such and all other types through the cosmic collective. Thought of which the universe is a material expression. Thus, every unit or atom of matter is a Puruṣa identifying itself with the solid (Pārthiva) "crust" of matter, which is the gross expression on the sensual plane of more subtle forces emanating from that Ground Substance, which is the source both of the experiencing subject and the object experienced. If the operation of gross matter gives the appearance of rigid mechanism, this does not imply that such operation is wholly unconscious and lifeless, but that life and consciousness are veiled by the Tamas Guṇa of Prakṛti in which Kalā, Niyati and other Kañcukas are operating to their fullest extent. But however intense may be their operation, life and consciousness can never be destroyed, for being Śakti Herself they are indestructible. Thus, every molecule of mineral substance is Puruṣa or Consciousness identifying itself with matter in its solid and apparently unconscious inert state. For Consciousness becomes that with which its identifies mineral matter it becoems that matter. What we think that we become. Nothing however is absolutely unconscious or inert. Every single atom in the unvierse is in constant movement and hence the world is called Jagat or that which moves. This scientific doctrine is in India an ancient inheritance. And so the Mantra runs "Hrīṁ. The Supreme Haṁsa dwells in the brilliant Heaven." The word Haṁsa is here said to be derived from the word Hanti which means Gati or motion. Sāyaṇa says that it is called Āditya because it is in perpetual motion. The Tattva Sandoha (VV. 13, 14) says:

"She is considered to be Prakṛti who is the collectivity of all the Śaktis, (Will, Knowledge and Action) who is the peaceful, that is, quiescent (Śāntā) Śakti of Him in contracted form (Saṅkucadrūpā); who is in the form of the equilibrium of Sattva, Rajas and Tamas Guṇas which again are Will, Knowledge and Action gathered together (Saṅkalita); who is in the nature of general unparticularised feeling (Citta) which is in the form of the undifferentiated Buddhi (and other Tattvas)."

*Icchādi-tri-samaṣṭiḥ*
  *śaktiḥ śāntā'sya saṅkucadrūpā.*
*Saṅkalitechādyātmaka*
  *sattvādika-sāmya-rupiṇī śaiva.*
*Buddhyādi-sāmarasya-*
  *svarūpacittātmika matā prakṛtiḥ.*

"Ham" or the male (Pumān) or Puruṣa is again in the same work (v. 6) described as:

He who having by Her become of limited form with all His powers contracted is this Male (Pumān or Puruṣa) like the sun which becoming red at even tide and His Power (of shining) contracted can scarce reveal Himself (by shining abroad).

*Sa tayā parimitamūrtiḥ*
*saṅkucita-samastaśaktir eṣa pumān.*
*Raviriva sandhyā-raktaḥ*
*saṁhṛtā-śaktiḥ svabhāsane' pyapatiḥ.*

Again in the same work (v.7) it is said.

His Śaktis are many consisting of complete Kartṛttva (power of action) and others, but on His becoming contracted (that is, limited) they also become contracted in the forms of Kalā and the rest and make him thus manifest (as Puruṣa).

*Sampūrṇa-kartṛtādya*
*bahvyaḥ santyasya śaktayas tasya.*
*Saṅkocāt saṃkucitāḥ*
*kalādirūpeṇa rūdhayanty evaṃ.*

Again in the Īśvara-Pratyabhījña it is said:

He who is Experiencer commencing with Śūnya (Śiva-tattva) and the rest, He being clothed by the five Kañcukas, Kāla and the rest, and becoming object to Himself, is then the Experiencer of objects as separate from Him.

*Yaśca pramātā śūnyādiḥ prameye vyatirekiṇi*
*Māta bhavati meyaḥ san kālādi-pari veṣṭitaḥ.*
(III.ii, 9)

That is, object is the Self appearing as such. He retains His own Self-hood and becomes at the same time the object of His own experience. Māyā, is not something apart from Brahman, for it is Brahman who through Māyā, an aspect of Brahman, Himself becomes His own object. In the first act of creation He commences to become His own object, but it is only when the subject as Puruṣa is clothed, that is limited, by the Kañcukas, that the latter sees objects as other than and outside Himself. At this stage duality is established and exfoliates in the Vikṛtis of Prakṛtis as the multiple experience of the World of Mind and Matter.

The Guṇas of Prakṛti are inadequately translated as "qualities", because the latter word involves some substance of which they are the qualities. But Prakṛti Śakti is, as Prakṛti, the Guṇas and nothing else, though Her Svarūpa, as that of all Śaktis, is Sat-Cit-Ānanda. The Guṇas Sattva, Rajas, Tamas are properly factors or constituents of Prakṛti. Of these it is commonly said that Tamas Guṇa is the veiling principle of Prakṛti. This is so. But nevertheless it is to be remembered that all the factors of Prakṛti in one way or another veil; the difference being that whereas Sattva to some degree veils (for Sattvaguṇa is not as such the same as absolute Sat) it is in its highest degree of potency, that is, predominance, the least degree of veiling, and therefore it represents the tendency to unveil, that is, to reveal and manifest Being (Sat) and Consciousness (Cit); whereas Tamas is in its highest potency the greatest degree of veiling and therefore specifically represents the tendency to veil. Rajas is the operative power in both cases. In all bodies there are the three Guṇas (for these cannot separately exist though one or other may predominate), and it is because of this and therefore of the presence of Sattva-Guṇa in organic matter that it exhibits the rudiments of sentiency and consciousness. But in inorganic matter Tamas Guṇa prevails. As bodies evolve, the strength of the operation of Tamas gradually diminishes and that of Sattva increases until in man it becomes predominant. The whole object of Sādhana is to increase Sattva-Guṇa until on man becoming wholly Sāttvika, his body passes from the state of predominant Sattva-Guṇa into Sat Itself. These Guṇas represent in the Jīva or Paśu the Icchā, Kriyā, Jñāna and Māyā-Śaktis of the Lord. As regards Māyā, the Lord (Māyin), as the Kulārṇava-Tantra says, wields and controls and is free of it; Jīva is controlled by it. So the Īśvara-Pratyabījñā (IV. I,4) says, "What are Jñāna and Kriyā (on the part) of the Lord (Pati) in all beings and things (Bhāveṣu) which (to Him) are really of the nature of His own body (or limbs) – it is these two (that is Jñāna and Kriyā) and nothing else (eva) which together with Māyā as the thrid are the Sattva, Rajas, and Tamas, (Guṇas in respect) of the Paśu."

*Svāṅga-rūpeṣū bhāveṣu patyurjñānaṁ kriyā ca yā.*
*Māyā tṛtīyā tā eva paśoḥ sattvaṁ rajas tamaḥ.*

Śiva-śakti has a threefold aspect as Icchā, Jñāna, Kriyā, which are inseparably associated, just as the Guṇas are, though, as in the latter case, one or other may be predominant. Of these again Icchā and Kriyā may be considered together; for as resolve is directed to action it is the preliminary of it. Icchā in the Śaiva-Śāstra is described as a state of wonder *(Sa camatkārā Icchāśaktiḥ)* in the Puruṣa. But Kiryā considered (for the purpose of analysis only) as apart from Jñāna is blind. For this reason Kriyā has been associated with Tamas. It is very clearly explained by Kṣemarāja in his Tattva-Sandoha (vv. 13-15), that Icchā or resolve to action becomes at a lower stage Rajas Guṇa, the principle of activity in Prakṛti; Jñāna becomes Sattva or the principle of manifestation in the same; and Kriyā becomes Tamas Guṇa or the specific veiling principle of the same form of Śakti. He says, "His Will (Icchā) assumed the form of Rajas and became Ahaṅkāra which produces the notion of "I" (Aham). His knowledge (Jñāna) likewise became Sattvarūpa and Buddhi which is the determining form of experience. His Kriyā being in the nature of Tamas and productive of Vikalpa (and Saṅkalpa) *i.e.*, rejection (and selection) is called Manas" *(Icchāsya rajo rūpāhaṅkṛti-rāsid ahampratitikarī jñānāpi śattvarūpā nirṇayabhodhasya kāraṇaṁ buddhiḥ, Tasya kriyā tamomaya-mūrtir mana ucyate vikalpakarī).*

The evolution of these Tattvas (Aśuddha) is the subject of a future chapter. But before dealing with these its is necessary, in the creative order, to further describe the Kāmakalā in which the Haṁsa arises and the Rosary or Garland of letters (Varṇamālā) which is the Mantra aspect of the Tāttvika evolution will come later.

# Chapter 17

# KĀMAKALĀ

In the previous chapters it has been shown that the Parabindu or Īśvara Tattva assumes in creation a threefold aspect as the three Bindus,— Bindu (Kārya), Nāda, Bīja. These three points constitute symbolically a Triangle which is known as the Kāmakalā. Kāma is of course not here used in the gross sense of desire, sexual or otherwise, but of Icchā, the Divine creative Will towards the life of form, which is here explicated from Bindu, the aspect previously assumed by Śakti through Nāda *(Bindutāṁ abhyeti)*. The undivided supreme Cit-śakti *(Akhaṇḍa-paracicchakti)* becoming desirous of appearing as all the Tattvas *(Samasta-tattva-bhāvena vivarttecchāsamanvitā)* assumes the Bindu aspect *(Bindubhāvam paryeti)* characterised by a predominance of activity *(Kriyā-prādhānya-lakṣaṇā)*. Here it may be observed that Icchā or Will is a form of Kriyā (action), in the sense that it is the preliminary to action and sets the self in motion. Śakti passes from potency through Will to action, which through Para Bindu manifests. Bindu-bhāva is that state (Īśvara-tattva) in which it is fully equipped to work and does so. Its threefold aspect as it works are Bindu Śivātmaka, Bīja, Śaktyātmaka and Nāda. Nāda is Samavāya, that is relationship of connection

(Sambandha) as exciter (Kṣobhaka) and that which is excited (Kṣobhya), which relation is the cause of creation (Sṛṣṭihetu). The Śāradā (I.10) then proceeds to deal with the appearance of the three Devīs and three Devas which are in the nature of the three Śaktis (Icchā, etc.) and Fire, Moon and Sun. Having then dealt with Śabda-sṛṣṭi it proceeds to describe Artha-sṛṣṭi (I.15), giving first the line of Devas from Śambhu who are the Lords of the Tattvas (Tattveśa) and then that part of Artha-sṛṣṭi which is Tattva-sṛṣṭi or the evolution of the Tattvas of mind and matter from Buddhi to Pṛthivī.

It is not easy in all cases to discover and set forth an accurate summary of the Devīs, Devas, Śaktis and so forth in Śabda-sṛṣṭi: because the Texts being in verse are not always to be read as they stand, the order of words being in some cases regulated by the meter. As the author of the Prāṇatoṣiṇī says in dealing with a citation from the Gorakṣa-Saṁhitā, the texts must not be read "Pratiśabdam", that is, according to the order of the words, but "Yathāsambhavam", according to the facts. But this does not relieve us from the difficulty of ascertaining what is the fact; that is the real order. Other elements may be also enter into the calculation: for instance, as Rāghava Bhatta points out, the order of Śaktis varies in Íśvara and Jīva. In the former it is Icchā, Jñāna and Kriyā and in Jīva, Jñāna, Icchā and Kriyā. In Īśvara's ideation *(Pratyabhījñā)* when He desires to do anything, an act of volition proceeds from Him *(Svecchyā kriyā)* to know or to do it *(Tat Jñātuṁ kartuṁ vā);* next there is the capacity for cognising such acts *(Tat kārya-jñāna-darśana-śahtitā)* which is Jñānaśakti; thirdly the gross efforts *(Sthūlaḥ samudyamaḥ)* is the Kriyā-śakti *(Kriyāśaktitā)* from which the whole world proceeds *(Tataḥ sarvaṁ jagat paraṁ)*. Rāghava also points out that there is a difference of order in Śabda-sṛṣṭi and Artha-sṛṣṭi. Thus in dealing with the Praṇava it is said, "A (the letter) which is Sun is Brahmā": but here in the Śāradā verse, "Viṣṇu is Sun." I will first give the order as it is given in the Śāradā Text (vl.10): "From Bindu came Raudrī; from Nāda Jyeṣṭhā, from Bījā, Vāmā. From these came Rudra, Brahmā, Ramādhipa (Viṣṇu)".

*Raudrī bindos tato nādaj jyeṣṭhā bījād ajāyata.*
*Vāmā, tābhvaḥ samutpannā rudrabrahmāramādhipāḥ.*

It then continues, "Who are in the nature of Jñāna, Icchā, Kriyā and Fire, Moon and Sun (v.11) *(Saṁjñanecchākriyātmāno vahnīndvarkasvarūpiṇaḥ),* who are in the form (Rūpa) of Nirodhikā, Arddhendu and Bindu." These are all different states of Śakti *(Śakterevāvasthaviśeṣāḥ),* for it is owning to their arising from Śakti *(Śaktitaḥ utpannatvāt),* that they are identified with the Śaktis Icchā and so forth.

According to the Yoginī-hṛdaya-Tantra (1) the order is (a) Icchā, Vāmā, Paśyanti; (b) Jñānā, Jyeṣṭhā, Madhyamā; (c) Kriyā, Raudrī, Vaikharī. It says that when Icchā-Śakti in the form of a goad (Aṅkuśakāra, that is, the bent line Vakrarekhā) is about to display the universe which is in seed (Bīja) form, She is Vāmā and in the form of Paśyantī Śabda. Paśyantī "She who sees," Īkṣaṇa. Vāmā is so called because this Śakti vomits forth the universe *(Vamanāt Vāmā)*. Jyeṣṭhā which is in the form of a straight line (Ṛjurekhā) attaining the state of Mātṛkā *(Mātṛkatvaṁ upapannā)* is Madhyamā vāk. Raudrī is Kriyā in triangular or pyramidal (Śṛṅgaṭaka,), this is, three-dimensional form, and is the manifested Vaikharī-Śabda. According to the Kāmakalāvilāsa (Comm. v. 22), Yoginī-hṛdaya-Tantra (Saṅketa1), and the Saubhāgyasudhodaya cited in Saṅketa (2) of the lst Śāstra, the order would appear to be (a) Icchā Rajas Vāmā Brahmā Paśyanti-Śabda; (b) Jñāna Sattva Jyeṣṭhā Viṣṇu Madhyamā-Śabda; (c) Kriyā Tamas Raudrī Rudra Vaikharī-Śabda.

I will not however here attempt a discussion, which would be both lengthy and technical, of the texts on this point. For present practical purposes it is sufficient to know that the three Bindus are Śiva, Śakti, Śivaśakti; Prakāśā, Vimarśa, Prakaśa-Vimarśa; White, Red and Mixed; Bindu, Nāda, Bīja; Supreme, Subtle, Gross; the three Devīs, the three Devas, and the three Śaktis of Will, Knowledge and Action. The Supreme at this point thus becomes a Trinity of Energy.

The division of the Mahābindu may be memorised by writing in Sanskrit the "Fire" Bīja or "Raṁ", that is Ra with Candra-bindu. Then invert the Nāda sign which will thus represent the Moon (Indu), the Bindu, the Sun (Ravi), and the Ra, Fire (Agni). The Triangle may be formed by drawing two sides or a bent line and then completing it with a straight line. At the apex place the Ravi-bindu (Sun) and at the left and right hand corners Vahni-bindu (Fire) and Moon, (Candrabindu). Between Sun and Moon place Vama Vakrarekha and Brahmā; between Fire and Moon, Jyeṣṭha, and Viṣṇu, and between Moon and Sun, Ṛaudrī, Ṛjurekhā and Rudra. between each of the points are lines formed by all the letters (Mātṛkāvarṇa) of the alphabet called the A-Ka-Tha triangle. The Pādukāpañcaka, a Hymn attribtued to Śiva, (See *The Serpent Power)* speaks of A-Ka-Tha in the second verse on which Kālīcaraṇa comments as follows: Here Śakti is Kāmakalā in form and the three Śakti (Vāmā, Jyeṣṭhā, Raudrī) emanating from the three Bindus are the three lines. The sixteen vowels beginning with A form the line Vāma, the sixteen letters beginning with Ka form the line Jyeṣṭhā and sixteen letters beginning with Tha for the line Raudrī. The abode of Śakti (Abalālaya) is formed by these three lines. The other three letters Ha, La, Kṣa are in the corners of the Triangle. Kāluyrādhvamaṇāya says, "The Tribindu is the Supreme Tattva and embodies in Itself Brahmā, Viṣṇu, Śiva (*Brahmā-viṣṇu-śivātmakam)*. The Triangle composed of the Letters has emanated from the Bindu;" also "The letters A to Visarga make the line Brahmā, the letters Ka to Tha the line Viṣṇu, and the letters Tha to Sa the Rudra. The three lines emanate from three Bindus. The Guṇas, as aspects of Śakti, are also represented by this threefold division. The Tantrojīvana says: "The lines Rajas, Sattva, Tamas surround the Yonimaṇḍala."Also "above is the line of Sattva, the line of Rajas is on its left and the line of Tamas on its right."

The Śabda-Brahman in its threefold aspect and Energies is represented in the Tantras by this triangular Kāṃakalā which is the abode of Śakti (Abalālaya). The Triangle is in every way an apposite symbol, for on the material plane if there are three form there is no other way in which they can be brought to interact except in the form of a trinagle in which whilst they are each as aspects separate and distinct from one another, they are yet related to each other and form part of one whole. In the Āgamakalpadruma it is said that the Bindu is Ham (one point) and Visargaḥ (two points) is Saḥ or Śakti. The Yāmala thus speaks of this abode. 'I now speak of Kāmakalā" and proceeding says, "She is the Eternal One who is the three Bindus, the three Śaktis and the three forms (Trimūrti)" The Maheśvarī-Saṁhitā says: "Sun, Moon and Fire and the three Bindus and Brahmā, Viṣṇu, Rudra the three lines. "The Lalitāsahasranāma calls the Devī

Kāmakalārūpā. Bhāskararaya in his commentary thereon (v.73) says that Kāma or creative will (Icchā) is both Śiva and Devī and Kalā is their manifestation. Hence, it is called Kāmakalā. This is explained in the Tripurasiddhānta: "On Pārvatī, Kalā is the manifestation of Kāmeśvara and Kāmeśvarī. Hence, She is known as Kāmakalā. Or, She is the manifestation (Kalā) of Desire (Kāma), that is, of Icchā-Śakti. The Devī is the great Tripurasundarī-Bhāskararāya's Guru Nṛsiṁhānandanātha wrote the following verse on which the disciple comments:

"I hymn Tripuré, the treasure of Kula, who is red of beauty; Her limbs like unto those of Kāmarāja who is adored by the three Devatās of the three Guṇas; who is the desire or Will of Śiva (according to the Anekārthadhvani-mañjarī lexicon, I=Manmatha=Kāma=Icchā) who dwells in the Bindu and who manifests the Universe." She is red because She is the Vimarśa-śakti. She is called (says the Commentator cited) Tripuré as She has three (Tri) Purās (literally cities or abodes), here meaning three Bindus, lines, angles, syllables and so forth. She has three angles (in the triangular Yoni, the source of the universe) as well as three circles (the three Bindus) and Bhūpura of her Yantra has three lines. Yoni does not here mean generative organ, but Kārāṇa – the Cause of the universe. She has three aspects and creates of the three Devatās through the three Śaktis, Vāmā and others, and manifests as Will, Knowledge and Action. Thus since She the Supreme Energy is everywhere triple, She is called Tripurasundarī. The three syllables of Her Mantra are the three divisions of the Pañcadaśī, namely Vāgbhava, Kāmarāja and Śakti Kūtas, which according to the Vāmakeśvara-Tantra are the Jñāna and other Śaktis. The Kāmabīja is Klīm and Klīṁ-kāra is Śivakāma. Here "Ī" is said to denote the Kāmakalā in the Turīya state through which Mokṣa is gained, and hence the meaning of the saying that "he who hears Bīja without Kā and Ī does not reach the place of good actions"-- that is he does not go to the region attainable by good actions but to that (Mokṣa) attainable by Jñāna alone. The Bhāva-cūḍāmaṇi says: "Meditate on the face in the from of Bindu, and below on the twin breasts (the two other Bindus, and below them the beauteous form of the Hakārarddha.The commentator on the Ānandalaharī says: In the fifth sacrifice (Yajña) let the Sādhaka think of his Ātmā as in no wise different from, but as the one and only Śiva; and of the subtle thread-like Kuṇḍalinī who is all Śaktis extending from the Ādhāra Lotus to Paramaśiva. Let him think of the three Bindus as being in Her body indicating Icchā, Jñāna, Kriyā; Moon, Sun, Fire; Rajas, Sattva, Tamas; Brahmā, Viṣṇu, Rudra; and then let him meditate upon the Cit-kalā who is Śakti below it." The Bindu which is the "Face" indicates Viriñci (Brahmā) associated with the Rajas Guṇa. The two Bindus which are the "Breasts" and upon which meditation should be done in the heart indicate Hari (Viṣṇu) and Hara (Rudra) associated with the Sattva and Tamas Guṇas. Below these meditate upon the subtle Cit-kalā which indicates all three Guṇas and which is all these three Devatās. Similar meditation is given in Yoginī (and other) Tantras winding up with the direction, "and then let the Sādhaka think of his own body as such Kāmakalā".

As regards this it is to be observed that in the Mūlādhāra there is a Traipura-Trikoṇa, so-called because of the presence of the Devī Tripuré within the Kā inside the triangle. This Kā is the chief letter of the Kāma-Bīja and Kam is the Bīja of Kāminī, the aspect of Tripurasundarī in the Mūlādhāra. Here also are the three lines, Vāmā, Icchā and so forth. Thus, the Traipura Trikoṇa is the Sthūla aspect of the Sūkṣma-Śakti in the region of the upper Sahasrāra called Kāmakalā. It is to this Kāmīnī that in worship the essence of Japa (Tejo-rūpa-japa) is offered, the external Japa being given to the Devatā worshipped in order that the Sādhaka may retain the fruits of his Japa. (*Nityapūjāpaddhati 8*). Man physically and practically is a limited manifestation of this threefold Śakti which resides within himself and is the object of worship. Such worship leads to identification and so the Śrītattvārṇava says: "Those glorious men who worship that Body in Sāmarasya are freed from the waves of poison in the untraversable sea of the universe (Samsāra)." Sāmarasya, I may here observe, is a term which is ordinarily applied to the bliss of sexual union *(Strīpumyogāt yat saukhyaṁ tat sāmarasyaṃ)*. For the benefit however of those who are always reading gross meanings into parts of the Śāstra necessary to explain that Sāmarasya is both gross (Sthūla) and subtle (Sūkṣma). Here the latter is meant. An erotic symbol is employed to denote the merger of the Jīva and Supreme Consciousness in Ecstasy (Samādhi). The Tantras largely employ such imagery which is to be found in the Upaniṣads and in non-Indian scriptures. Thus, the highly sensual imagery of the Biblical "Song of Songs" is said (whether rightly or not, I will not here inquire) to symbolise Christ's love for His Bride, the Church. Spiritual union is symbolised by terms borrowed from the world of man. By Mantra-yoga is sought that perfection and unity of Bhāva which leads to Jñānayoga Samādhi.

"On the division of the Supreme Bindu (into the three-fold Kāmakalā) there was the Unmanifested Sound" *(Bhidyamānāt parād bindor avyaktātmā ravo'bhavat,* Śarada-I-11). This is the Śabda-brahman or the Brahman as the cause of manifested Śabda and Artha and therefore of Mantra. This causal "Sound" is the unmanifested (Avyaktātmā), undifferentiated (Akhaṇḍa) principle of Śabda (Nādamātra), composed of Nāda and Bindu (Nādabindumaya) devoid of all particularity such as letters and the like (Varṇādiviśesa rahita). Some, as the Śāradā says (V.12), have thought that the Śabdabrahman was Śabda and others Śabdārtha, but this cannot be, for both are unconscious (Jadatvāt). "In my opinion," its author says (v. 13), "Śabda-brahman is the Consciousness in all beings" *(Caitanyaṁ sarvabhūtānaṁ Śabda-brahmeti me matiḥ)*. For if Śabdārtha or Śabda be called Śabda-brahman then the meaning of the term Brahman is lost *(Brahmapadavācyatvaṁ nopapadyate);* for the meaning of the term Brahman (Brahmapadārtha) is Sat-Cit-Ānanda (Saccidānandarūpa), whilst these are unconscious (Jada). Rāghava-Bhatta says that Śabda-brahman is Nāda-bindumaya Brahman (Brahmātmaka), Sound (Śabda), unmanifested (Avyakta), undifferentiated (Akhaṇḍa), all pervading (Vyāpaka), which is the first manifestation of Paramaśiva in creative mood *(Sṛṣṭyunmukhaparamaśiva-prathamollāsamātraṁ)*. He also cites a passage from some work unnamed which says that out of Prakṛti in Bindu form in whom Kriyā-Śakti prevails *(Kriyāśaktipradhānāyo prakṛter bindu-rūpinyaḥ)* arose the Supreme Śabda-brahman, the cause of Śabda and Śabdārtha (Śabdaśabdārthakāraṇaṁ). The sound (Rava) here spoken of is in the form of Bindu-rūpa), which later appears in all bodies as the Mātṛkās and Varṇas in their respective places. The Śāradā (1,14) having thus dealt with Paraśabdāsṛṣṭi concludes in a general way, "Consciousness which is the svarūpa of, and appears as, Kuṇḍalī-Śakti in the bodies of all living beings manifests as Letters in prose and verse, having obtained the instruments for utterance which are the throat and so forth."

*Tat prāpya kuṇḍalīrūpaṁ praninām dehamadhyagam.*
*Varṇātmanāvirbhavati gadyapādyādibhedataḥ.*

The subsequent Śabdasṛṣṭi is derived from Kuṇḍalinī. The Kāmakalā is thus called the root (Mūla) of all Mantras, for it is the threefold aspect of the Śabdabrahman, the cause of all manifested Śabda and Artha and therefore Mantra. In a future article I will continue the account of the creative process, namely, the Artha-sṛṣṭi in which are included the Tattvas from Buddhi to Pṛthivī and the Lords (Tattveśa) or forms of Consciousness which preside over them. These are necessarily dealt with in connection with Tattvas over which they preside. In the same way Paśyantī, Madhyamā, and Vaikharī states of sound are also dealt with, because Paśyantī and the others only exist in the created body. Paraśabda is unmanifested Caitanya, but the other three Feet of the One Brahman are set in the manifested world of Mind and Matter.

## Chapter 18

# THE GROSS TATTVAS AND THEIR LORDS

The Śāradā-Tilaka (Chapter I) having first dealt with Śabdasṛṣṭi on account of its priority *(Prādhānyadyotanāya prathamoddiṣṭaṃ)* commences with the fifteenth verse to speak of the creation of objects (Artha-sṛṣṭi), for Paśyantī and the other Bhāvas assume the existence of the manifested body. It says that from Śambhu who is in the nature of Kalā *(Kalātmanaḥ)* and Bindu *(Bindvātmanaḥ)* and friend of Kāla *(Kālabandhu)*, issued (Ajāyata) the "Witness of the World" (Jagatsākṣī), the all-pervading (Sarvavyāpī) Sadāśiva. Rāghava says Kalā is here either used generally, or as refering to the Nivṛtti and other Kalās which Śambhu is in the nature of Nāda (Nadātmā), because in unbeginning and unending Time. He is the helper of Kāla which is Sṛṣṭi *(Anādyanante kale sṛṣṭ irūpakālasahāyāt)*. The connection again is one between cause and its possessor. Again "friend" indicates the causality (Nimittatvam) of Kāla. For it has been said: "It has its beginning in Lava and ends in Pralaya and is full of Tamas Śakti." Lava is the time taken to pierce with a needle a lotus-petal. Thirty Lavas=one Truṭi. This Kāla is

Apara, for there is also Para Kāla. Kāla or Māyā is the cause of the occurrence of birth and destruction, Raghava concludes that Prakṛti and Kāla exist in even Mahāpralaya. But their permanence (Nityatā) is a dependent one (Apekṣakanityatā). For the permanence of the Puruṣa in which all things have their goal is alone independent (Svatahnityatvaṁ).

From Śambhu emanated the Sadāśiva who is the Doer of the five forms of work, namely Creation, Preservation and Destruction, Favour (Anugraha) and Disfavour (Nigraha). From Sadāśiva comes Īśa, from Him Rudra, from Rudra Viṣṇu, from Viṣṇu, Brahmā (v.16). On this verse Rāghava says: "It has been said before how they arise in Śabda-sṛṣṭi. Here they arise in Artha-sṛṣṭi."

The five Śivas are known in the Tantras as the "Five great corpses" (Pañca-mahāpreta). Śiva is constantly represented in corpse-like (Savarūpa) form. This symbolises that Consciousness in Itself (Svarūpa) is actionless and inert. All action is by Śakti. Hence, the Devī is in pictures imaged as standing on the inert corpse-like body of Śiva. The same notion is represented by *Viparīta-maithuna,* a prominent example of the use of erotic symbolism in the Śākta-Śāstra. These Pañcamahāpreta form the couch on which the Devī, Wave of Consciousness and Bliss, rests in the house of Cintāmaṇi adorned with a garden of Nīpa trees, which is in the Island of Gems, surrounded with a grave of celestial trees, in the midst of the ocean of nectar (Ānandalaharī). This is the well-known Tāntrika meditation on the Heart-lotus of worship below the Anāhata-cakra. The Bahurūpāṣṭaka and Bhairavayāmala say: "There is the supreme abode (Mandira) of Devī full of Cintāmaṇi stones (which grant all desires). The great couch is Śiva, the cushion or mattress (Kaśipu) is Sadāśiva, the pillow the great Īśāna. The four support (Pada) are Iśāna, Rudra, Hari, and Brahmā. On that bed reclines the supreme Tripurasundarī." Hence, the Devī in the Lalitāsahasranāma (v. 73) is called Pañcabrahmāsanasthitā. The "Jewelled Island" is a high state of Consciousness in that ocean of nectar which is the infinite all prevading Consciousness Itself. The Devī is united with Paramaśiva in the Praṇava the Nāda over the Oṁkāra being the couch on which is resting Para-śiva in His Bindu form. A,U,M, Nāda, Bindu, the five component parts of ṁ and the Śrī-cakra Yantra are here referred to.

The supreme Paramaśiva abides in Satyaloka beyond mind and matter. Śambhu presides over mind and his abode is Maharloka. Ether, air, fire, water, earth are presided over by Sadāśiva, Īśa, Rudra, Viṣṇu, Brahmā whose abodes are Tapoloka, Janaloka, Svarloka, Bhuvarloka, Bhūrloka; and their centres in the human body are in the Ājñā, Viśuddha, Anāhata, Maṇipūra, Svādhiṣṭhāna and Mūlādhāra-Cakras, respectively. Kuṇḍalī-Śakti manifests as the six. But notwithstanding all Her subtle and gross manifestations, She remains ever the same Cit and Ānanda; for the Ātmā in its own nature (Svarūpa) as distinguished from its Powers and their products is the same in all times and places.

Turning then to the Tattvas the Śāradā says (v. 17) that from the unmanifest Mūlabhūta (Prakṛti or root of all creation) of the Supreme (Paravastu-Bindu) when subject to change (Vikṛti) issued, through inequality of the Guṇas, the Sāttvika-Tattva Mahat in the form of the Antaḥkaraṇa and Guṇas.

Mahat is the cosmic Buddhi which is said to be in the form of the Āntaḥkaraṇa (Buddhi, Ahaṅkāra, Manas) for all three are implicitly contained in the first (Upacārādubhayātmakaḥ), as also the Guṇas which here mean the Tanmātras of sound, touch, sight, taste and small. According to Nyāya the Guṇas appertain each to each (Tattadviśeṣaguṇaḥ); or according to Sāṅkhya. Ether has one Guṇa, Air has two, Fire three and so forth. From Mahat was derived Ahaṅkāra which is threefold as Vaikārika, Taijasa, and Bhūtādi or the Sāttvika, Rājasa, and Tāmasa-Ahaṅkāras (v.18), Rāghava says that it is called Vaikārika because it issues from Parameśvara when His Sāmarasya with Śakti becomes Vikṛta or disturbed. The Devas also are Vaikārika because produced from it. According to Sāṁkhya the Vaikāṛika nature is due to its generation from Pradhāna when Vikṛta. The Vaikārika Devas are Dik, Vāta, Arka, Pracetā (Varuṇa), Aśvins (two Aśvinīkumāras), Vahni, Indra, Upendra (Viṣṇoreka-ṃūrtiḥ), Mitra (the third sun) and Ka (Candra). These are the Presiding Devatās of the senses (Indriyas). From the Taijasa-Ahaṅkāra were evolved the Indriyas. The five Tanmātras and the derived Bhūtas came from Bhūtādi-Ahaṅkāra.

The Text and Commentary speak of the derivation of Ākāśa from Śabda tanmātra, Vāyu from Sparśa-tanmātra and so forth. But as the word Purva occurs, others read this as meaning that each becomes cause of what follows in association with what had gone before. Thus, Śabda-tanmātra produces Ākāśa. From Śabda-tanmātra together with Sparśa-tanmātra come Agni and so forth.

The Śāradā then gives the colours of the Bhūtas namely transparent (Svaccha ether, black air, red fire, white water, and yellow earth, the Ādhāras of which are the Tanmātras and the Guṇas of which are sound, touch, sight, taste and smell. Rāghava Bhatta says that it is for the purpose of worship (Upāsanā-sthānam) in pursuance of Śāstra *(Svaśā-stranuro-dhena)* that certain invisible things are here said to have colours *(Atra keśāṁcit arūpidravyānāṁ varṇakathanam)*. This might perhaps seem to suggest to some that the colours are not real. But if this be so, is it correct? Ether is transparent which is no colour, black is the absence of colour. With Rūpa there must be colour. For what is colourless is formless. Form is only perceived by means of colour: and the last three Bhūtas are with form. Their colours are widely adopted. Thus in China also yellow is the colour of earth, and red white are generally assigned to fire and water, respectively. Possibly what is meant is that the colours are here mentioned for the purpose of worship: that is the mentioning is for such purpose. Else how could the Yogī perceive them? For it is said: "Tāni vastūni tānmātrādīni pratyakśaviśsayāni" (that is to Yogīs). Elsewhere it is said that ether is hollow or pitted (Suśiracinaṁ), air is moving (Calanaparaḥ), fire is digesting (Paripākavān), water is tasteful (Rasavat) and earth is solid (Ghana). All the universe is composed of the four Bhūtas entering into one another *(Parasparānupraviṣṭaiḥ māhābhūtaiś caturvidhaiḥ)* pervaded by either (Vyāptākāśaiḥ).

Thus, Consciousness as Śakti evolves mind and matter. The principles (Tattvas) of these are not always clearly understood. They may, and indeed must be, considered from the point of view of evolution— that is according to the sequence in which the limited experience of the Jīva is evolved— or from that in which they are regarded after creation when the experince of concrete sence objects has been had. According to the former aspect, Buddhi is the state of mere presentation; consciousness of being only, without thought of "I" (Ahamkāra) and unaffected by sensations (Manas, Indriya) of particular objects which *ex hypothesi* do not yet exist. It is thus a state of impersonal Jīva consciousness. Ahaṁkāra of which Buddhi is the basis is the personal Consciousness which realises itself as a particular "I", the experiencer. The Jīva wakes to world experience under the influence of Māyā-Śakti. In the order of awakening he first experiences in a vague general way without consciousness of the limited self, like the experience which is had immediately on waking after sleep. It then refers this experience to the limited self and has the consciousness "I am so and so." Manas is the desire which follows on such experience, and the senses and their objects are the means, whereby that enjoyment is had which is the end of all will to life. The cosmic mind projects its content as ideas and desires on to the gross sensual plane and there the individual mind enjoys them as such.

I may here observe that the same scheme exists in Buddhism where the root is given as Avidyā, from which arises Saṁskāra. This gives birth to Vijñāna (which is Buddhi) and then to Nāmarūpa that is an external world at first vaguely perceived. The desire take cognisance of this gives rise to the six sense organs (Ṣaḍāyatana) namely Manas and the Indriyas. From this follows contact (Sparśa) of the sense organs with the external world giving rise to feeling (Vedānta) called forth by such contact in the form of pleasure and pain. This experience produces Desire (Tṛṣṇā) which a recent work on the Unconscious calls Libido, for pleasant sensations resulting in attachment and enjoyment (Upādāna), and then the individual Jīva consciousness (Bhāva) is born (Jāta), ages and dies and is again reborn until Nirvāṇa is attained. Throughout it is the will to life, the root of which is in Avidyā which produces the instruments namely the mind and senses whereby enjoyment is to be had and which creatively imagines the content of its experience from out of the store of past lives in past universes. True experience therefore can only be had by destroying the root which is Avidyā. One of the tasks which yet remains to be done is to show the essential similarities of Buddhism and Hinduism instead of dwelling, as it usually done, on their differences, alleged or real. When it is fully realised that Buddhism took its birth in India and the implications necessary therein truer notions will be entertained of it then generally prevails.

An example from science has been given which illustrates the process stated. In some animals there are no specialised sense organs but when stimulus is often given to particular part of a body that part gets specially sensitive to it and a particular organ is developed. The illustration of course assumes that objects have been already created. But in the evolution of the world similar principles come into as those which exist after it has been evolved. The effect exists in its cause. Consciousness awakening to world-experiences reaches forth and as it seeks to come by recollection to its limited self, its desire evolves the instruments of enjoyment into the sensual world. This is the action of the Saṁskāra operating and upon consciousness.

Whilst however in the order of evolution Buddhi is the first principle, in the actual working of the Antaḥkaraṇa, after creation has taken place it comes last. It is more convenient therefore for ordinary exposition to commence with the sense objects and the sensations they evoke. Matter as the objective cause of perception is not, in its character, as such, under the cognisance of the senses. All that can be predicated of it is its effect upon these senses which is realised by the instrumentality of mind in its character as Manas. In science the notion of indestructible matter in atomic form is no longer held, for all matter it is now shown can be dissociated and the atom is dematerialised. The old duality of Force and Matter disappears, these two being held to be differing forms of the same thing. The ultimate basis is now recognised as Māyā or Prakṛti-Śakti. Matter is a stable form of force into which on disturbance of its equilibrium it disappears. Sensible mater (Bhūta) affects the expriencer in five different ways giving rise to sensations of hearing (Ākāśa), touch and feel (Vāyu: not in the sense of all forms of contact, for form and solidity are not yet developed), colour and form and sight (Rūpa), taste (Rasa) and smell (Gandha). Sensible perception however exists only in respect of particular objects. But there exist also general elements of the particulars of sense-perception. There is an abstract quality by which sensible matter (Mahābhūta) is perceived. This abstract quality is Tanmātra the "mere thatness" or abstract quality of an object.. These are the general elements of sense perception which necessarily come into existence when the senses (Indriyas) are produced. This is supersensible (Atindriya) matter, the existence of which is ordinarily only mediately perceived through the gross particular objects of which they are the generals and which proceed from them. Sensations aroused by sense objects are experienced by the outer instruments (Bāhya-karaṇa) or senses (Indriyas), whether of cognition (Jñānendriya) or action (Karmendriya) which are the afferent and efferent impulses respectively. The Indriyas are not however sufficient in themselves. In the first place unless attention co-operates there is no sensation (Ālocana) at all. Nextly as the experiencer is at every moment besieged by countless sensations from all sides, if any of these is to be brought into the field of consciousness it must be selected to the exclusion of others. Lastly, the manifold of sense or "points of sensation" must be gathered together and made into a whole. These three functions are those of Manas the function of which is said to be Saṅkalpa-vikalpa, that is selection and rejection of material provided by the Jñānendriya. These sensations, to affect the experiencer, must be made his own and this is done by Ahaṅkāra or "Self-arrogation." It is then passed on to Buddhi which determines either by way of forming percepts and concepts of resolutions *(Kartavyaṁ etat mayā)*. Thus all the Tattvas work for the enjoyment of the Self or Puruṣa. They are not to be regarded as things existing independently by themselves but as endowments of the Spirit (Ātmā). They do now work arbitarily as they will but represent an organised co-operative effort in the service of the enjoyer, the Experiencer or Puruṣa.

The Tantras speak of three Tattvas manely of Ātmā, Vidyā, Śiva. The first includes those Tattvas of the Thirtysix which are called impure (Aśuddha) namely Pṛthivī to Prakṛti; the second the pure-impure (Śuddha-Aśuddha) or Māyā, the Kañcukas and Puruṣa; and the third, the pure Tattvas (Śuddha) from Śuddhavidyā to Śiva-Tattva. I have dealt with the last two in previous Chapters and deal with the first in the present one. It is also said (see Jñānārṇava-Tantra XXI-1-22) that there are four Ātmās constituting the Citkuṇḍa or Maṇḍala in the Mūlādhāra where the inner Homa is made. By knowledge thereof there is no rebirth. These are Ātmā Jñānātmā, Antaratmā and Paramātmā.

The Ātmā (Prāṇarūpī) which is in all creatures (Jantu) as the basis of their Prāṇa or vital principle is their Ātmā. It is Hamasāsvarūpī and is manifested in individual bodies by inspiration and expiration (Śvāsa, Ucchvāsa). This is Jīvātmā. It is like the Ākāśa seperated in a pot which when broken becomes mingled with the total Ākāśa. Jñānātmā is said to be Śākṣāt-sākṣirūpaka. That is, it is that aspect of Ātmā which witnesses all and by which the unity of all is known. It is thus the basis os Buddhi and all mental Tattvas derived therefrom. By "Antar" in Antarātmā is meant the subtle Ātmā of atomic dimension *(Rahasyasūkṣma-rūpaka-paramāṇu)* which pervades every object. It is the "inner bodiness" (Antaraṅgatā) the spark of Paramātmā. It is Haṁsa known only by Yogīs. Its beak is Tāra (Mantra Om). Its two wings are Āgama and Nigama. Its two feet are Śiva and Śakti. The three Bindus are Its three eyes. When this Paramahaṁsa is spread (Vyāpta) throughout Creation then all Bhūtas spring up in the their order (Ākāśa, Pavana etc). Of these five the root is citta. This Haṁsa Bird disports Itself in the Lake or Ignorance (Avidyā) in the mud of illusion and infatuation (Mohapaṅgka) which is the world. When this Haṁsa becomes other-worldly (Niṣprapañca) and dissolving (Saṁhārarūpī), then it reveals the Self *(Ātmānaṁ pradarśayet)*. Then its "Birdness" (Pakṣitva) ceases. Then the Śohamātma is established which is the Supreme Experience or Paramātmā.

To complete the creative process it is now necessary to resume the creation of Śabda (Śabdasṛṣṭi) from its supreme state (Para-śabda or Parabrahman) through its three Bhāvas, Paśyantī, Madhyamā and Vaikharī manifesting in bodies composed of the Tattvas above described; for in this way the birth of the letters composing Mantras is shown. I will deal with this in Chapter 21 under the title "Garland of Letters" (Varṇamālā), a subject or primary importance in the Tantras, after a description of the Causal Śaktis of the Praṇava or Mantra Om and an explanation of the Kalās.

# Chapter 19

# CAUSAL ŚAKTIS OF THE PRAṆAVA

The present Chapter is but a short summary of the result of some enquiries recently pursued in Kashmir with a view to ascertain the notions of the Northern Śaiva school on several matters which I have been studying in connection with my work on the awakening of the spiraline energy or Serpent Power. I was already aware as the Kulārṇava-Tantra (one of the foremost Tantras of the "Bengal" school) indicates, that the Ṣaiva-Śākta-Darśana and not Śaṅkara's exposition of Vedānta is the original philosophical basis of the Śākta faith, though some who call themselves Śāktas seem now-a-days to have forgotten, if they were ever aware of that fact. In Kashmir, Kula-Śāstra is, I believe another name for the Trika. But amongst several other objects in view I wished to link up the connection of certain Śaktis mentioned in the Kriyā portion of the Śāstras with the thirtysix Tattvas of the Śākta school, their position in the scheme not being in all case clear to me according to the information previously at my disposal. I have worked the matter out in more detail and present Chapter will summarise conclusions on the certain points.

Being (Sattā) is of two kinds, formless (Arūpa) and with form (Rūpa). In the first the "I" *(Aham)* and the "This" *(Idam)* or universe representing the Prakāśa and Vimarśa aspects of experience are one. Śiva and Śakti exist in all he planes. But they are here undistinguishably one in the embrace of the Lord (Śiva) and the Heart of the Lord" (Śakti). Śiva is *Cit*. Śakti is *Cidrūpiṇī.*" He is Parā and She, Parā. This is the Perfect Experience which is Ānanda or "Resting in the Self" (Svarūpa-viśrānti). Śiva then experiences the universe and Parāśakti, that is, Paranāda and Parāvāk. This is the Love of the Self for the Self. The Supreme experience is the bliss of unalloyed Love. The Idam then exists as Parā-śakti. The two aspects are as it were one *(Ekaṁ tattvaṁ iva),* to use a phrase in the Ahirbudhnya-Saṁhitā of the Pāñcarātra Āgama. The "Supreme Sound" and "Supreme Speech" are thus the perfect Universe which is the supreme Kailāsa. This is the supreme unitary experience in which, though the "I" and the "This" do not cease to exist they are both in their *Svarūpa* and thus mysteriously coalesce in one unity of Being which is the "Two in one." The whole process then of creation, that is the rise of imperfect or dual experience, is the establishment through the negation of Śakti *(Niṣedha-vyāpārā-rūpā-Śakti)* of a diremption in the one unitary consciousness whereby the Aham and the Idam, which had then existed, coalesced in one, diverge, in consciousness, until in our own experience the "I" is separated from the "This" seen as objects outside ourselves.

The process of manifestation of Mantra is that of cosmic ideation *(Sṛṣṭi-kalpanā)* in which Jñana-Śakti first merely formulates as though the outlines of the limited universe which is about to emerge from, and for, consciousness, and which is called the "thinkable"

*(Mantavya),* which through Nāda which is *Kriyāśaktirūpa* moves towards the "speakable" *(Vācya),* with which again consciousness identifies itself as Bindu which is characterised by a predominance of activity *(Kriyāprādhānyalakṣaṇā).* Diversity *(Pṛthagbhāva)* is then produced by Bindu as Ma-kāra in the Māyā-Tattva. Śakti as U-kāra creates objects *(Prameya)* as separate existences and by the completion of the Tattvas objectivity is completely revealed as A-kāra. To describe however adequately this grand system of Ābhāsa, as it is called, would require a full exposition of the Northern and monistic Śaiva and the allied Śākta-Darśana on which the Śakta doctrine and practice of the Āgamas is based. I can here only indicate shortly the Śaktis of the Mūla-Mantra or Praṇava, which are the correspondences from the Śakti aspect of Śaiva-Śākta-Tattvas. The account of the Śakti vary, but such variance is rather due to the fact that some accounts are fuller than others than to any substantial difference in principle.

The gist of the matter may be shortly stated as follows: In creation, the three Śaktis, Jñāna, Icchā, Kriyā manifest. These are manifested powers of the supreme Bindu. "What is here is there," and these Śaktis of the Lord (Pati) appear as the Guṇas of Prakṛti in the Paśu; or as it has also been said, Jñāna and Kriyā with Māyā as the third appear as Sattva, Rajas, and Tamas of the Puruṣa-Prakṛti stage which is the immediate source of the consciousness of the Paśu.

*Svāṅga-rūpeṣu bhaveṣu patyur jñānaṁ kriyā ca yā*
*Māyā tṛtīyā tā eva paśoḥ sattvaṁ rajas tamaḥ.*
(Īśvara-Pratyabhījñā, IV 1,4)

The creative consciousness (Śakti) projects the universe as all-diffusive Consciousness *(Sadākya-Tattva),* which considered from the Mantra aspect is all-duffusive "Sound" that is movement or Nāda. Here the emphasis is on the Aham, which is yet coloured by the Idam as the universe faintly rises into the field of the changeless consciousness. Consciousness then identifies itself with the clearly perceived Idam and becomes Bindu. Here the emphasis is on the Idam with which consciousness becomes a point (Bindu). Then the evolving consciousness holds the "I" and the "This" in equal balance *(Samānādhikaraṇa),* at which point Māyā Śakti, which is the sense of difference *(Bhedabuddhi)* intervenes to separate the Aham (as Puruṣa) and Idam (as Prakṛti) hitherto held as parts of the one Consciousness, and the divisive power of Kalā-Śakti breaks up the universe so separated from the Self into the plurality of objects which is our ordinary worldly experience. The universe which in the Puruṣa Prakṛti stage was seen as whole, though different from the Self, is now also seen as separate but as a multitude of mutually exclusive beings.

There is first a fivefold division of the "five rays" of Om, namely, A, U, M, Nāda Bindu, Śānta. The Prapañcasāra-Tantra says that Jāgrat is Bīja, Svapna is Bindu, Suṣupti is Nāda, Turīya is Śakti and the Laya beyond is Śānta. This is the simplest form of statement setting forth one Śakti for each of the Varṇas, and the Candra-Bindu. In other words from Śiva-śakti (which includes all the Tattvas down to the appearance of the three Devatās) these latter are produced. There is next a sevenfold division. Parā-saṁvit of Paramaśiva is not technically accounted a Tattva, for the Supreme Experience is Tattvātīta. But if we include it as the transcendental aspect of the Śaivatattva from which the Ābhāsa proceeds, we get the number seven counting Puruṣa and Prakṛti as two. The number seven is of frequent occurrence; as in the case of the seven Śivas, namely, Paraśiva, Śaṁbhu and the five Mahāpretas; the seven Śaktis of the Oṁkārā as given in the Śāradā-Tilaka; the seven Śaktis Unmanī and the rest as given in the Commentary of Kālīcaraṇa on the Ṣaṭcakranirūpaṇa chapter of Pūrṇānanda-Śvamī's work entitled Śrītattva-cintāmaṇi *(The Serpent Power)*; and the three and half coils of Kuṇḍalinī of which the Kubjikā-Tantra speaks, namely Puruṣa, Prakṛti, Vikṛti, which it may be observed when uncoiled and divided by its diameter given seven divisions.

The Śāradā speaks of six Śaktis which with Parameśvara who is Saccidānanda make seven, namely: Śiva, Śakti, Nāda, Bindu (Kāraṇa), Bindu (Kārya), Nāda (Kārya) and Bīja. The other seven Śaktis above mentioned are Unmanī (or Unmanā), Samanī (or Samanā), Āñjī, Mahānāda (or Nādānta), Nāda, Arddhacandra and Bindu. If in the first series we take Kārya-Nāda which is discribed as the Mithaḥ-Samavaya (mutual relation) of Śivarūpakārya-Bindu and Bīja, which is Śaktirūpa, as the correspondence in this scheme of the Śaiva Śuddhavidyā-Tattva with its Samānādhikaraṇa, then this series repręsents all the Śaiva Tattvas up to and including Puruṣa-Prakṛti. The same remarks apply to the second series of Śaktis or causal forms (Kāraṇarūpa). The first is described by Kālīcaraṇa as the state in which all-mindness (Manastva), that is ideation ceases. Here there is neither Kalā nor Kāla, for it is "the sweet pure mouth of Rudra" (Śivapada). The second is the cause of all causes (Śarvakāraṇakaraṇaṃ). The third which is also called by him Vyāpikā-Śakti appears in the beginning of creation. Mahānāda is the Kāraṇa-Nāda which is Kriyā-Śakti and the first appearance of Nāda. Śakti as Nāda is a development of the latter which is transformed into Ardhacandra and then Bindu.

These Śaktis (as well as two others with A U M, making altogether twelve) are explained according to Śaiva views in an account extracted from the Netra Tantra with Kṣemarāja's Commentray and from the Tantrāloka. There the Śaktis are given as Unmanā, Samanā, Vyāpika, (or Vyāpinī), Añjanī, Mahānāda, Nāda, Nirodhinī, Ardhacandra, Bindu, Ma-kāra, U-kāra, A-kāra. The Sanskrit passages here given are the summary in his own language made for me by the Kashmirian Paṇḍit Harabhaṭṭa Śāstrī of Srinagar.

"When the Supreme Śiva beyond whom there is nought, who is in the nature of unchanged and unchangeable illumination moves forth His will, such (willing movement as) Śakti, though in fact inseparable from Him, is called Unmanā; Her place is the Śiva-Tattva" *(Anuttara-paramaśiva avicalaprakāśātmā yadā svecchayā prasarati sā śaktiḥ śivād abhinnaiva Unmanā ityucyate; tatsthānaṁ śiva-tattvaṁ iti).*

"When the Unmanā-Śakti displays Herself in the form of the universe beginning with the Śūnya and ending with Dharā, formulates as mere thought the thinkable, then She is called Samanā as well as Śaktitattva" *(Yadā unmana-śaktir ātmānaṁ kṣobhayati śunyadinā dharāntena jagat-atmanā sphurati mantavyaṁ mananamātreṇa āsūtrayati, tadā Samanā ityucyate Śakti-tattvaṁ iti ca).* "This Samanā-Śakti Herself is called Vyāpinī when She operates as the Power which withdraws into Hereself all thinkables which are Her creation. She resides in the Śakti-tattva" *(Samanā śaktir eva svamāntavye saṁhāra-prodhānatvena Vyāpīni ityucyate, eṣā Śakti-tattva-tiṣṭhati).* "It is again the same Samanā Herself who is called Śakti when her operation is chiefly creative in regard to her own thinkables. She resides in the Śakti-tattva and is also called Āñjanī because of Her being associated with the thinkable" *(Samanaiva svamantavya sṛṣṭipradhānatvena śaktirityucyate eṣā Śakti-tattva tiṣṭhati mantavyā-paraktatvāc ca Āñjanī ityapi ucyate)* "When Śabda-brahman moves forth with great strength from Its Śiva form then the very first sound (produced thereby) like the vibration produced by a sounding bell is called Nādānta *(i.e.* Mahānāda). It resides in the Sadāśiva-tattva". *(Yadā śabdabrahma śiva-rūpad ativegena prasarati tadā prathamataraṁ ghantānurāṇatmā Śabdo Nādānta itucate, sa Sabdā-śiva-tattva tiṣṭhati).* When Śakti fills up the whole universe with Nādānta then She is called Nāda And this also is the sadāśiva-Tattva because of the equality therein of the "I" and the "This" *(Nādāntena yadā viśvaṁ āpūrayati tadā Nāda ityucate, sa ca ahamte-damtayoḥ samānādhiharanyena Sadāśiva-tattvamiti".* Samānādhikaraṇa in its technical sense is the function of the later developed Śuddhavidyā-Tattva. Apparently its original is here represented to be the function of the earlier Sadāśiva-Tattva in which the duality of the Aham and Idam first manifests.

"When Nāda, after having ceased to operate in its universal scope, does so limitedly (or particularly) then it is called Nirodhinī. This Śakti rests in the Sadāśiva-Tattva" *(Nādo yadā aśeṣavyāptiṁ nimajjya adharaṁ upyāptiṁ unmajjavyati tadā Nīrodhinī ityucyate sā Sadāśivatatvaṁ ālambate).* " When Nāda is slightly operative towards the creation of the "speakable," it is called Ardhacandra which is Īśvara-Tattva." *(Nādo yadā īṣadvācyonmeṣaṁ śrayati tadā Arddhacandra ityucate Īśvaratattve).* Then " Para-Śakti

Herself is called Bindu when She is in the nature of inseparate illumination in regard to the whole range of the speakable" *(Paraiva śaktiḥ yadā samastavācye abheda-prakāśa-rupatām gṛhṇāti tadā Bindur ityucyate, sa Īśvara-tattva tiṣṭhati)*

Ma-kāra or Rudra-Devatā is defined: "When Bindu causes diversity to manifest it is called Makāra and It moves in Māya-Tattva". *(Yadā binduḥ pṛthagbhāvaṁ ābhāsayati tadā Ma-kāra ityucyate, saca Māyātattve).* When Śakti creates objects as separate existences then She is called U-kāra. It resides in the Prakṛti-Tattva" *(Yadā prameyaṁ pṛthag-bhāvena-unmeṣayati, tadā U-kāra ityucyate, saca Prakṛti-tattve tiṣṭ hati).* When the creation of the Tattvas has come to an end, then because objectivity is completely revealed, (Śakti as) Māntrī-Kalā ( that is the creative are or process considered as "Sound" or Mantra) is called A-kāra" *(Tattvasargasya nivṛttir yadā jāyate, tadā prameyasya pūrṇatyā prakāśanat A-kāra iti Māntrī-kalā ucyate).*

The extra five Śaktis enumerated in this account are due firstly to the inclusion of A U M; secondly to counting Vyāpinī and Āñjanī separately instead of as being the Nimeṣa and Unmeṣa aspects of one Śakti, and thirdly the sevenfold series would appear to include Nirodhinī, also called Nirodhikā, in Nāda of which it is a more particularised development. Nāda would appear in the fuller series to represent Sāmānya-spanda of the sound emanation. For just as in the region of ideation the evolution is from infinite consciousness to the general and thence to particular ideas; so from the corresponding objective or Mantra aspect, which is that of Śāktopāyayoga, motion commences from the unextended point first as general, then as particular movement, at length developing into the clearly defined particularity of speech and of the objects which speech denotes. The rhythmic vibration of objects is the same as that of the mind which perceives them, since both are aspects of the one Śakti which thus divides itself.

*Namaste ravatvena tattvābhidhāne.*

## Chapter 20

# THE KALĀS

*Kalā* is a common term in Tāntrika literature for which it is difficult to find an appropriate English rendering. Śiva has two aspects Niṣkala (Nirguṇa) and Sakala (Saguṇa). The former is therefore without Kalā. The latter is with Kalā. Śiva is never without Śakti, for the two are one and the same, and Śakti in Herself, according to her proper nature (Śakti-Śvarūpa), is Consciousness or Caitanya (Caitanyarūpiṇī). Thus, there are said to be no Kalās in Unmanī which is in the Śiva-Tattva. Thereafter with Samanī in Śakti-Tattva the Kalās appear. Thus in Śrī-Netra-Tantra (Ch. 22) seven Kalās are assigned to Samanī. The Śakti of a Devatā is divided into sixteen Kalās or "parts" of power. That aspect of Devatā which has full power is called Pūrṇa-Kalāmūrti. One sixteenth of that or any part of the whole (Pūrṇa) is Kalāmūrti. A fraction again of that is Aṁśamūrti and a fraction of Aṁśamūrti is Aṁśāṁśa-mūrti. Śiva is partless. Śakti has parts (Kalā). But parts as we know them do not exist until after the universe has evolved from Prakṛti: that is, part in the literal sense of the Māyik world. When therefore mention is made of Kalā in connection with so high as Śakti as Samanī or any other Śakti which precedes Prakṛti, what is meant is something which may be best expressed by modes or aspects of Śakti. Kalā, in short, is a particular display of power or Vibhūti. Kalā is also one of the Kañcukas which go to the making of the Puruṣa consciousness and is the product of higher Śaktis and Kalās. The Kañcukas or enveloping Śaktis cut down the natural perfections as they exist in the Supreme Self and thus constitute the evolved Self or Puruṣa. The four Kalās called Nivṛtti, Pratiṣṭhā, Vidyā, Śānti are specific modes of Śakti well defined. These are explained later. As regards the other Kalās there is greater difficulty. In the first place the texts are not consonant. This may be either due to inaccuracy in the MSS. or real variances or to both. Then explanations of the terms are in general wanting though sometimes they are given by the commentators. The Sanskritist will however perceive that these latter Kalās are variant aspects (like Āvaraṇa-Devatās of worship), descriptive of the nature and functions of the Śakti whose Kalās they are and as such may have been set forth for Upāsanā; the lengthy lists being in conformity with the taste of the age in which these Śāstras were promulgated. Thus, Kalās have been called Jyotsnā (moonlight) and the like on account of their Sarvajñāta-dharma, that is, Prakāśa-rūpatā-dharma; that which being in the nature of manifestation is white and brilliant as moonlight. So again Indhikā (kindling) Kalā is so called because it is Jñānarūpa or in the nature of knowledge; and Rundhanī is so called because of its opposing or staying quality as explained later. This great elaboration of Śaktis is also in conformity with a psychological principle on which Tāntrika Upāsanā is based into which I can not enter here.

The above remarks are illustrated by the lengthy list of Kalās of the Varṇas and Praṇava given in Ch.3 of the Prapañcasāra-Tantra. The Kalās of Nāda, Bindu, A U M are there given and I will not repeat them here; but I will relate instead an account obtained from the Kashmirian Paṇḍit Hara Bhatta Śāstrī and taken by him from Śrī-Netra-Tantra which has not been published. The reader of the Prapañcasāra will observe that the account vary both as to the names and numbers of the Kalās. In Śrī-Netra-Tantra seven Kalās are given of Samanī-Śakti, *viz.*, Sarvajña, Sarvagā, Durgā, Savaraṇā, Spṛhanā, Dhṛti, Samanā; five of Āñjanī, *viz.*, Sūkṣmā, Sūsukṣma, Amṛtā, Amṛta-sambhavā, Vyāpinī; one of Mahānāda *viz.*, Urddhva-gāminī; four of Nāda, *viz.*, Indhikā, Dipikā, Rocikā, Mocikā. Some texts speak of Recikā. Nirodhini-Śakti has five Kalās called Rundhinī, Rodhini, Raudrī, Jñāna-bodhā, Tamo'pahā. The Ṣaṭcakra-nirūpana (V.38) speaks of Bandhatī, Bodhinī, Bodhā. Rodhinī and Rundhanī, which mean "opposing," indicate the opposition encountered by lower Experiencers such as Brahmā and other Devas attempting to enter into the higher state of Nāda. These Śaktis (like the "Dwellers on the Threshold" of Western occult literature) oppose all those to whom they do not extend their grace (Anugraha) by the Kalās Jñānabodhā (Wisdom) and Tamo'pahā (Dispeller of darkness). These Kalās are therefore called Sarvadeva-nirodhikā, that is, they oppose entrance into the higher state of consciousness and they oppose the fall therefrom of such Devas as have attained thereto. Of Arddhacandra there are five Kalās, *viz.*, Jyotsnā, Jyotsnāvatī, Kānti, Suprabhā and Vimalā, which are said to be Sarvajña-pada-saṁsthitā. For She is Knower of all. If one can remain in Arddhacandrapada then all things are known— past, present and future. I am informed that according to Śrī-Netra-Tantra (Ch. 22) and Svacchandra-Tantra (Ch. 20), the four Kalās of Bindu are the very important ones Nivṛtti, Pratiṣṭhā, Vidyā, Śānti; which however are said in Prapañcasāra to be Kalās of

Nāda, the four Kalās of Bindu being there given as Pitā, Śvetā, Aruṇā and Asitā. These five modes of Śakti are described later. The number and name of the Kalās of A U M differ in these several texts. According to the former the Kalās of the Destructive Ṛudra, are Tamomohā, Kṣudhā, Nidrā, Mṛtyu, Māyā, Bhayā, Jadā; of the Protective Viṣṇu the Kalās are Rajas, Rakṣā, Rati, Pālyā, Kāmyā, Buddhi, Māyā, Nāḍī, Bhrāmaṇī, Mohinī, Tṛṣṇā, Mati, Kriyā; and of the Creative Brahmā there are Siddhi, Ṛddhi, Dyuti, Lakṣmī, Medhā, Kānti, Dhṛti, Sudhā. The three Bindus of the differentiating Parabindu form the Kāmakalā. The Kalās Nivṛtti and the rest are the generalities (Sāmānya) of the Tattvas issuing from Prakṛti; that is the Tattvas are subdivisions or differentiations of these four Kalās. Nivṛtti-Kalā is the working force and essential element in the Pṛthivī-Tattva or Solidity; and is so called because here the stream of tendency is stopped and the manifesting energy turned upwards. When Pṛthivī has been reached by process of evolution, Śakti becomes Kuṇḍalī (coiled; at rest). Her next movement which is that of Yoga is that of Yoga is upwards by involution, retracing the steps of descent. The Pṛthivī *Aṇu* or point of solidity is in-exhaustible potentiality in, and as a physical, that is, sensible manifestation, of, the Spiraline Power welling up from and coiling round the Śiva-bindu. This aspect of the Power supplies (as a friend learned in Śiva literature informs me) the curving and circular motion which manifests as the rounding and spherical skin and flesh with which all Prāṇis are supplied. According to the same view Pratiṣṭhā which is the same force in all the Tattvas from Ap to Prakṛti (Tantrāloka Āhn. 10) is so called, because whilst Nivṛtti supplies the outer covering Pratiṣṭhā, as its name, indicates supplies the basis and inner framwork on which the outer physical universe is laid. Vidyā-Kalā, which is so called because it is limited knowledge, is the dominant Kalā in the Tattvas from Puruṣa upwards together with five Kañcukas to Māyā. These are related to the Śaktis Vām, Jyeṣṭhā and Raudrī which manifest as the three motions which go to make the universe, which in terms of consciousness are the movements of the Antaḥkaraṇa towards the objects (Viṣaya) of its experience, such objects being the combination of lines on various planes, in curves and circles. The three-dimensional framework affords the basis (Pratiṣṭhā) for the outer solid covering (Nivṛtti) supplied by the spiraline Śaktis as the manifested sensible and physical. Beyond Māyā there is the consciousness which is peace (Śānti), for it is free of the duality which is the the source of sorrow. The last Kalā is therefore called Śāntā and is dominant in the glorious experience of the Tattvas from Salvidyā to śakti-Tattva. Thus, the Tattvas are only the manifestations of Śakti as three typical forms of movement starting from the kinetic state. It is these moving forces as the Kalās which are the inner life and secret of them. The Kalās are not dead forces; for the universe does not proceed from such. They are realised in direct experience as Devatās in and beyond all natural manifestations and may be made to serve the purpose of Sādhanā. As Divine Beings they are modes of the one Divine Mother worshipped diagrammatically in Yantras. As the inner forces in the Tattvas the Kalās group together the latter into four great "Eggs" (Aṇḍa), that is, Spheroids comprising those Tattvas only of which a Kalā is the common dominant feature and inner force. These are the Brahmāṇḍa comprising Pṛthivī-Tattva in which all others are involved, the bounding principle or envelope of which is ether (Ākāśa); Prakṛtyaṇḍa or Mūlāṇḍa and Śaktyaṇḍa of which the envelopes are Prakṛti, Māyā and Śakti respectively. Beyond all these in the centre thereof and pervading all is the Śiva-Tattva in regard to which the

Divine Śakti as a Kalā is an utter negation (Śūnyati-śūnya), an empty space giving or vacuity-producing power (Avakāśadā), which is the negative pole of the conjoint Śiva-Śakti-Tattvas. The Śiva-Tattva is thus the Paramaśiva or Parāsaṁvit, the great Bhairava experience with its supreme experience of the universe negatived.

Regarding them this ultimate Śakti also, in so far as it is a manifestation, as a Kalā or moving Power, the thirtysix Tattvas of which the universe consists are but manifestations of five forces (Śakti) or Kalās into which the one partless Divine Śakti differentiates Herself in an infinite variety of permutations so as to produce the universe with parts: namely, Śāntātitā or Avakāśadā, Śāntā, Vidyā, Pratiṣṭhā, Nivṛtti.

According to the account given in the Śaṭcakra-nirūpaṇa *(The Serpent Power)* and the Commentaries of Kālicaraṇa and Viśvanatha, there is a Śakti called Nirvāṇa-Śakti with two Kalās, which are Nirvāṇa-Kalā and Amā Kalā, known as the seventeenth and sixteenth Kalās respectively. Unmanī is Śivapada which is beyond Kalā and Kalā. In Śakti-Tattva these have their source. The highest Śakti in this Tattva is Samanī; Nirvāṇa-Śakti is, according to Viśvanātha, Samanāpada or Samanī, the life and origin of all being (Sarveṣāṁ yonirūpiṇī). According to Kālīcaraṇa, Nirvāṇa-Śakti is Unmanī. Śakti as seventeenth Kalā is Cinmātrā and is called Nirvāṇa-Kalā. Viśvanātha identifies it with Vyāpinī-Tattva which is Śakti-svarūpā and above (Parātparā) the sixteenth Kalā. It is Antargatā of, that is, included within, Amākala, just as Nirvāṇa-śakti is Antargatā of Nirvaṇa-Kalā. Kālīcaraṇa identifies it with Samanāpada. Amā is the sixteenth Kalā. She is the receptacle of the nectar which flows from the union of Para

(Bindurūpa Śiva) and Para (Śakti). Viśvanātha cites the Yoginīhṛdaya-Tantra to show that Amā is Vyāpikā-Śakti. Kālīcaraṇa agrees as to this. But it has been said by Viśvanātha that Nirvāṇa-Kalā is Vyāpinī-Tattva. We must take it then that according to this view Nirvāṇa-Kalā are the two aspects, supreme and creative, of Vyāpinī-Tattva as Vyāpikā and Āñjanī. Beyond or more excellent than Āmā-Kalā is Nirvāṇa-Kalā, and then this last, Nirvāṇa-Śakti or Samanī in Śakti-Tattva wherein is bondage (Pāśajāla). Thus, Nirvāṇa-Kalā is the Cinmātra-svabhāvā or pure consciousness aspect of what in the creative aspect is called Amā, the receptacle of necter, that is, the blissful current which flows from the union of Śiva and Śakti. This is the rapture of creation which is known to us also. The same Śakti is in differing aspect Amṛtākararūpiṇī as the seventeenth and the receptacle of Amṛtā as the sixteenth Kalā. Amā is both Sṛṣṭyunmukhī (looking towards creation) and Ūrddhva-śaktirūpā (looking upwards, that is towards Liberation). The former is the meaning of the expression "downward-turned-mouth" (Adhomukhī). This is the position of the Petals before Kuṇḍalinī ascends.

This is my reading of Tests which are not devoid of discussion. Thus apart from difficulties in the Texts cited I was informed in Kashmir that Śakti is called the seventeenth Kalā or Amā when Cinmatrāsvabhāvā; and Amṛta-Kalā when Puruṣa is with the sixteen Kalās, which in this case are said to be the Jñānendriya, Karmendriya, Tanmātra and Manas (which includes Ahaṁkāra and Buddhi). This may be a difference of terminology only. What seems clear is that in Śakti-Tattva (of the thirty-six Tattvas) there are two Kalās which represent the supreme and creative modes of Śakti whether we call them Nirvāṇa and Amā or Amṛtākāṛā and

Amṛta-Kalā. The sixteenth is the creative Śakti and the Kalā which is in the nature of ever-existent changeless cit (Cinmātrasvabhāvā) is the seventeenth.

To sum up. Paramaśiva (Parā-saṁvit) in his aspects as Śiva-Tattvas is the Śūnyāti-śūnya, so called because in His experience there is not the slightest trace of objectivity whatever. Both these aspects are Śāntātīta. Śakti then gradually unveils again the universe for the consciousness of Śiva who is Prakāśa or the Illuminating Consciousness which is the subjective aspect of things; and the experience which is summed up as Śāntā-Kalā arises, extending from Śakti-Tattva to Sadvidyā, with the Śaktis, Saminī, Vyāpinī, Āñjanī and their Kalās; and the Śaktis of the Nadā and Bindu groups with is their Kalās. This is the Spheroid of Śakti (Śaktyaṇḍa) which is the abode of those glorious Beings who are called Mantra-māheśvara, Mantreśvara, Mantra and Vidyeśvara. The Vijñāna-kalās who are below Śuddha-vidyā are also above Māyā. From the unfolding of Bindu the other Spheroids emanate, which manifest the three principal forms of movement which go to the making of the universe. Next, in concentric circles arise the Spheroid of Mayāṇḍa, the field of operation of Vidyā-kalā, which is the Śakti producing the limited dual consciousness of all experiencers (Pralayākala, Sakala) below Sad vidyā and in or below Māyā. Lastly, the Spheroids of Prakṛti and Brahmā, provide the vehicles in which the Experiencer called Sakala functions. These Experiencers comprise all things from Brahmā down-wards who are not liberated. Brahmā, Viṣṇu and Rudra are the Lord of the spheres from Pṛthivī to Māyā; Īśa and Anāśṛta Śiva of higher Tattvas; and lastly Śiva of Śiva-Tattva, which is the ultimate source of, but is Itself beyond, all Kalās.

# Chapter 21

# THE GARLAND OF LETTERS OR VARṆAMĀLĀ

We now speak of "Vak"– "The World" – a great concept of the Śāstras. Śurti says: "Four are the steps measured by Vāk. The wise Brāhmaṇa knows them. There being hidden in the cave do not issue. The fourth is spoken by men in their speech."

The Para-bindu is the Śabda-Brahman: for on its differentiation arises the "unmanifest sound" (Avyakta-rava), the Hidden Word from which all manifested speech and the objects which it denotes are derived. This is the state of Supreme Śabda (Para-śabda), the evolution of which (Para-śabda Sṛṣṭi) has been shown in the previous Chapters. In its further development the existence of mind and body is assumed. This has been discussed in the account of the evolution of the objects (Arthasṛṣṭi) which man thinks and in uttered speech names. This Śabda-Brahaman as appearing in bodies is Kuṇḍalini-Śakti (Kuṇḍalinī Śabda-Brahmamayī). The Śāradā-Tilaka says (1-108,109):

*Sā prasūte Kuṇḍalini śabdabrahmamayī vibhuḥ.*
*Śaktiṁ tato dhvanis tasmān nādas tasmān nirodhikā.*
*Tato' ṛdhendus tato bindus tasmād āsīt parā tataḥ*

"She who is Kuṇḍalinī, all-pervading Śabda-brahman, produces Śakti. From this came Dhvaṇi; from Dhvani, Nāda; from Nāda, Nirodhikā; from Nirodhikā, Ardhendu; from Ardhendu, Bindu; and then comes Parā."

It will be observed that just as there is a sevenfold comic development, it is repeated here in the case of individual bodies. Kuṇḍalinī is Śabdabrahman, an aspect of Caitanya or Consciousness (Cit). By Śakti is here meant Cit entered into by Sattva (Sattva-praviṣṭā), which is the Paramākāśāvastha. By Dhvani is meant that same Cit when entered into by Sattva (Sattvapraviṣṭā), penetrated by Rajas (Rajo'nuviddhā),which is Akśarāvasthā. By Nāda is meant the same Cit penetrated by Tamas (Tamo'nuviddhā) or Avyaktāvasthā. By Nirodhikā is denoted that same Cit with abundance of Tamas (Tamaḥ-prācuryā) ; by Ardhendu the same with abundance of Sattva (Sattvaprācuryā). By the term Bindu is denoted that same Cit when in it there is a combination of the two (Tadubhayasamyogāt). This development appears to indicate the gradual process whereby Śakti passes through subtle to more gross forms of potency until it reaches that full potency for manifestation which is the Ghanāvasthā State or Bindu in which Kriyā exists in full creative perfection. So it is said, "Moved by the strength of Icchā-śakti (Icchā-śakti-balākṛṣṭaḥ)," illumined by Jñāna-śakti (Jñāna-śakti-pradīpitaḥ)," that Śakti (Sā śaktiḥ) in male form (Pumrūpiṇī) who is the Lord (Prabhu) puts forth Her who is called Action (Kriyākhyā) that is, Kriyā-śakti.

The Śāradā then continues:

*Paśyanti madhyamā vāci vaikharī śabda-janmabhūḥ.*
*Icchājñānakriyātmā'sau tejorūpa guṇātmikā.*
*Krameṇānena srjati Kuṇḍalī varṇamālikāṃ.*

"(Then Parā) and then came Paśyantī, Madhyamā and Vaikharī-Śabda. In this order Kuṇḍalī who is Will (Icchā), Knowledge (Jñāna) and Action (Kriyā), who is both Light (Tejorūpā) and Cidrūpā (in Herself consciousness) and in the form of the Guṇas (Guṇātmikā, that is, Prakṛti) creates the Garland of Letters."

Parā is Śabda as Para-bindu and is motionless (Niṣpanda).This as already explained becomes three fold and the threefold aspects from the Śabda stand-point are Paśyantī, Madhyamā,Vaikharī. Each of these is a manifested form of the Unmanifested Para-bindu or Śabda-brahman. It is, as Rāghava says, by shifting to another place in Her *(Asyāṁ eva binduḥ sthānānta-rāgataḥ)* that Bindu which is Parā when un-manifested and motionless is called Paśyantī, Madhyamā and Vaikharī speech (Vāk). Parā is in the Mūlādhāra cakra, Paśyantī in Svādhiṣṭhāna (and upwards), Madhyamā in Anāhata (and upwards), and Vaikharī in the throat. In Kuṇḍalī, Śakti is subtle (Sukṣmā) and in the form of mere light *(Jyotirmātrātmarūpī)* and not an object of hearing (Aśrotra-viṣayā). Thence She goes upward (Urddhvagāmiṇī) and becomes Paśyantī, self-manifesting (Svayaṁprakāśā) in the Suṣumnā-Nāḍī (Suṣ umnāṁ āśritā). She again becomes Madhyamā as a form of Nāda (Nādarūpiṇī) when reaching the Heart Lotus (Anāhata). Then She goes upward as a mere undifferentiated "hum" *(Saṁjalpamātrā avibhaktā)*. It is She who appearing at the chest, throat, teeth, nose, palate and head assumes the form of all letters (Varṇa) issuing from the root of the tongue and lips, and thus becomes Vaikharī, the Mother of all sounds, audible to the sense of hearing (Rāghava Bhatta). The same commentator then say, citing the Kādimata section of Tantrarājā, "Under the influence of one's own will *(Svatmecchāśaktighātena)* a high (Uttama) form of the Nāda called Para generates in the Mūlādhāra as Prāṇavāyu *(Prāṇavāyusvarupataḥ)*. This when carried up by will (Icchā) and made to appear in the Svādhiṣṭhāna is called Paśyantī associated with Manas. Gradually led up by Her it is called Madhyamā associated with Buddhi in the Anāhata. Carried still further upward it is called Vaikharī in the Viśuddha in the region of the throat. Thence it is generated as the Letters from A to Kṣa through its presence at the head, throat, palate, lips, teeth, tongue (root, tip and back), nose, palate and throat (together), lips and teeth (together), and throat and lips (together). Their letter-hood (Akṣaratva) is said to be due to their being divided into different parts beginning with the letter A and ending with Kṣa."

It is Cit-Śakti which is called Parā, that is to say, it is Para-Vāk not moved to vibration by the Māyā which reveals *(Parāprakāśikā Māyā niṣpandā)* on account of its bearing the reflection of Caitanya *(Caitanyābhā-saviśiṣtattyā)*. The vibratory states are Paśyantī and the other two *(Saspandāvasthāḥ paśyantyādyāḥ)*. Paśyantī which is in the nature of Bindu *(Bindutattvātmikā)* is the form of a general (that is, not particularised) motion *(Sāmānya-praspanda-prakāṣarūpiṇī)*, which is manifested in the region between the Mūlādhāra and the Navel *(Mūlādhārādi-nābhyantara-vyaktisthānā)*. It is called Paśyantī because of its being Jñāna *(Jñānatmakatvāt)*. It is associated with Manas. Madhyamā is in the form of the internal and external instruments *(Bāhyāntahkaraṇatmikā)* and manifests as Nādabindu *(Nādabindumayī)*. Hiraṇyagarbha sound *(Hiraṇyagarabharūpiṇi* is in the region extending from the navel to the heart *(Nābhadi-hṛdayāntabhivyaktisthāna)*. It is associated with the Tattvas of specific ideation and so forth *(Viśeṣasaṁkāl-pādisatattvā)*. She is Madhyamā when Buddhi is Madhyamā. Madhyamā is middle, that is, "in the midst" between Paśyanti which is "Seeing" (Īkṣaṇa) and Vaikharī which is utterance. She is neither like Paśyanti nor does She proceed outward like Vaikharī with articulation fully developed. But she is in the middle between these two. Vaikharī is a form of Bīja *(Bījatmikā)* as Madhyamā is of Nāda *(Nadarupiṇī)*, and as Paśyantī is of Bindu *(Bindūatmikā)*. Vaikharī is manifested in the region from the heart to the mouth *(Hṛdayādhyāsyāntābhivyaktisthānā)*. It is called Vaikharī according to Rāghava on account of its particular (Viśeṣa), hardness (Kharatva). Bhāskararāya (Lalitā. v. 81) derives it from Vai=very ; Khara=hard. According to the Saubhāgya-Sudhodaya, Vai=certainly; Kha=cavity (of the ear) : R=to go or enter. But according to the Yogaśāstras the Devī who is in the form of Vaikhari *(Vaikharīrūpā)* is so called because She was produced by the Prāṇa called Vikhara. This is Virātśabda, that is, the manifested letters which singly, or in combination, make certain sounds which are called Mantras. Strictly speaking all uttered sounds are Mantras, all uttered speech having a common origin or development: but in the more usual sense, Mantra means those letters or combination of letters which are used in Upāsanā and Mantrayoga and are the Mantras of the Devatās of Śastrik worship. The Arthasṛṣṭi of Kuṇḍalinī are the Kalās which arise from the letters such as the Rudra and Viṣṇu Mūrtis, their Śaktis and so forth.

The root "Man" means "to think" and the suffix "tra" indicates the saving character of Mantra. I have elsewhere spoken of Mantra as "thought-movement vehicled by and expressed in speech" and as being a "power in the form of idea clothed with sound." I find that this has led to misunderstanding. I will therefore make my meaning clearer. The one supreme Śakti appears in dual aspects as the Word, the Sence by which as uttered sound it is heard, and as the Object or Artha which the world denotes. The child is taught the meaning of words. Such and such an objects is pointed out as being indicated by a word. But a Mantra *is* the Devatā. The Sādhaka is taught who that Devatā is. He does not however at once see that Devatā. At this stage that Devtā exists for him clothed with or as an audible sound, which evokes a particular thought-movement or transformation of mental substance. The next stage is by Mantra-Sādhanā to realise that Devatā; to know it not only as a word and its mental counterpart, but as a form of that Power of which they are but a faint reflection in the world of mind and matter. That Power is infinitely greater than either, and the Mantra is a particular form of Devatā vehicled as all else in the world by mind and matter. The power by which the Devatā is realised is also Śakti, that is, Sādhana-Śakti, that is again the power of the individual Sādhaka to realise by Sādhanā. The Devatā whom he is taught to realise is infinitely greater than that. All is Śakti, but what is sought to be realised is Śakti Herself presented to the Sādhaka in the Mantra form. Brahman is of course in all things as their substance and all forms of *becoming* are without exception Śakti. But these forms are only Śakti as such. As such limited forms we realise them at once. For this we require mind, senses, and attention only in their functioning. But the Devatā, which the Mantra is, cannot be realised in this way only, since in

Itself (that is other than as the sound heard, and the idea it evokes) it is not an object in the ordinary material universe. The Sādhaka has to pierce through the vehicle of the audible Śabda and realise the Devatā whose form the Mantra is. He is enabled to do this by the co-operation of the Mantra-Śakti with his own Sādhana-Śakti. The latter gives to those who exert their own power (Sādhana-Śakti) the ability to achieve. At length and by striving, the Consciousness which manifests as Sādhana Śakti unites both, and the Consciousness, which is the Devatā, is thus realised and in this sense appears to the Sādhaka. This is the Saguṇa or Vācaka form of Devatā, and this when realised at length procures for the Sādhaka a realisation of the Vācyā-Śakti which the Saguṇā-Devatā indicates. In short the Devī or Supreme Śakti has two "forms", Her gross (Sthūla) Saguṇa form as Mantra (Mantramayī) and Her subtle (Sūkṣma) from as "light" (Jyotirmayī). Realisation is the passage from that indirect knowing, through word and its mental counterpart, to that direct knowledge which is union with the Devatā whose form a particular Mantra is.

Śabda-Brahman is all-pervading, undifferentiated Śakti, and Mantra is Its particular manifestation. It is Varṇātmaka-śabda (Lettered sound) manifested by Ākāśa caused by the contact of the surrounding air with the vocal organs, the formation of which in speech is in response to the mental movement or idea, which by the will thus seeks outward expression as audible sound. All Śabda has its corresponding Artha, for neither can be dissociated from the other. The word "Artha" comes from the root "Ri" which means to get, to know, to enjoy. Artha is that which is denoted by Śabda and is that which is known and enjoyed. This Artha is either subtle (Sūkṣma) or gross

(Sthūla). The latter is outer physical object which speech denotes and the former is the Vṛtti (modification) of the mind which corresponds to the gross Artha; far as an object is perceived the mind forms itself into a Vṛtti which is the exact mental counterpart of the object perceived. The mind has thus two aspects, in one of which it is the perceiver (Grāhaka) and in the other the perceived (Grāhya) in the shape of the mental impression. That aspect of the mind which cognises is called Śabda or Nāma (name) and that aspect in which it is its own or cognised is called Artha and Rūpa (Form), Śabda being associated with all mental operations. In the evolution of the universe the undifferentiated Śabda divides itself into subtle Śabda and subtle Artha which then evolve into gross Śabda and gross Artha. For the Cosmic Mind projects its subtle Artha on the sensuous plane which is then a physical gross Artha named in spoken speech. Thus, the subtle Śabda associated with cognition is called Mātṛkā and the subtle Artha is the mental impression; whilst the gross Śabda are the utterd letters (Varṇa) denoting the gross other physical object (Sthūla-Artha).

Just as the body is causal, subtle, gross, and as there are three cosmic and individual states, dreamless seep, dreaming, waking; Prajña, Taijasa, Visva; Īśvara, Hiraṇyagarbha, Vaiśvānara or Virāṭa; and a fourth transcendent state or Turīya; so there are three states (Bhāva) of sound Paśyantī, Madhyamā, Vaikharī developed from a fourth supreme and undifferentiated state (Parā). This last and Paśyanti represent the causal aspect of Śabda, for Pasyantī represent the causal aspect of Śabda, for Paśyantī is the actual moving aspect of the unmoving Parā. Madhyamā is Hiraṇyagarbhaśabda. This Sūkṣma-śabda and its corresponding Artha belong to the subtle body

(Liṅga-Śarīra). In creation the Cosmic Mind first develops Paśyantī-śabda and Artha, and then projects this subtles Artha into the world of sensuous experience and names it in spoken speech developed in the throat and issuing from the mouth. Vaikharī is Virāt-Śabda belonging, as well as the physical objects it denotes, to the gross body (Sthūla-Śarīra). This last gross Śabda is language, that is, sentences (Vākya), words (Pada) and letters (Varṇa) which are the expressions of ideas and Mantra. Paśyantī is characterised by non-particular general movement (Sāmānyaspanda), the first undefined push of the Vāyu towards manifestation; Madhyamā is specific movement (Viśeṣaspanda), the Vāyu commencing to differentiate; and Vaikharī is Spaṣṭ ataraspanda, that is, the clear separate movements of articulate speech. Mental Arthā is a Saṁskāra, an impression left on the subtle body by previous experience and which is recalled when the Jīva re-awakes to world-experience and re-collects the experience temporarily lost in the cosmic dreamless state (Suṣupti) which is dissolution (Pralaya). The Cause (Kāraṇa) which arouses this Saṁskāra is the Śabda or Nāma, subtle or gross, corresponding to that particular Artha. There is thus a double line of creation from the Śabda-Brahman, namely, language expressive of ideas and the objects which these denote. Uttered speech is a manifestation of the inner "naming" or thought which is similar in men of all races. Possibly for this reson a thought-reader whose cerebral centre *is en rapport* with that of another may read the hidden "speech," that is, the thought of one whose spoken speech he cannot understand. Vaikharī-śabda however differs in various races owing to racial and climatic conditions, the physical formation of the vocal organs and so forth. But for each particular man speaking any particular language, the uttered name of any object is the gross expression of his inner thought movement. It evokes that movement and again expresses it. It evokes the idea and that idea is consciousness as mental operation. That operation can be so intensified as to make itself creative. This is Mantra-caitanya when thought is not only in the outer husk but is vitalised through its conscious centre.

The above is but the Mantra way of saying that the homogeneous Consciousness differentiates as Śakti and appears as subject (Śabda) and object (Artha), at first in the subtle form of mind and its contents generated by the Saṁskāra and then in the gross form of language as the expression of ideas and of physical objects (Arthā), which the creative or Cosmic Mind projects into the world of sensuous experience to be the source of impressions to the individual experiencer therein. The natural name of anything is the sound which is produced by the acion of the moving forces which constitute it. He therefore, it is said, who mentally or vocally utters with creative force the natural name of anything brings into being the thing which bears that name. Thus, "Ram" is the Bija of fire; and is said to be the expression in gross sound (Vaikharī-śabda) of the subtle sound produced by the activity of, and which is, the subtle fire-force. The mere utterance however of "Ram" or any other Mantra is nothing but a movement of the two lips. When however the Mantra is awakened (Prabuddha), that is, when there is Mantra-caitanya, then the Sādhaka can make the Mantra work. However this may be, in all cases it is the creative thought which ensouls the uttered sound which works now in man's small magic, just as it first worked in the grand magical display of the World-Creator. His thought was the aggregate, with creative power, of all thought. Each man is Śiva and can attain his power to the degree of his ability to consciously realise himself as such. Mantra and Devatā are one and the same. By Japa the presence of the latter is invoked. Japa or repetition of Mantra is compared to the action of a man shaking a sleeper to wake him up. The two lips are Śiva and Śakti. Their movement is the coition (Maithuna) of the two. Śabda which issues therefrom is in the nature of Bindu. The Devatā thus produced is as it were the son of the Sādhaka. It is not the Supreme Devatā (who is actionless) who appears, but in all cases an emanation produced by the Sādhaka for his benefit only. The boy-Śiva (Bāla-Śiva) who thus appears is then made strong by the nature which the Sādhaka gives to his creation. The occultist will understand all such symbolism to mean that the Devatā is a form of the consciousness of the pure Sādhaka, which the latter arouses and strengthens and gains good thereby. It is his consciousness which becomes Bāla-Śiva and which when strengthened is the full-grown Divine Power Itself. All Mantras are in the body as forms of consciousness (Vijñānarūpa). When the Mantra is fully practised, it enlivens the Saṁskāra and the Artha appears to the mind. Mantras are thus a form of the Samskāras of Jīvas the Artha of which appears to the consciousness which is pure. The essence of all this is concentrate and vitalise thought and will-power. But for such a purpose a method is necessary, namely, language and determined varieties of practice according to the end sought. These Mantra-vidyā (which explains what Mantra is) also enjoins. For thought in the sense previously stated, words (gross of subtle) are necessary. Mantra-vidyā is the science of thought and of its expression in language as evolved from the Logos or Śabda-Brahman Itself.

It is in this sense that the universe is said to be composed of the letters. It is the fifty (or as some count them fifty-one) letters of the Sanskrit alphabet which are denoted by the Garland of severed heads which the naked Mother Kāli, dark like a threatening rain-cloud, wears as She stands amidst bones and carrion, beasts and birds, in the burning ground,, on the white corpse-like (Śavarūpa) body of Śiva. For it is She who "slaughters," that is, withdraws all speech and its objects into Herself at the time of the dissolution of all things (Mahāpralaya). From Her in Her aspect of Mahā-kuṇḍalī coiled round the Śiva-bindu they are derived. Mahā-kuṇḍalī when with one coil is Bindu; with two Prakṛti Puruṣa; with three Śaktis (Icchā, Jñāna, Kriyā and the three Guṇas: Rajas, Sattva, Tamas); with three and a half She is then actually creative (Sṛṣṭyunmukhī) with Vikṛti. Then with four coils and so on to 51. She is according to the Śakti-saṁgama-Tantra (Utpatti-Khāṇḍa, Ullāsa 1 ) Ekajatā, Ugratārā, Siddhakālī, Kālasundarī, Bhūvaneśvarī, Caṇḍikeśvarī, Daśamahāvidyā (ten coils), Śmaśānakālikā Caṇḍabhairavī, Kāmatārā, Vaśikaraṇa-kālikā, Pañcadaśī Ṣoḍasī, Chinnamastā, Mahāmadhumatī, Mahāpadmāvatī, Ramā, Kāmasundarī, Dakṣiṇakālikā, Vidyeśī, Gāyatrī (24 coils), Pañcami, Śaṣṭhi, Mahāratneśvarī, Mūlasañjīvanī, Paramākalā, Mahānīlasarasvatī, Vasudhāra, Trailokyāmohinī, Trailokya-vijayā, Mahākāmatāriṇī, Aghorā, Samitamohinī, Bagalā, Arundhatī, Annapūrṇā, Nakulī, Trikaṇṭakī, Rājeśvarī, Trailokyākarśiṇī, Rājarājeśvarī, Kukkutī, Siddhavidyā, Mṛtyuhāriṇī, Mahābhagavatī, Vāsavī, Phetkarī, Mahāśrīmatṛsundrī, and Śrīmātṛkoṭpattisundarī (coils 51) respectively. Each coils is said to represent the Mātṛkā or subtle form of each of the letters (Varṇa) and to denote the number of Kūtas of divisions in the Mantras of each of these Devatās. Mahākuṇḍalī coiled round the Śiva-bindu, as it were a mathematical line without magnitude,, makes with it one point. When the time for creation comes She uncoils Hereself and creates the whole universe in the form of the Letters and the objects which they denote Having so created it, She again rests as Kuṇḍalī in the root centre of the body (Mūlādhāra) of all living creatures from which She issues as Paśyantī, Madhyamā, and Vaikharī Śabda. Man's body is called in the Tantras a microcosm (Kṣudra-Brahmāṇḍa), containing within itself all which is in the universe (Mahā-Brahmāṇḍa) of which it is a part. The Yoginī-hṛdaya-Tantra (Chap. I. 36) says that when Śakti first "sees" (that is, ideates), She is Paramākāla in the Mother form (Ambikārūpa) which is both supreme Peace (Paramā-Śāntā) and Supreme Speech (Parā-vāk). She sees the manifested Śabda from Paśyantī to Vaikharī. The Paśyantī state is that in which Will (Icchā-Śakti) is about to display the universe then in seed (Bīja) form. This is the Śakti-Vamī. Madhyamā-Vāk which is knowledge (Jñāna) is Jyeṣṭhā. Here there is the first assumption of form as the Mātṛkā *(Mātṛkātvaṁ-āpanna)*, for there is particular motion (Viśeṣa-spanda). Vaikharī state is that of Kriyā-Śakti (action) whose form is that of the gross universe. As the former Śakti produces the subtle letters of Mātṛkā which are the Vāsanā, so the latter is the Śakti of the gross letters (Varṇa) of words and their objects. These letters form the Garland of the Mother (Varṇamālā), issuing from Her as Kuṇḍalī and absorbed by Her in the Yoga which bears Her name.

As the Yoga-kuṇḍalī-Upaniṣad says: "That Vāk (Power of speech or Logos) which sprouts in Parā, gives forth leaves in Paśyantī, buds in Madhyamā, and blossoms in Vaikharī. By reversing the above order sound is absorbed. Whoever realises the great Lord of Vāk, the undifferentiated illumining Self is unaffected by any word (Śabda), be it what it may." As the Haṭha-yoga-pradīpikā

(IV. 101-102) concisely says: "Whatever is heard in the form of sound is Śakti. The absorbed state (Laya) of the Tattvas (Prakṛti's evolutes) is that in which no sound exists. So long as there is the notion of the, so long is the sound (that is, vibration) heard. The soundless is called Parabrahman or Paramātmā." Śabda-Brahman is thus the Brahman in its aspect as the cause of the manifested Śabdārtha. It is the ideating kinetic aspect of the undifferentiated Ether of Consciousness, the Cidākāśa of Philosophy and the Saguṇa-Brahman of worship. It is Cit-Śakti vehicled by undifferentiated Māyā-Śakti or the manifesting Godhead uncreated, unborn, eternal, evolving the changing worlds of name and form (Nāmā-rūpa) by its wondrous and inscrutable Māyā. Therefore, as Caṇḍī says, "Reverence to Her Who is eternal, Raudrī, Gaurī, Dhātrī, reverence and again reverence; to Her who is the Consciousness in all beings, reverence and again reverence."

## Chapter 22

# OM

The ancient Hindu had an aptitude, much to be appreciated in these often verbose days, of saying a great deal in a few words. The Mantra "Om" is an instance. For this short syllable contains a whole philosophy which many volumes would not suffice to state-- an Eastern philosophy I may add which is gaining increased support from Western science. These two will before long be reconciled when the latter has cast aside what a friend calls its "habit blinkers." The beneficial result will, it is hoped, be a science which is religious, and a religion which is scientific.

The Mantra "Om" is composed of three latters A, U, M, -- of which the first two vowels coalesce into O. over the Om is written the sign Candranbindu or Nāda and Bindu, shown as a crescent with a dot or point over it. Nāda and Bindu, are two of many aspects of That which in India is called the mother, or great Power (Mahāśakti), as it was by the near East called Mangna Mater and by the Gnostics Megale Dunamis. This is both the efficient and material cause of the universe which is Its form or body. Nāda, is the Mantra name for the first going forth of power which gathers itself together in massive strength (Ghanībhūta) as Bindu to create the universe, and which bindu, as so creating, differentiates into a Trinity of Energies which are symbolised by A,U,M. Nāda and Bindu thus represent the unmanifested "fourth" (Turīya) state immediately before the manifestation of the world, in which animate life exists in the three conditions of dreamless sleep, dream, and waking. Man always anthropomorphises. In the west he calls the creator the father. More aptly Supreme creative Being in the East and by the Śāktas is called the mother, for this power conceives in its womb, which is consciousness, gives birth to and nourishes, the Universe. The first mantra into which a child is initiated is Mā or Mother, for that is its first world, and Mother is often the last word on the lips of the dying. Reverence to the natural Mother is reverence to the Mother of all and they who in life and at death drink the milk of that mother attain to her. Moreover, in the world the mother aspect of Her who is Brahman is alone fully manifested. What she is Herself (Svarūpa) is not known to mind or senses. The Yoginī-hṛdaya-Tantra says: "What man knows the heart of women? Only Śiva knows the Hearts of Yoginī." This is the cosmic Heart of the universe whose systole and diastole is the going forth and return of millions of worlds. This process Brahmanism called Pravṛtti and Nivṛtti and Taoism (which is perhaps a Chinese adaptation of the doctrine of the Upaniṣads) names it Yang and Yinn. Relatively to man's knowledge the Supreme Power is said to be in Itself Being (Sat), Consciousness (Cit) and Bliss (Ānanda). The Primordial Power or Ādyā Śakti is inconceivably beyond manifested presonailty, for this limited experience hedged in by mind and matter. Though not in itself a Person as we understand that term, It is ever *personalizing* in the form of all individual (Vyaṣṭi) things in the world. It is also a Person as the aggregate (Samaṣṭi) of all such personalities.

Whilst infinite, it contains in itself the sum of all human and other experience. Whilst the power (Mahāśakti is in Itself beyond mind and senses in that darkness (as man thinks it to be) which is the body of Mahākālī, its manifestations are seen. It is with reference to such manifestation inferred to be the Radical Vital Potential which is, as it were, the thread (Sūtrātmā) of the whole series of being, which form one Vital Continuity, a principle on which Indian Monistic philosophy is based. Nothing has an absolute commencement or end. All is transformed. Birth and death are modes thereof. Each existence is as it were a knot tied in an infinite rope which knot is made at birth and united at death. Something does not come from nothing, and something never becomes nothing. An absolute beginning or end is inconceivable. Particular universes come into being and go. Birth, life and death are modes of the universal transformation governing all organic life "from a blade of grass to Brahmā Himself". The divine infinitude is ever such, but appears as limited function and its effects, and as apparently discontinuous, because of the limitation of the senses which perceive its working. The whole fact is never present to consciousness, but only that section to which pragmatic attention is for the moment given, and therefore appears localised and in succession of time, Nevertheless there is an infinite Vital Continuity stretching from the Radical potential to its actualisation as the crust of matter, which is but an infinitesimal portion of the effect produced by the function of substance relative to whole universal efficiency. For ether (Ākāśa) is more continuous than matter which is but the outer crust of the General Power. Ether is continuous and all- pervading and is said to be more than a thousand times denser than gross pondrable matter. The visible earth is therefore but a microscopic point evolved by the vital power (Śakti) of substance (Śiva) in the midst of the invisible, perpetually active, but in its own nature (Svarūpa) unaffected Divine substance pervading all space. Therein nothing truly exist independently of another, but all are transformation of the one power. And as that power is itself vital and creative, its products or rather transformations of itself are that. As it is being with the potentialities of all life in form, none of its manifestations is "dead" though in common parlance we concede, "life" only to that which displays evolutionary growth. The search therefore for the origin of life is futile, since life is eternal and had no beginning.

All things are part of the one mother who is life itself. It displays itself in innumerable forms, but the vastest generalisation of its working discloses three movements of creative upbuilding, of destructive disintegration and the holding of these two opposing force in equilibrium. Nādabindu differentiates into the Trinity of will (Icchā), knowledge (Jñāna) and Action (Kriyā), "Sun", "Moon", and "Fire", and this self-explicating power manifest in matter in the threefold manner described. These three powers are A,U,M, or the Devatās Brahmā, Viṣṇum, Rudra. These are not "Gods." There is only one God. They are Devas or "Shinning ones," being aspects and specific manifestations of the One divine Power whose feet (in the words of Śāstra) even Brahmā, Viṣṇu and Rudra worship. They are scientific concepts deified, and rightly so, for their content refer to aspects of the supreme power which is God. Scientifically they stand for the three functions of Vital Substance. It is incorrect to suppose that God in his aspect as Brahmā created the world some millions of years ago and has since done nothing, or that He in his form as Rudra has a yet had no opportunity of displaying his power of dissolution. Brahmā is always creating and recreating the elements of manifested substance which Rudra is ever breaking down. Throughout Nature there are these twin forces upbuilding and destroying forms, integrating and disintegrating, anabolism and catabolism, tending to change and conservation of tissues and so on. The three aspects A, U, M, of the Primordial Power (Nāda-bindu) are always operating. Whilst Rudra is, by chemical destruction, breaking down the combinations of matter and thus working towards the final dissolution of things, that is the disintergration of forms into ether its more general elements (Mahābhūta) or into the formless substance (Prakṛti) the material cause of all, Brahmā creates it anew by his ever rejuvenescent molecular activity, thus rescuing organised vitality from the processes which are ever at work to consume its forms. Viṣṇu again is the power which stabilises matter in the midst of these conflicting forces and thus maintains all Existences. Things only possess relative stability. So, it is that the power of Rudra works its purpose at the end. Matter itself is only a relatively stable form of Energy from which as Supreme Will it appears and into which, on the attainment of its terminal state, it again merges. It is Viṣṇu who holds it together in equilibrium. Again leaving individual existences and looking at the sum total of manifest Energy, Viṣṇu, the Maintainer, throughout Space and time, is a theological statement of the general conservation of Energy. To these intuited laws and truths objective science is giving increasing support. In this sense "Om" is the Pratīka or representative of the Radical vital potential of the universe and of the Trinity of Energies by which it actualises and materialises itself as the five forms of "matter" (though ether is not ponderable matter), namely ethereal (Ākāśa), aerial (Vāyu), fiery (Agni), liquid (Ap) and solid (Pṛthivī). Through worship of and meditation on this Pratīka, with all its implications, man, according to Advaita-Vedānta, realises himself as the one vital Śakti who is the Mother of all.

## Chapter 23

# THE NECKLACE OF KĀLĪ

The world has never been altogether without the Wisdom– the Mūla Veda nor its Teachers. The degree and manner in which it has been imparted have, however, necessarily varied according to the capacities of men to receive it. So, also have the symbols by which it has been conveyed. These symbols further have verying significance according to the spiritual advancement of the worshipper. This question of degree and variety of presentation has led to the superficial view that difference in beliefs negatives the existence of any commonly established Truth. But if the matter be regarded more deeply, it will be seen that whilst there is one essential wisdom, its revelation has been more or less complete according to symbols evolved by, and, therefore, fitting to, particular recial temperaments and characters. Symbols are naturally misunderstood by those to whom the beliefs they typify are unfamiliar, and who differ in temperament from those who have evolved them. To the ordinary western mind the symbols of Hinduism are often repulsive and absurd, it must not however, be forgotten that some of the symbols of western faiths have the same effect on the Hindu from the picture of the "Slain

Lamb," and other symbols in terms of blood and death, he naturally shrinks in disgust. The same effect on the other hand is not seldom produced in the Western at the sight of the terrible forms in which India has embodied her vision of the undoubted Terrors which exist in and around us. All is not smiling in thus world. Even amongst persons of the same race and indeed of the same faith we may observe such differences. Before the Catholic Cualtus of the "Sacred heart" had overcome the opposition which it at first encountered, and for a considerable time after its imagery was regarded with aversion by some who spoke of it in terms which would be today counted a shocking irreverence. These differences are likely to exist so long as men vary in mental attitude and temperament, and until they reach the stage in which having discovered the essential truths, they become indifferent to the mode in which they are presented. We must also in such matters distinguish between what a symbol may have meant and what it now means. Until quite recent times the English present folk and others danced around the flower-wreathed Maypole. That the pole originally (like other similar forms) represented the great Liṅga admits of as little doubt as that these folk, who in recent ages denced around it, were ignorant of that fact. The Bishop's mitre is said to be head of a fish worn by ancient near eastern hierophants. But what of that? It has no such associations now.

Let us illustrate these general remarks by a short study of one portion of the Kālī symbolism which affects so many, who are not Hindus, with disgust or horror. Kālī is the Deity in that aspect in which it withdraws all things which it had created into itself. Kālī is so called because she devours Kāla (Time) and then resumes Her own dark formlessness.

The Mahānirvāṇa-Tantra says (IV.30-34) of the Supreme Mother: "Thou the supreme yoginī moved by his mere will doth create, maintain and withdraw the world with all that moves and is motionless therein. Mahā-kāla (Great Time) the Dissolver of the universe is Thy form. At the dissolution of things it is Kāla (Time) who will devour all and by reason of this He is called Mahā-kāla and since Thou devourest Mahā-kāla Himself it is Thou who art called the supreme primordial Kālikā.

"Because Thou devourest Kāla, Thou art called Kālī and because thou art the origin of and devourest all thing Thou art called the Ādyā-Kālī. Resuming after dissolution thine own nature dark and formless, Thou alone remainest as one, ineffable, and Inconceivable. Though appearing in form Thou art yet formless; though Thyself without beginning, multiform by the Power of Māyā, Thou art the beginning of all, Creatrix. Protectress and Destructress that Thou art". From Her then, in her nature one with Śiva, the state which is Aśabda, issue all letters and words (Śabda) and the world of things (Artha) which they denote. Into her as Kālī they are dissolved.

The scene is laid in the cremation ground (Śmaśāna) amidst white sun-dried bones and fragments of flesh, gnawed, and packed at by carrion beasts and birds. Here the "heroic" (Vīra) worshipper (Sādhaka) performs at dead of night his awe-inspiring rituals. Kāli is set in such a scene for she is that aspect of the Great power which withdraws all things into Herself at, and by, the dissolution of the universe. He alone worships without fear, who has abandoned all worldly desires, and seeks union with Her as the One Blissful and Perfect Experience. On the burning ground all worldly desires are burnt away. She is naked and dark like a threatening raincloud. She is dark, for she who is Herself beyond mind and speech, reduces all things into that worldly "nothingness," which as the Void (Śūnya) of all which we now know, is at the same time the All (Pūrṇa) which is Light and Peace. She is naked,being clothed in space alone (Digambarī), because the great power is unlimited; further She is in Herself beyond Māyā (Māyātītā); that power of Hereself with which She covers Her own nature and so creates all universes. She stands upon the white corpse like (Śavarūpa) body of Śiva. He is white because he is the illuminating (Prakāśa) transcendental aspect of consciousness. He is inert because he is the changeless aspect of the Supreme, and She the apparently changing aspect of the same. In truth She and He are one and the same, being twin aspects of the One who is changelessness in, and exists as, change. Much might be said in explanation of these and other symbols such as Her loosened hair, the lolling tongue, the thin stream of blood which trickles from the corners of the mouth, the position of her feet, the apron of dead men's hands around Her waist, her implements and so forth. Here I take only the garland of freshly-severed heads which hangs like a Varṇamālā low from her neck.

Some have conjectured that Kālī was originally the Goddess of the dark-skinned inhabitants of the Vindhya Hills taken over by the Brāhmaṇas into their worship.

One of them has thought that she was a deified Princess of these folk, who fought against the white incoming Aryans. He pointed to the significant fact that the severed heads are those of white men. The Western may say that Kālī was an objectification of the Indian mind, making a Divinity of the Power of the Death. An Eastern may replay that She is the Samketa (symbol) which is the effect of the impress of a spiritual Power on the Indian mind. I do not pause to consider these matters here.

The question before us is, what does this imagery mean, and what has it meant for centuries past to the initiate in Her symbolism? An esoteric explanation describes this Garland as made up of the heads of Demons, which She as a power of righteousness, has conquered. According to an inner explanation given in the Indian Tantra-Śāstra this string of heads is the Garland of Letters (Varṇamālā), that is the fifty, and as some count it, fifty one letters of the Sanskrit Alphabet. The same interpretation is given in the Buddhist Demchog Tantra in respect of the Garland worn by the great Heruka. (See *Śrī Cakra Sāmbhara.* – A Buddhist Tantra). These letters represent the universe of names and forms (Nāma-rūpa), that is Speech (Śabda) and its meaning or object (Artha). She the Devourer of all, "slaughters," that is withdraws, both into Her undivided Consciousness at the Great dissolution of the Universe. She wears the letters which, She, as creatrise, bore. She wears the Letters which She, as the Dissolving Power, takes to Herself again. A very profound doctrine is connected with these Letters, which space prevents me from fully entering into here. I have set it out elsewhere in greater detail. The movement of Her creative projection are indicated by the letters subtle and gross which exist on the petals of the inner bodily centres or Lotuses.

Very shortly stated. Śabda which literally means Sound-here lettered sound- is in its causal state (Parā-Śabda) known as "Supreme Speech" (Parā-Vāk). This is the Śabda-brahman or Logos; that aspect of Reality or

Consciousness (Cit) in which it is the immediate cause of creation, that is of the dichotomy in consciousness which is "I" and "This", subject and object, mind and matter. This condition of causal Śabda is the Cosmic Dreamless State (Suṣupti). This Logos awakening from its causal sleep "sees", that is, creatively ideates the universe, and is then known as Paśyantī-śabda. As Consciousness "sees" or ideates, forms arise in the Creative Mind, which are themselves impressions (Saṁskāra) carried over from previous worlds, which ceased to exist as such when the universe entered the state of causal dreamless sleep on the previous dissolution. These re-arise as the formless consciousness awakes to enjoy once again sensuous life in the world of forms.

The Cosmic Mind is at first itself both cognising subject (Grāhaka) and cognised object (Grāhya); for it has not yet projected its thought into the plane of Matter : the mind as subject-cogniser is Śabda and the mind as the object cognised, that is the mind in the form of object is subtle Artha, This Śabda called Madhyamā-Śabda is an "Inner Naming" or "Hidden Speech letters" (Varṇa) are the "Little Mothers" or Mātṛkā, the subtle forms of gross speech. There is at this stage a differentiation of Consciousness into subject and object but the latter is now within and forms part of the self. This is the state of Cosmic Dreaming (Svapna). The cosmic Mind then projects these mental images on to the material plane and there they become materialised as gross physical objects (Sthūla Artha) which make impressions from without on the mind of the created consciousness. This is the cosmic waking stage (Jāgrat). At this last stage the thought-movement expresses itself through the vocal organs in contact with the air as uttered speech (Vaikharī Śabda) made up of letters, syllables and sentences. This lettered sound is manifested Śabda or name (Nāma) and the physical object denoted by speech are the gross Artha or form (Rūpa).

This manifested speech varies in men, for their individual and racial characteristics and the conditions, such as country and climate in which they live, differ. There is a tradition that there was once a universal speech before the building of the Tower of Babel, signifying the confusion of tongues. Of these letters and names and their meaning or objects, that is concepts and concepts objectified the whole Universe is composed. When Kālī withdraw the world, that is the names and forms which the Letters signify, the dualism in consciousness which is creation, vanishes. There is neither "I" (Aham) nor "This" (Idam) but the one non-dual Perfect Experience which Kālī in Her own true nature (Svarūpa) is. In this way Garland is understood.

"Surely" I hear it said "not by all. Does every Hindu worshipper think such profundities when he sees the figure of Mother Kālī?" Of course not, no more than, (say) an ordinary Italian peasant knows of, or can understand, the subtleties of either the Catholic mystics or Doctors of theology. When however, the western undertakes to depict and explain Indian symbolism, he the interest both of knowledge and fairness, understand what it means both to the high as well as to the humble worshipper. Salutation is thus made to Her from whom the mind and its thoughts proceed and the language (Vāk) in which they are expressed. Vāk is Prakāśa, the illuminating consciousness, and Artha is Vimarśa its objects. Vāk is in the form of Varṇa (letters), Pada (syllables) Mantra. Artha is Kalā,

Tattva, and Bhuvana the other so-called Adhvas. (See Ch. 27). Out of Vāk and Artha the whole world, consisting of six Adhvās (Ṣadadhvātmaka) originated. Round the neck of Kāli the letters (Varṇa) which make the syllables (Pada) and Mantra are hung. In Her they are dissolved in the fiery ending of the worlds.

# Chapter 24

# DHVANI

Motion may be either produced or unproduced. The latter is the causal stress itself, and the former the effect of it. In the world, sound is produced by the contact of one thing with another – of (say) the hand and the drum in case of unlettered sound and the vocal organs and air in the case of uttered speech. Causal stress itself is uncreate, is self-produced and not caused by the striking of one thing against another. For this reason it is called Anāhata. This Anāhata-Śabda which is Brahman-movement is heard in the heart which It has produced and which It causes to pulse, a movement which we can feel and hear.

This uncreated self-existing Śabda as causal stress manifests in double form as unlettered sound or Dhvani and is thus called Dhvanyātmaka-Śabda and as lettered sound or Varṇa which is Varṇātmaka-Śabda. And so the *Bhāṣā-pariccheda* says (164,165):

*Śabdo 'dhvaniśca varṇaśca mṛdaṇgādibhavo dhvaniḥ'*
*Kaṇṭha-saṁyoga-janmāno-varṇaste kādayo matāḥ.*

That is Śabda is of two kind – Dhvani and Varṇa. The first is illustrated in the sound given forth by a drum and the like. In the production of the second the organ is exercised and it is manifested as Ka, Kha, and the other letter of the Alphabet . That is in certain sound such as the beating of a drum, the roar of thunder, the sounds of laughing, crying and so forth no letters appear to be manifested *(Varṇaviśeṣāna-bhivyañjaka)* but that in certain others, letters or Varṇas are manifested as in the case of sound of articulate speech. The former class are called Dhvanis and the latter Varṇas.

In both cases it is to be observed that sound is produced by the clashing (Abhigāta) of two created things, *viz.*, the drum and the hand or drumstick and the vocal organs in contact with the circumambient air.

The distinction therefore between the two classes does not depend upon this -- (1) that whilst Varṇas are produced by the mutual impact of the throat, air, and the ear, the Dhvanis are produced by an assemblage of condition of which the throat is not one. In other words the Vyāpāra or functioning of the vocal organ does not constitute the distinction between Dhvanyātmaka and Varṇātmaka-Śabda. For the vocal organ is exercised in laughing, crying, and so forth and also in the cries of animals, but in them we hear no Varṇātmaka-Śabda or articulate speech. Thus, Dhvanis may be produced by the vocal organs.(2) Nor can it be said that the exercise of the vocal organs is the sine qua non of the Varnātmaka-Śabda. Thus, when we hear articulate sounds over the telephone or from the gramo-phone, the immediate cause of the sounds is not the Vyāpāra of the vocal organ, though the non-immediate cause may be so. (3) Nor again can we say that the Varṇātmaka-Śabdas are in all cases significant or expressive of meanings and that the Dhvanyātmakas are in all cases insignificant. In a general sense this is so, and thus, in common parlance, we speak of Varṇātmaka-Śabda as having a meaning and Dhvani as being without it. But this is not necessarily and always so. Doubtless to Īśvara every Dhvani has a meaning, and even to us unlettered sound may express a meaning. Again some Varṇātmaka-Śabda may not for even to a man who know a particular language *any* combination of letters or any combination of words will not be expressive language- but only letters in certain order and combination. Thus, the sound of laughter or crying is Dhvanyātmaka yet the sound may express a meaning in the sense that it is recognised at once from the sound that a particular person is happy or in trouble. Many of the Dhvanis of animals may be significant in this sense. The sound of a bell, bugle, or drum may be suggestive of meaning as in the case of the midday gun. On the other hand many Varṇātmakas may not express a meaning. Thus the combination M, A, N, has a meaning and spells "man" in English but M,A,N, and other combinations (except N, A, M which may have some sort of meaning) do not express meaning. Each letter separately may have a meaning. According to the Vyāsa-Bhāṣya on Yoga, each Varṇa is capable of expressing all Arthas or meanings. But any arbitrary combination of separate letters will not give a meaning. A special combination of varṇas is necessary to express a special meaning. Electricity may be latent in all material objects but we require to make special combinations of such objects *(e.g.*, zinc, copper and sulphuric acid in a cell) to make such electricity patent. Any arbitrary combinations *(e.g.*, of wood, water, and oil) will not effect this. In an unsuitable combination of Varṇas, their Śaktis check the one the other.

The distinction between the two classes is therefore a

distinction between sounds which manifest themselves as letters and others which do not. The former are usually produced by the throat *(Kaṇṭha-saṁyoga-janmānaḥ)* but not invariably. On the other hand, as we have seen, Dhvanis too may be so produced. Both Varṇas and Dhvanis again are momentary (Kṣaṇika). Both therefore are produced by the contact (Abhighāta) of two or more created things. Let the letter "Ka" be uttered a hundred times. Each time it is a different sound which is uttered. Again one person says 'Ka' and then another says Ka. The sounds again are different. The sounds produced and heard in these cases are indeed different. Nevertheless we may still recognise that one Varṇa sound, *e.g.,* 'Ka' is being uttered by oneself all those hundred times and by oneself and the other person. We recognise here oneness in the midst of all differences of the individual sounds produced and heard. The recognition (Pratyabhījñā) takes this form:

"It is the same 'Ka' that I utter now and that I uttered moment before. It is the same Ka that you have uttered and I have uttered." Western psychology may attempt an explanation of this recognition of Varṇa identity by comparison, abstraction and assimilation. Thus, if Ka is uttered by one person ten times, actually different sounds are produced varying in pitch, softness, harshness and so on. If another person utters the same letter ten times, then each of them is a different sound and the sounds are also different from the sounds produced by the first person. But though all these Dhvanis are different in pitch, timbre and the like, it will be admitted that both persons have uttered the same letter. Western psychology would explain this as follows:

The Dhvanis *are* different but we make a rapid *comparison* of them and find that though they have differences in pitch, timbre, etc., still they have a *great* deal of *similarity*. The differences are then thought away or abstracted and then the twenty sounds are *assimilated* so as to give us a geneeric sound which we recognise as the Varṇa sound "Ka". It is in this way also we form the generic notion of "Man" or "Book". The generic sound Ka is not something that actually exists apart from the twenty variations which either of the two persons mentioned have heard. On the contrary the variations are the actual phenomena. The type (the generic sound) is simply our mental construction through comparison, abstraction and assimilation. To a mind which cannot compare, abstract and assimilate, the sounds are different sounds and it cannot recognise any typal sound in their midst. The Indian theory on the subject is, on the other hand, as follows:

The Varṇas or letters have imperishable and invariable (Nitya) forms. As the Paramāṇus or prime "atoms" of matter are imperishable so are the Varṇa-śabda. "Nitya" however here means "imperishable" so long as the cosmic order itself lasts. *(Natu madhye varṇānām, utpatti-vināśan.* -Vedānta-Paribhāṣā). That is in the period of cosmic life beginning with creation (Sṛṣṭi) and ending with Dissolution (Laya) the Varṇa sound persist. They are compared to a jar in a dark room which cannot by reason of darkness be seen *(Andhakārastha-ghaṭānupalambhavat*-Vedānta-Paribhāṣā). Just as the jar existing in the dark may not be seen with the eyes, as the prime Śabda or Varṇas, though always given, may not be always manifested as acoustic phenomena. To be thus manifested they require a manifestor (Abhivyañjaka) or vehicle of expression. This vehicle (Abhivyañjaka) through which an eternal exiting letter become an acoustic phenomenon *now* and *then* is called Dhvani. The period of cosmic life (Madhye) is a 100 years of Brahmā when the world dissolves (Laya). The Varṇas persist during all these years of Brahmā – a time which is called Kalpa. In Laya they enter the germinal state as seeds of potency. This view is thus essentially different from that of ordinary western psychology. Plato's doctrine of ideal archetypes and their sensible variations comes nearer the Vedānta doctrine.

According to this the Varṇa-śabdas are always *(i.e.,* during a Kalpa) actually going on (Nitya and Anāhata *i.e.,* continuous and uninterrupted.) – produced by artificial means. But they are often unmanifest (Avyakta) to the gross perceptive organs. They become manifest (Vyakta) to gross sensibility through certain manifestors (Abhivyañjaka) which are the Dhvanis. Thus the Śabda "om" is uninterruptedly going on, but this it is said, one can only hear in certain stages of Sādhanā, or in a quiet place particularly during night time when there is little promiscuous interference of the sound-waves. The Kālī-Mūrti is an eternal symbol of the world-process (involving Cit and the play of Śakti) and the Garland of Letters (Mātṛkās) on the breast of the mother is also an eternal possession. Whether the Varṇas are uttered and heard or not, they are Anāhata sound-forms and according to Indian ideas they are more real and more actual than the variations (differing in pitch, timbre and so forth) which are uttered and heard. Thus, the variations alone are not the actual phenomena as the ordinary western empiricist would hold.

Therefore a Dhvani as an acoustic manifestation of a Nitya Śabda is subject to all conditions of place, time and circumstance and is non-permanent (Anitya) and variable

(Vikārī). This variableness and transitoriness which really pertain to the Abhivyañjaka-Dhvani are transferred by us (through association) to the manifested letter (Varṇa). Thus, we say "Ka is now produced and is no more." But really that which comes to be or ceases to be is the vehicle (Dhvani) and not the Varṇa-Śabda. As the Vedānta-Paribhāṣā (Ch.IV) says:

*Utpanno gakāra ityādipratyakśatu so'yam gakāra ityādi-pratyabhijña-virodhād apramāñaṁ. Varṇābhivyañjaka- dhvani-gatotpatti-nirūpita-parampara-sambandha-viśayatvena pramāṇam vā.* "The apprehension (Pratyakṣa) that "Go" is now produced is not right apprehension because it conflicts with the recognition (Pratyabhijñā) of the present 'Go' *(i.e.,* at present uttered and heard by me) being identical with all other 'Ga' (i.e., those uttered and heard in the part). 'Or' we may take it as a correct apprehension if we ascribe the idea of production to the Varṇas (which are manifested but not produced) seeing that the Dhvanis which manifest them are produced and using a characteristic which really belongs to the manifestor for the manifested.

Śamkarācārya discusses the theory of Varṇa and Sphoṭa in his Śārīraka-Bhāṣya (1-3-28). He describes Dhvani in these words:

*"Kah punarayam dhvanir nāma, yo dūrād ākarṇayato varṇavivekam apartipadyamānasya karṇapathaṁ avatarati, pratyasidataśea mandatvapatutvādibhedaṁ varnesvasanjayati, tannibhandhanaścodattādayo viśeṣā na varṇasvarūpanibandhanāh, Varnāṇāṁ pratyabhījñayamānatvāt,* etc." By Dhvani is to be understood that which is heard by a person listening from a distance without distinguishing the separate letters

and which in the case of a person standing near-by affects the letters with its own distinctions of high and low pitch and so forth. It is on this Dhvani that all the distinctions of Udātta, Anudātta and the like depend and not on the intrinsic nature of the letters which are recognised to be the same whenever pronounced.

When a man is heard shouting from a great distance we do not catch his actual words and yet we can hear the pitch, modulation and so forth of his voice. When he speaks close to us we catch his words as well as the modulation, pitch sweetness or outherwise and so forth of his voice. In both cases the pitch, etc., of the sound constitute its Dhvani. These qualities of pitch, sweetness and the like do not inhere in the Varṇas themselves but belong to their acoustic expression, the Dhvanis. Thus, Dhvanis are: (1) gross embodiments (Anitya, Vikārī) or Nitya, Avikārī Varṇa-Śabdas; (2) other gross sounds (either produced in nature such as the sound of the storm or produced by ourselves such as laughter or the sound of musical instruments) which do not appear to us as embodying Varṇa-Śabdas. Those who believe (such as the Grammarians) in Sphoṭa regard Dhvani as its Abhivyañjaka. Śaṁkara however contests the necessity of assuming Sphoṭa or that which causes the apprehension of the sense of a word.

Dhvani however is used also in a sense different from that in which it is defined in Nyāya or Vedānta as expounded aby Śaṅkara and different from Dhvani as conceived by those Garmmarians who regard Dhvani as the manifestor (Vyañjaka) of the ideal sound called 'Sphoṭa.'

In the Tantras Dhvani is a form of Causal Śabda. Thus, we hear of the "sweet murmuring Dhvani of Kuṇḍalinī," the Creatrix of all Śabdas and Arthas.

The Śāradā-Tilaka to which I have repeatedly referred (1,108-109) says:

*Sā prasūte* Kuṇḍalinī *Śabda-brahmamayi vibhuḥ.*
Śaktim *tato* Dhvanis *tasmān nādas asmān* Ṅirodhikā.
*Tato'rdhendus tato* Bindus *tatmādāsāt parātataḥ.*
*Paśyantī Madhyamā vāci Vaikharī śabdajanmabhuḥ.*

The words in roman type are various forms of Śakti, producing one another in the order in which they are mentioned in the verse. From Kuṇḍalinī issued Śakti, from Śakti, Dhvani and so on. From the order of evolution it will appear that Dhvani in such Śāstra is a subtle causal principle and not a gross manifestation of Śabda which is its ordinary sense. It is Vaikharī which is the gross manifestation of Śabda. Here the Śabda manifests from its subtle state as Madhyamā, which issued from the causal state as Parā, Paśyantī, through the Dhvani caused by the contact of the vocal organs and air. Parā and the rest are located in various Cakras and tracts of the bodily organism. Rāghava Bhatta quoted by Vācaspatya (page 60) says-

*Saivoraḥ-kāṇṭha-talusṭhā śiro-ghrāṇa-radastitā.*
*Jihvā-mūloṣṭha-nisyūta-sarva-Varṇa-parigrahā.*
*Śabda-prapañca-jananī srotra-grāhya tu vaikarī.*

She (Kuṇḍalinī) being in the heart, throat and palate and going through the passages of the head and nose and teeth and coming out from the base of the tongue and the lips becomes audible Vaikharī – the Kuṇḍalinī who has invested herself with the Varṇas and is the Mother of all varieties of Śabda.

Śakti, Dhvani, Nāda and the rest are described as verious aspects of Cit due to its varied association with the Guṇas – Sattva, Rajas and Tamas. Thus, Śakti is defined as the Śattva predominant (Sāttvika) condition of Cit.; Dhvani as the Rājasika-Sāttvika condition *(Rajo'nu-viddha)* Sāttvika of Cit, that is a Sāttvika condition in which there is also a trace of Rajas; and Nāda a state of Causal Śabda in which there is a trace of Tamas *(Tamo'nuviddha)*. These are called Paramākāśāvasthā, Akṣarāvasthā, Avyaktāvasthā. Whether then we have to deal with Dhvani in the sense of a form of causal Śabda or as a gross manifestation of Śabda depends upon the context.

## Chapter 25

# SUN, MOON AND FIRE

These words do not refer to the heavenly luminaries of Fire in the three worlds of Birth and Death, but are technical terms of the Mantra-śāstra denoting the creative Trinity.

In the Brahmasvarūpa is merged Vimarśa (Antarlīnavimarśa). Śruti says that there was first merely One without a second or Brahman. It became inclined towards creation (Śṛṣṭi-mukha). The material cause out of which the world is made is, according to the Vaidika Text, "May I be many." Vimarśa is that which is the object of experience as "This" (Idam) and this Idam is the Universe. The "Idam" is thus the world as object of experience (Prapañca-parāmarśa). Vimarśa-Śakti is thus the Power which produces and exists in the form of the universe. Before the world existed it was in the Brahman in the form of Brahma-Śakti. Then alone was the Light which is beyond Sun, Moon and Stars which in the Āgama is known as the imperishable Supreme World *(Anapāyini, Parā-Vāk)*.

She the supreme Vimarśa-Śakti is our Supreme Lady (Parā-bhaṭṭārikā) Mahā-tripura-Sundarī, in whom are all the 36 Tattvas beginning with Śiva and ending with Kṣiti, who is in the form of all worlds (Sarva-prapañcātmikā) and also transcends them (Taduttīrṇā). She is beyond the three Śaktis who are Sun, Moon and Fire. She is the causal seed of all, with whom Śiva unseparately is. For Śiva cannot create without Śakti nor Śakti without Śiva. As between moon and moonbeam there is no defference so there is none between Śiva and Śakti. The Svarūpa of Śiva is "I" (Aham), for it is said in the Kama-kalāvilāsa from which this account is, in general, taken *(Śivasya svarūpam aham-ityeva-mākaram)*. The Vimarśa of that is the experience of "I-ness." She the primordial Vimarśa-Śakti is the pure mirror which manifests that Experience *(Tasya prakāśane nirmalādarśaḥ)*. The work cited illustrates this as follows:

A handsome King looking at his reflection in a mirror which is before him knows "I am he who is thus reflected." So, the Supreme Lord loking at His own Power within Himself knows His own Self as "I am all *(Paripūrṇo'ham),*" that is, the whole or Perfect "I". This is the union of A = Śiva and Ha = Śakti, A+Ha= Aham or "I". Śiva indicates Jñāna-Śakti, and Śakti, Kriyā-Śakti--Knowledge and Action. Śiva is illumination (Prakāśa). The Vimarśa mirror is composed of a mass of His rays and Vimarśa-Śakti is impulse (Visphuraṇa-Śakti) maturing in action. The Rays being reflected back on the foundation of Consciousness there is the Mahābindu. So, when the Supreme Lord who is Illumination (Prakāśa) is connected with the mirror-like Vimarśa there shines forth the Parameśvara as Pūrṇo'ham (The Lord Experience as "I am all.") The Supreme "I" is thus the massing together of Śiva and Śakti. This "I-ness" (Ahambhāva) arises upon the gaze of Śiva upon His own luminous Śakti or Power. So it has been said that in the notion of 'I' Illumination rests in itself (Ātmaviśrānti). So, Śruti (Śvet.4-1) says, "That which in letterless (Avarṇa) generates many letters (Varṇa)." This supreme "I" is Cittamaya.

We have spoken of the Aham or "I" and Idam or "This". The first is known as the white (Sīta) Bindu or "Moon" and represents the Śiva aspect of the supreme "I", and the second is the red (Śoṇa) Bindu or "Fire," the Śakti aspect. They are in conjunction known as the Divine Husband and Wife (Kāmeśvara and Kāmeśvarī). The union of both is the Mixed (Miśra) Bindu or "Sun". The "Sun" is Kāma and Kalā is "Moon" and "Fire," the three Bindus being known as the Kāmakalā. This mixed Bindu becomes creative and is the cause of the manifested Word (Vāk) and its meaning (Artha). From this Bindu issues Nāda-Śakti in seed form. The Bindu is the union of the letters A and Ha, which denote the union of Prakāśa and Vimarśa, that is, white and red Bindus.

Kāma is that which is desired (Kāmyate) by the great Yogis who knew the Paramārtha as their self. Mahātripurasundarī, inseparable from Kāmeśvara, is the collectivity of the Bindus and Kāmakalā. The Bindu above is Her Face (Sun) and the two Bindus below are Her two breasts (Moon and Fire) and the Kalā below it, which is half of Ha, is Her womb (Yoni). Nāda which comes forth is the cause of the origin of all sounds. This Nāda is eventually divided into all the particular letters and words their compounds and the subtle elements and all objects, their compounds. For both the world of speech and of objects have ultimately the same origin. A letter or word is the Brahman as such, just as an object denoted by the word is the Brahman as such object.

The two Bindus are inseparate, that is, Prakāśa and Vimarśa. For this reason it is said that Śiva and Śakti are one Tattva. In the same way there is no difference between Vidyā or Mantra as indicator (Vedaka, Vācaka) and the Ḍevatā thereby denoted (Vedya, Vācya). Vāk and Artha are always united. This is realised in Sādhanā when the Devatā, the Artha of the Mantra, appears and leads the Sādhaka to a realization of the Vācyā-Śakti, the Brahma-Svarūpa. So Naṭanānandanātha in his Commentary on Puṇyānanada's Kāma-kalā-vilāsa (VV. 6,7) says that great Yogis worship the Mother Mahātripura-sundari, who is Kāmakalā, the collectivity of the three Bindus. For "Pura" here means Bindu, the three (Tri) which are Sun, Moon and Fire, which are Illumination and Bliss: within whom is the Power (Vīrya), which is the endless mass of letter (Anantākṣararāśi) and great Mantras. In the worship of the great Śrīcakra-Yantra (figured in my Edition of the Kāma-kalā-vilāsa) the gross letters, in Vaikharī form, are in the outer Maṇḍalas, and passing though the subtler forms of Śabda, the Śabda-brahman and the Śūnya are attained. He therefore cites the Vijñāna-Bhaṭṭāraka as saying: "By passing through the different Maṇḍalas (of the Śrīcakra) where the gross (Sthūla) letters (Varṇa) are, and rising up to Ardhendu, Bindu Nādānta and to the Śūnya in the Bindurūpacakra, one becomes Śiva." This is the worship which a Missionary author describes as worship of *pudendum muliebre.* The Yantra is composed of intersecting triangles, some upright and some inverted. The letter only are symbollic of the Yoni, which is here not the Yoni of any woman. Here it is the womb of the Divine Mother of the world. Here is the seat of the secret play of Śiva and Śakti as "Moon," "fire" and as the "Sun" which is the union of both-- the Divine Energy, whence proceeds the world of name (Nāma=Śabda) and Forms (Rūpa=Artha).

# Chapter 26

## BĪJA-MANTRA

Action necessarily implies movement. Whenever threfore, there is action, there is Spanda or movement and therefore what to the perceiving subject (when heard) is called Sound. This may or may not be heard . One person may have a sharpened natural faculty of hearing; so that he may hear what escapes the ear of another. There is Sound though the latter may not hear it. Similarly, there is Sound which is not heard by any natural ear until assisted by the extension of the faculty procured by a material scientific instrument. Similarly again, there is Sound which cannot be heard by any material instrument, but which is apprehended by the Yogic Mind as part of its experience. In the beginning of things the natural Principle (Prakṛti) was in a state of equilibrium (Sāmyavāsthā). Then there was no Sound, for there was no movement of the objective world. The first Vibration which took place at the commencement of creation, that is, on the disturbance of equilibrium (Vaiṣamyāvasthā) was a general movement (Sāmānya- Spanda) in the whole mass of Prakṛti. This was the Praṇava-Dhvani of Om Sound. It is not that the Sound is represented as it is by the Sound of the letters Om. Om is only the *approximate* representation or gross utterance to gross ear of the Subtle Sound which is heard in Yoga experience of the first movement which is continuously taking place, for at each moment the creative movement is present. From out of this general movement and Sound special movements (Viśeṣa-Spanda) and Sounds arise. The following apt illustration has been given (see "World's Eternal Religion"). If a vessel of water is shaken, there is first a general movement of the whole water in every part of the water, now this way, now that So, the evenly balanced Guṇas or factors of Prakṛti equally vibrate throughout their whole mass, and as the movement continues, the equilibrium is disturbed and the Guṇas act and re-act on one another as in the second state of the water in the illustration. Diverse vibratory condition being set up, diverse Sounds are given forth. The first equally distributed motion throughout the mass is Om, which is the great seed-mantra (Mahābīja), for it is the source of all others and of all compounded Sounds. Just as Om is the general Sound, the other Bīja-mantras are the particular Sounds which are the letters of the alphabet. These are evolved out of the general Sound which underlies all particular Sounds. Both the Oṁkara or Praṇava and the Bīja-Mantras as pronounced by the mouth are thus the articulate equivalents of the inarticulate primal Dhvani. They become articulate at the last stage called Vaikhari or Spaṣṭatara-Spanda of the four stages, known as Para (Rest passing into movement), Paśyantī (general movement), Madhyamā or special movement of subtle character heard by the subtle ear, and Vaikharī or special movement which as speech is the fully articulated Sound heard by the gross ear; The Praṇava-Mantra is thus the Sound Equivalent of Brahman and the Bīja-Mantras are the various forms with attribute (Saguṇarūpa) of the Devas and Devīs. It is true that the approximate Sound Om is said to be constituted of the letters a, u, m. This is not to say that the primordial Dhvani was these letters or their combination, For these letters are the product of the primordial Dhvani which precedes them. What is meant is that Om as a gross Sound heard by the gross ear is the Saṁdhi or combination of these letters: A European Sanskritist told a friend of mine that *Om* said before a Mantra is simply the "clearing of the throat" before utterance ; and I suppose he would have said – the clearing of the throat after utterance; for *Om* both precedes and follows a Mantra. Why however should one clear the throat them? *Om* has nothing to do with hawking sounds, or the throad. *Om* is, according to Indian belief, a sound actually heard by Yogīs as above described. If moreover, the learned man had ever heard the Mantra *Om* recited he would have felt that it could not be explained in so shallow and materialistic a way. For *Om* is sounded as from the navel with a deep rolling and continuous Sound ending at the upper part of the nostrils where the Candra-bindu is sounded. Moreover, how are we to account for the other Bija Sounds on this hypothesis, such as Am, Ām, Eṃ and so forth, except by supposing that the unpleasant and unmannerly act of clearing the throat had undergone an unaccountably varird development? Be the doctrine true or false, it is more profound than that.

Mantras are given various names according to the number of their syllables. A Bīja or Seed-mantra, is strictly speaking, a Mantra of a single letter such as Kam, which is composed of the letter K (Ka) together with Candrabindu which terminates all Mantras. Even here there is in a sense another letter. The reason is that the vowel cannot be interminably pronounced and is therefore terminated by a consonant. In fact, as Pāṇini says, the function of a consonant is to interrupt a vowel sound. The consonant cannot be pronounced without a vowel, which is hence known as the Śakti of a consonant. Here the termination is M in the form of the nasal breathing called Candrabindu which is Nāda and Bindu. The M which ends the Bija is sounded nasally, high up in the bridge of the nose, and never reaches the lips. In all the other letters one or other of the five Bhutas or forms of sensible matter (Ākāśa, Vāyu, Agni, Ap, Pṛthivī,) predominates. For this reason, in the selection by the Guru of the Mantra for his disciple the letters are chosen according as an examination shows that there is an excess or deficiency of any particular Bhūta. Where there is excess of a Bhūta, the letter in which it is predominant is said with the outbreathing. Where there is deficiency it is said with the inbreathing. M is chosen to end the Bīja because here Bhūtas are said to be in equipoise. Though strictly the Bīja is of one letter as the seed from which the Mantra springs, popularly other short unetymological vocables such as Hrīm, Śrīm, Krīm, Hūm, Aim, Phaṭ are called Bījas. In these there are two or more letters, such as in the first H, R, I and Candrabindu. Thus a Mantra may or may not, convey on its face its meaning. Bījas have no meaning according to the ordinary use of language and for this reason they have formed the subject of ridicule to those ignorant of the Mantra-śāstra. The initiated however know that their meaning is the own from (Svarūpa) of the particular Devatās whose Mantra they are, and that they are a form of the Subtle Power as creative Dhvani which makes all letters sound and which exists in all that we say or hear. Each Devatā has His ir Her Bīja. Thus the Devatās of Krīm, Hrīm and Ram are Kālī, Māyā and Agni respectively. The primary Mantra in the worship of any Deva or Devī is known as the Root Mantra (Mūlamantra). Every letter, syllable and Mantra is then a form ( Rūpa) of the Brahman, and so is the image and all the lines of the Yantra and all objects in the universe. And so the Śāstra says that they go to Hell who think that the image is merely a stone and that the Mantra is merely a letter of the alphabet. All letters are forms of Śakti as sound-powers. The Śakti of which they are a manifestation, is the living Energy which projects itself into the form of the universe. The Mantra of a Devatā is the Devatā. The rhythmical vibrations of its sounds not merely regulate the unsteady vibrations of the sheaths of the worshipper, thus transforming him, but through the power of striving (Sādhana-śakti) of the worshipper, there arises the form of the Devata which it is. And thus the Bṛhad-gandharva-Tantra (Ch. V) says:

*Sṛṇu devi pravakśyami bījānām deva-rūpatāṁ.*
*Mantroccāraṇamatreṇā deva-rūpam prajāyate.*

The Bījas thus have a meaning. They indicate the Artha or Devatā which they are. What that Devatā is, is taught to the Sādhaka, just as the child learns that rose means a particular flower, and that rice and milk are the names for particular forms of food and drink which he takes.

The Bījas of the five Bhūtas, that is, of the Devatās of the four forms of sensible matter, are Ha, Ya, Ra, La, Va, with Candra-bindu. Where there is more than one letter, each has its meaning. As examples I here select twelve Bija-mantras (in their popular sense), the meanings of which are given in the 6th Chapter of the *Varadā-Tantra* as quoted in the well-known Bengali compendium known as the *Prāṇatoṣiṇī*. I may here observe that the meaning of individual letters is given in the Bijakośas, such as the Tantrābhidhāna. The Varadā-Tantra, Ch. 6, says :

### Haum

Śivavāci *hakārāstu aukārah* syat Sadāsivāḥ.
*Śunyaṁ* duhkhahararthaṁ tu tasmattena Śivaṁ yajet.
That is,

*Ha* meaṇs Śiva. Au is Sadāśiva. The *Śūnya* is that which dispels sorrow. Hence with that Śiva should be worshipped.

### Dum

*Da* durgāvācakaṁ devī *ukāraścāpi* rakṣaṇe.
Viśvamātā *nāda*rūpā kurvartho *bindurū*pakaḥ.
Tenaiva Kālikādevim pūjayedduhkhaśāntaye.

That is,

*Da,* O Devī, means Durgā. *U* also means to save. *Nāda* is the mother of the Universe. *Bindu* means (pray) do.

### Krīm

*Ka* Kālī brahma *ra* proktam Mahāmāyārthakaśca ī.
Viśvamātārthako *nādo bindu*rduhkhaharārthakaḥ.

That is,

*Ka* is Kālī. *Ra* is said to be Brahma. *Ī* means Mahāmāyā *Nāda* means Mother of the universe. *Bindu* means Dispeller of sorrow . With that Devi Kālika should be worshipped for cessation of sorrow.

### Hrīm

*Hakāraḥ* śivavāci syād *rephaḥ* prakṛtirucyate.
Mahāmāyārtha *ī*-śabda *nādo* viśvaprasūḥ smṛtaḥ.
Duhkḥaharārthako *bindu*bhuvanāṁ tena pūjayet.

That is,

*Ha* means Śiva. *Ra* is said to be Prakṛti. *Ī* means Mahāmāyā. *Nāda* is said to be mother of the universe. *Bindu* means dispeller of sorrow. With that Bhuvaneśvarī should be worshipped.

### Śrīm

Mahālakṣmyārthakaḥ Śaḥ syād dhanārtho *repha* ucyate.
Ī tuṣtyartho' *paronādo bindu*rduhkhaharārthakaḥ.
Lakṣmīdevyā bījam etat tena devīṁ prapūjayet.

That is ,

*Śa* means Mahālakṣmī. *Ra* is said to mean wealth. Ī means satisfaction. *Nāda* is Apara (which may mean Aparabrahma or Īśvara). *Bindu* means Dispeller of sorrow. This is the Bīja of Devī Lakṣmī. With it the Devi should be worshipped.

### Aim

Sarasvatyārtha *ai*-śabdo *bindu*duhkhaharārthakaḥ.
Sarasvatyā bījaṁ etat tena Vāṇīṁ prapūjayet.

That is,

*Ai* means Sarasvatī. *Bindu* means Dispeller of sorrow. This is the Bija of Sarasvati. With it Vāṇi or Sarasvatī should be worshipped.

Klīm

*Kaḥ* Kāmadeva uddiṣṭo' pyathava Kṛṣṇa ucyate .
*La* Indra ī tuṣṭivāci sukhaduhkhapradā *ca am.*
Kāmabijārtha uktaste tave snehan maheśvarī.

That is,

*Ka* refers Kāmadeva, or according to some to Kṛṣṇa. *La* means Indra. *Ī* means contentment. *Am* is that which grants happiness and sorrow. Thus, O Maheśvarī, the meaning of Kāmabīja is spoken unto Thee out of my love for Thee.

Hūm

*Ha* śivaḥ kathito devi ū Bhairava ihocyate.
Parārtho *nāda* śabdastu *Bindu*rduhkhaharārthakaḥ.
Varmabījatrayo hyatra kathitas tava yatnataḥ.

That this ,

*Ha,* O Devī, is said to be Śiva. Ū is said to be Bhairava. *Nāda* means Para, Supreme. *Bindu* means Dispeller of sorrow. Here the three composing the Varmabīja (armour-bīja) are spoken unto Thee owing to Thy solicitation.

Gam

Ganeśārthe *ga* uktas te *Bindu*rduhkhaharārthakaḥ.
Gaṁbījārthaṁ tu kathitaṁ tava snehān maheśvarī.

That is,

*Ga,* I speak unto Thee, means Ganeśa. *Bindu* means Dispeller of sorrow. Thus, O Māheśvarī, the meaning of Gam-bija is spoken unto Thee out of love for Thee.

Glaum

*Ga* Ganeṣo vyāpakārtho *lakā*rasteja *au* mataḥ.
Duh khaharārthako *bindu*rganeśaṁ teṇa pūjayet.

That is,

*Ga* is Gaṇeśa, *La* means what pervades. *Au* means tejas. *Bindu* means Dispeller of sorrow . With it Gaṇeśa should be worshipped.

Kṣraum

Kśa, Nṛsimho Brahma *raśca* urdhvadantārthakaśca *au*.
Duḥkhaharārthako *bindur* Nṛsimhaṁ tena pūjayet.

That is,

*Kṣa* is Nṛsiṁha and *Ra* is Brahma. *Au* means teeth pointing upwards, *Bindu* means Dispeller of sorrow. With it Nṛsiṁha should be worshipped.

Strīm

Durgottāranavācyaḥ *sa* tārakārthastakārakaḥ.
Muktyārtho *repha* ukto'tra mahāmāyārtnakaśca *ī*.
Viśvamātārthako *nādo Bindu*rduhkhahararthakaḥ.
Vadhūbījārtha ukto'tra tava snehān maheśvarī.

That is,

*Sa* means deliverance from difficulties. *Ta* means Saviour. *Ra* here means salvation or liberation. *Ī* means Mahāmaya. *Nāda* means Mother of the universe. *Bindu* means Dispeller of sorrow. Thus, the meaning of Vadhūbīja is spoken unto Thee, O Maheśvarī, out of love for Thee.

A close examination of the above may raise some difficulties, but must, in connection with what is elsewhere written, remove the charge that the Bīja is a meaningless saying to the worshipper. It is full of meaning to him.

# Chapter 27

## ṢADADHVĀS

Adhvā means a path, and Mantrādhvā is all knowledge relating to Mantra. The Six (Ṣat) Adhvās are, on the Śabda side, the three Varṇa (letter), Pada (syllable) and Mantra (combination of syllables), each being dependent on one another, Pada on Varṇa, and Mantra on Pada, which are said, in the work from which I take the following table,to be 51,81,11 respectively. On the Artha side the three other Adhvās are Kalā (5), Tattva (36) and Bhuvana (224), each similarly dependent. The science of the Ṣadadhvās is referred to in both Śaiva and Śākta works, but seems peculiarly characteristic of the Śāmbhava-Darśana in which Śaiva and Śākta Darśanas are synthetised. The Śākta doubtless worships Śiva as well as Śākti with emphasis on the latter aspect. The ordinary Śaiva worships Śakti as well as Śiva with emphasis on the latter aspect. In Śāmbhava Darśana both are raised into a higher synthesis. In the same way Kula = Śakti and Akula =Śiva, and therefore Kulīna means one who worships the two in one.

Kalā means Śakti either generally in its higher aspect and more commonly some specific aspect and function of Śākti. The five chief Kalās which sum up in themselves groups of Tattvas are Śāntyātita-kalā, Śāntikalā, Vidyā-kalā, Pratiṣṭhā-kalā, Nivṛtti-kalā. These have been already referred to. These are the Powers of certain Tattvas or Principles, and two stages in the emanative process. They (the Tattvas) are 36 in number and are divided into 3 classes, *viz.*, Pure (Śuddha-tattva); Pure-Impure (Śuddhāśuddha-tattva) and Impure (Aśuddha-tattva). Three groups of tattvas are also called Śiva, Vidyā, Ātma Tattvas, The first as stated in the Siddhānta-Sārāvali and other works comprise the Śiva-Tattva and Śakti Tattva; the Second the Tattvas from Sadāśiva-Tattva to Śuddha-vidyā-Tattva; and the third the Tattvas for Māyā to Pṛthivī.

The word Bhuvana means world or region. Bhuvana = *Asmāt bhavati iti bhuvanaṁ,* or "what comes from this," that is, "what is produced" is Bhuvana. These Bhuvanas or Regional Bodies are also Pure, Pure-Impure, and Impure. These are shown with the corresponding Kalā and Tattva in the accompanying table which I have extracted with the permission of the owner of the copyright from pp. 392-367 or Part II, Vl. II of the late T.A. Gopinātha Rao's *"Elements of Hindu Iconography"* where they are conveniently tabulated. I have made one or two verbal corrections.

| Kalās | Tattvas | No. of Bhuvanas | Name of the Bhuvanas |
|---|---|---|---|
| (a) Śāntyātīka-kalā | i. Śuddha-tattvas. 1. Śiva-tattva | 10 | Anāśrita, Anātha, Ananta, Vyomarūpinī,. Vyāpiṇī, Ūrddhavagāmini, Mocikā, Rocikā, Dīpikā, and Indhikā – (Five of these are śākta- bhuvanas and The remaining five Nādorddhva-bhuvanas.) |
| | 2. Śakti-tattva | 5 | Śāntyātītā, Śānti, Vidyā, Pratiṣṭhā and Nivṛtti (These are called the Baindavapuras). |
| | Total | 15 | |
| (l) Śānta-kalā | 3. Sadāśiva-tattva | 1 | Sadāśivabhuvana. |
| | 4. Īśvara-tattva | 8 | Śikhaṇadī, Śrīkaṇṭha, Trimūrti, Ekaruda, Ekanétra, Śivottama, Sūkṣma and Ananta. |
| | 5. Śuddhavidya – tattva | 9 | Manonmanī, Sarvabhūta-damanī, Balapramathanī, Balavikaraṇī, Kālī, Raudrī, Jyeṣṭhā and Vāmā. |
| | Total | 18 | |

| Kalās | Tattvas | No. of Bhuvanas | Name of the Bhuvanas |
|---|---|---|---|
| (d) Vidyā-kalā | ii.Śuddhāśud ha tattvas | | |
| | 6. Māyā | 8 | Aṅguṣṭhamātra, Īśānta, Ekekṣaṇa, Ekapingala, Udbhava, Bhava, Vāmadeva and Mahādyuti. |
| | 7. Kāla | 2 | Śikhesa and Ekavīra. |
| | 8. Kalā | 2 | Pañcāntaka and Śūra. |
| | 9. Vidyā | 2 | Piṅga and Jyoti. |
| | 10. Niyati | 2 | Saṁvarta and Krodha, |
| | 11. Rāga | 5 | Ekaśva, Amanta, Aja, Umāpati and Pracaṇḍa. |
| | 12. Puruṣa | 6 | Ekavīra Īśāna, Bhava, Īśa, Ugra, Bhīma and Vāma. |
| | Total | 27 | |
| (d) Pratiṣṭhā-kalā | iii Aśuddha-tattvas | | |
| | 13. Prakṛti | 8 | Śrīkaṇṭha, Auma, Kaumāra, Vaiṣṇava, Brahma, Bhairava, Kṛta and Akṛta. |
| | 14. Buddhi | 8 | Brahma, Prajeśa, Saumya, Aindra, Gandharva, Yakṣa, Rākṣa, Rākṣasa and Piśāśca. |
| | 15. Ahaṅkāra | 1 | Sthaleṣvara. |
| | 16. Manas | | |
| | 17.Śrotra | | |
| | 18. Tvak | 1 | Sthūleśvara. |
| | 19. Cakṣus | | |
| | 20. Jīhva | | |

| *Kalās* | *Tattvas* | *No. of Bhuvanas* | *Name of the Bhuvanas* |
|---|---|---|---|
| (e) Pratiṣṭhā-kalā | 21. Nāsā<br>22. Vāk<br>23. Pāni<br>24. Pāda<br>25. Pāyu<br>26. Upastha | | Śaṅkukarṇa |
| | 27. Śabda<br>28. Śparśa<br>29. Rūpa<br>30. Rasa<br>31. Gandha | 5 | Kālañjara, Mandaleśvara, Mākota, Drāvinda and Cakalaṇḍa. |
| | 32. Ākāśa | 8 | Sthāṇu, Svarnākṣa, Bhadrakarṇa, Gokarṇa, Mahālaya, Avimukta, Rudrakoṭi and Vastrapāda. |
| | 33. Vāyu | 8 | Bhīmeśvara, Mahendra, Attahāsa, Vimaleśa, Nala, Nākala Kurukṣetra and Gayā. |
| | 34. Tejas | 8 | Bhairava, Kedāra, Mahākāla, Madhyameśa, Amāra–tāka, Jalpeśa, Śrīśaila and Hariścandra. |
| | 35. Jala | 8 | Lakuliśā, Parabhūti, Diṇḍi, Mundī, Vidhi, Puṣkara, Naimiṣa, Prabhāsa, and Amaresa. |
| | Total | 56 | |

| Kalās | Tattvas | No. of Bhuvanas | Name of the Bhuvanas |
|---|---|---|---|
| (f) Nivṛtti-kalā | 36. Pṛthivī | 108 | From Bhadrakālī to Kālāgni. |
| | Grand Total | 224 | |

Thus to take the first and highetst of Śiva-tattva and the associated Śakti-tattva, the Bhuvanas are Anāśrita, the Region or Bhuvana without support and self-sustaining, Anātha or Lordless because there is no higher Lord here, Anānta or endless, Vyomarūpiṇī in the form of the all-spreading Ether, Vyāpini all- spreading Ūrddhva-gāminī upward going, Mocika freed of all bonds, Rocika Beautiful or source of Beauty, Dīpikā illuminating, Indhika destroyer of all impurity. Such are the Bhuvanas of the Kalā Śāntyātītā (Beyond even the high abode of peace) and the conjoined Śiva and Śakti-Tattvas. Five of these are called Sakta and the remaining five Nādorddhva (above Nāda) Bhuvanas. The rest are various other divine bodies named after their divine residents. All these regions have been created by Parama-śiva for the enjoyment of the Beings therein; there being an immense variety of beings in an ascending hierarchy from man up to the supreme Lord and Lady af all. The beings in the Pure regions are wholly Pure and the others Pure Impure or Impure. Impurity or Mālā is ignorance and is of three kinds, namely, Mala, Māyā and Karma. There are thus three classes of Paśus or created beings, namely, Vijñānakalās enveloped by that ignorance which is called Mala, Pralaya-kalās enveloped in both Mala and Māyā, and Sakalās or those surrounded by the three forms of ignorance Mala, Māyā and Karma. Above the Vijñānna-kalā are the beings called Mantras. The Mala envelope when in the stage at which it is about to leave the being is said to have undergone Paripaka. The Vijñānakalās, whose Mala is in a high state of Paripaka, are the eight Vidyeśvaras. They are eight in number and are variously coloured as in the following table, for which I am indebted to the same work.

| *No.* | *Name* | *Colour* |
|---|---|---|
| 1. | Ananteśa | Blood-red |
| 2. | Sūkṣma | White |
| 3. | Śivottama | Blue |
| 4. | Ekanetra | Yellow |
| 5. | Ekarudra | Black |
| 6. | Trimūrti | Crimson |
| 7. | Śrīkaṇṭha | Red |
| 8. | Śikhaṇḍi | Dark-brown |

The author cited refers to several southern Āga-mas, such as Pūrva-Kāraṇa, Aṁśuma-bhedāgama, Kāmilka and other works for their Dhyāna. From these it would appear that the colours and so forth are not always given in the same way.

These Vidyeśvaras are higher spiritual Entities, by whose aid the lower orders of beings attain the higher stage of spiritual evolution. Next to the Vidyeśvaras come the Mantreśvaras. Having been given pure bodies (Tanu), instrument (Karaṇa), regions (Bhuvana) and enjoyment (Bhoga), these gradually get rid of all Mala. Above the Mantresvaras are the Mantra-maheśvaras and beyond these are the Eternal and unproduced Śiva-Tattva and Śakti-Tattva.

In the Vimarśinī on Īśvara-pratyabhījñā (III) Sadāśiva-Tattva is described as that particular specialisation (Cid-viśeṣatvam) which consists in the experience of that Bhyāvarāsi or mass of ideation belonging to the collectivity (Varga) of Caitanya called Mantra-maheśvara. Of the Vidyeśvaras it is said (*cf.* III, 1-6) that whilst the Ego-side is pure, yet unlike the experience of higher states they perceive the objects as different from themselves in the same way as the Īśvaras, as recognised by the Dvaitavādins, perceive theirs. The various locations of the Jīvas in the various Tattvas is given as follows: Mantramaheśvara in Sadākhya-Tattva, Maheśvara in in Īśvara-Tattva, Mantras in Suddhāvidyā-Tattva (the eight Vadyeśvaras Ananta and the rest are different from the Mantras), Vijñānakalās below Śuddhavidyā but above Māyā Pralayā-kalās in Māyā and Sakalās include all other beings from Brahmā downwards who are not Mukta.

The whole of the Śāmbhava-Darśana rests on a principle of the specialisation of Consciousness, stages of descent form Pure Cit to the consciousness of the gross material world. Each stage is more bound in ignorance than the former unitl gross matter is reached. The Śāstra speaks of the eight called Cit, Citi, Citta, Caitanya, Cetana, Indriyakarma, Deha and Kalā. The first is consciousness in the pointed or Bindu state, the second out-spreading (Vyāpinī), the third with inward and outward activity, the fourth the Bodha or experience which is from outwards inwards, the fifth is the retention (Dhāraṇā) of that Bodha, the sixth is experience through action of the senses, and the seventh and eighth are the Body and its inherent subtle moving forces such as the 38 Kalās of Moon, Sun and Fire. In moon Sattva is dominant and in fire Tamas. The Rājasik activity of the Sun mediates between these opposites. The Lords of the Tattvas proceeding form "Earth" (Pṛthivī) upwards are Brahamā form Pṛthivi to Pradhāna (Prakṛti), Viṣṇu from Puruṣā to Kalā, Rudra in Māyā. Īśa in the regions extending to Sādākhya-Tattva. Then follow Anāśrita Śiva and Paraśiva.

## Chapter 28

# MANTRA-SĀDHANA

In the Gayātrī-Tantra it is said-- "that is called Mantra, by the meditation (Manana) on which the Jīva acquires freedom from sin, enjoyment of heaven and Liberation and by the aid of which he attains in full the four-fold fruit (Cāturvarga)." Elsewhere it is said "Mantra is so called because it is achieved by mental process". *"Man"* of "Mantra" comes from the first syllable of *Manana* or thinking and *"tra"* from Trāṇa of liberation from the bondage of the Saṁsāra or phenomenal world. By the combination of *"man"* and *"tra"* that is called Mantra which "calls forth" (Amantraṇa) the four aims of being (Cāturvarga) .

A Mantra is composed of letters. Letters and their combinations as syllables and words are all forms of manifested Śabda, that is, Brahman-forms. They are each and all forms of the Creative Stress as uttered by the mouth, heard by the ear, and apprehended by the mind; but what are ordinarily called Mantras are those particular sounds which are used in worship and practice (Sādhanā) which consist of certain letters, or arranged in a definite sequence of sound of which the letters are the representative signs. The relations of Varṇa, Nāda, Bindu, vowel and consonant in a Mantra constitute the Devatā in varying forms. Certain *Vibhuti* or aspects of the Devatā are inherent in certain Varṇas. The Mantra of a Devatā is that letter or combination of letters which reveals the Devatā to the consciousness of the Sādhaka, who has evoked it by Sādhanā-śakti. The form of a particular Devatā therefore appears out of particular Mantra of which that Devatā is the Adhiṣṭhātri Devatā. The mantra is intoned in the proper way according to letter (Varṇa) and rhythm (Svara). For these reasons a Mantra; when translated ceases to be a Mantra; that is, the sounds heard and utterd in the translation are not the body of and do not evoke, the Devatā. We are then not dealing with the same sound; but with a translation in another language; with other sounds giving the meaning to the intellect of the Sanskrit Mantra. This shows that Mantra is not mere individual thinking but a particular sound-body of consciousness

A particular Mantra therefore (such as the Gāyatrī) is not a mere collocation of words. Though to a non-believer it may seem but a string of mere letters bearing on their face a particular meaning or in the case of Bīja Mantras apparently no meaning at all, to the Sādhaka it is a very mass of radiant *Tejas* or energy. An ordinary collection of works is something gross. These as all else, are forms of Śakti. But the Mantra of which we speak is the Devatā Himself or Herself in Mantra-body. Mantra is thus a mass of radiant Energy. Sayings give information and advice to men of the world, whilst Mantras awaken super-human power or Śakti. A mere saying is therefore, like a Jīva, subject to birth and death, whilst a Mantra is directly Brahman in sound-body, unwasting and undecaying. A Mantra again is not the same thing as prayer of self-dedication (Ātma-nivedana). Prayer is conveyed in what words the worshipper chooses and bears its meaning on its face. It is only ignorance of Śāstrika principles (See

"Principles of Tantra" as to what precedes and follows) which supposes that Mantra is merely the name for the words in which one expresses what one has to say to the Divinity. If it were, the Sādhaka might choose his own language without recourse to the eternal and determined sounds of Śāstra.

Śabda is Śakti. The Viśvasāra-Tantra (Ch. II) says that Śabda-brahman which is Mantra (Mantra-maya) exists in the body of Jīva and is the subtle aspect of the Jīva's vital Śakti. As the Prapañcasāra Tantra states, the Brahmāṇḍa spheroid (universe) is pervaded bny Śakti as Dhvani, called Nāda, Prāṇa and the like. The manifestation in of the gross (Sthūla) form of Śabda would not be possible unless Śabda existed also in subtle (Sūkṣma) form.

Śabda is the Guṇa of Ākāśa, but is not produced by it. It manifests in it; and Śabda-svarūpa is the Brahman. In the same way, however, as in outer space waves of sound are produced by movements of air (Vāyu), so in the space within the Jīva's body, waves of sound are produced according to the movements of the vital air (Prāṇavāyu) and the process of inhalation and exhalation. The Śabda which first appears in the Mulādhāra (See *The Serpent Power*) is in fact the Śakti which gives life to the Jīva. The Jīva who inbreathes and outbreathes utters a great Mantra. This is the Ajapā-Mantra of Hamsah, called "Ajapā", because it repeats itself naturally without any effort on the part of the Jīva. It is the heaving of the Dhvani which cause alternate inspiration and expiration. Śakti it is who is the Cause of the sweet, indistinct and murmuring Dhvani (See Ch. 24) which sounds like the humming of black bees. This sound is Parā and then Paśyanti, which becomes subtle as Madhyamā and gross as Vaikharī. Kuṇḍalinī, who is

Varṇamayī and Dhvanimayī is the manifestation in bodies of the Paramātmā. So the substance of all Mantra is Cit manifested as letters syllables, words and their sentences. In fact the letters of the alphabet which are known as Akṣara are nothing but the Yantra of the Akṣara or imperishable Brahman. It is the gross or Sthūla form of Kuṇḍalinī appearing in different aspects as different Devatās, which is the presiding Devatā (Adhiṣṭhātrī) of all Mantra though it is the subtle (Sūkṣma) form at which all Śadhakas aim. For in every Mantra there are two Śaktis. The Vācya-Śakti and the Vācaka-Śakti. The Devatā who is indicated (Pratipādya-Devatā) as the ultimate Svarūpa is the Vācya-Śakti, and the Devatā who is that Mantra (Mantramayī-Devatā) is the Vācaka-Śakti. Thus if Durgā is the Devatā of a Mantra, then Mahāmāyā is the Vācyā-Śakti. The latter is without attribute and Vācaka-Śakti is with attribute. The latter is the object of worship and is a support and means whereby the Vācya-Śakti is realised. For worship assumes as its object some form. When the Śakti with attribute, resident in and as the Mantra, is by dint of Sādhanā awakened, then She opens the gate of monistic truth, revealing the true nature and essence of the universe.

There are thus two Śaktis, *viz.*, the Mantra-Śakti and the Sādhanā-Śakti, that is the Śakti of the Sādhaka generated by Sādhanā. It is the uniting of these two Śaktis which accomplishes the fruit of Mantra-sādhanā. How? The Saguṇa-Śakti is awakened by Sādhanā and worshipped. This Saguṇa-Devatā is the Presiding Deity (Adhiṣṭhatri-Devatā) of the Mantra as the Nirguṇa (formless) Iśvara of Iśvarī is the Vācya-Śakti. Both are one, but the Jīva by the laws of his nature and its three guṇas must first meditate on the gross (Sthūla) form before he can realise the subtle (Sūkṣma) form which is liberation.

The utterance of a Mantra without knowledge of its meaning or of the Mantra method is a mere movement of the lips and nothing more. The Mantra sleeps. There are various processes preliminary to, and involved in, its right utterance, which processes again consist of purification of the mouth *(mukha-śodhana),* (See Chapter 10, Śāradā-Tilaka, *japa of Praṇava* or the mantra *Om* varies with the Devatā- *e.g.,* Om Hsau for Bhairava), purification of the tongue, *Jihvā śodhana*, (seven *japa* of one-lettered *Bīja* triplicated, *Praṇava* triplicated, then one- lettered *Bīja* triplicated, and of *Aśauca-bhanga, Japa of Mula-mantra* preceded and followed by *Praṇava*. As to the "birth" and "death" defilements of a *mantra,* see Tantra-sāra 75. *et seq., Kullūka,* see Śāradā *loc. cit.* Thus *Kullūka,* which is done over the head of Kālikā is Māyā (see Puraścaraṇa Bodhinī., p. 48, and Tantra-sāra); *Nirvāṇa Japa of Mūla and Mātṛkā-bīja* in the *Maṇipura Setu* (Generally the Mahāmantra *Om* or *Māyābīja* Hrīm, but it also varies. Thus *Setu* of *Kālī* is her own *Bīja Krīm,* of Tārā, *Kurca* etc.); *Nidrā-bhaṅga*, awakening of mantra *(Japa of the Mantra* preceded and followed by *Im* seven time); *Mantra-caitanya,* or giving of life or vitality to the *mantra* (Japa of *Mūlamantra in Maṇi-pūra* preceded and followed by Mātṛkā-bīja. Meditating on the *Mūla-mantra* in the *Sahasrāra, Anāhata*, *Mūlādhāra,* with *Hum*, and again in Sahasrāra. The Mūla is the principal *mantra,* such as the *Pañcadāśi); mantrārtha-bhāvanā,* forming of a mental image of the Divinity (Lit., thinking of meaning of *mantra* or thinking of the Matrika in the mantra which constitutes the Devatā from foot to head.). There are also ten *Saṁskāras* of the *Mantra* (See Tantrasāra, p. 90). *Dīpanī* is seven *Japa of the bīja,* preceded and followed by *Om*. Where *Hrīm* is employed instead of *Om* it is Prāṇayoga. Yoni-mudrā is meditation on the *Guru* in the head and on the Iṣṭadevata in the heart, and then on the *Yoni-rūpa Bhagavatī* from the head to the *Mūlādhāra*, and from the *Mūlādhāra* to the head making *japa* of the *Yonī Bīja (Em)* ten time (See Purohitadarpaṇam).

The Mantra itself is Devatā that is, the Supreme Consciousness (Cit-Śakti) manifesting in that form. The Mantra is awakened from its sleep (Mantra-caitanya) through the Sādhanā Śakti of the mantrin. It is at base one and the same Śakti which appears as Sādhanā Śakti and Mantra Śakti the latter however being the more powerful manifestation. The consciousness of the Sādhaka becomes *en rapport* and in union with the Consciousness in the form of the Mantra; and the Devatā who is the Artha of the Mantra appears to the Sādhaka, whose mind has been cleansed and illumined by devotion. Though the substance of the Mantras is Consciousness, that fact is not realised without the union of the Sādhaka's Śakti derived from Sādhanā with Mantra-śakti. The Devatā is then revealed. In the case of Pūjā, Dhyāna and other Sādhanās, it is only the Sādhaka's Sādhanā-Śakti which operates, whilst in the case of Mantra-sādhanā, Sādhanā-śakti works in conjunction with Mantra-sakti which is all-powerful and reinforces Sādhanā-Śakti which is imperfect and meets with obstacles. The individual Śakti is like fire. Just as wages of air, when struck and restruck by flames of fire, set up a blaze with redoubled force, so the Sādhaka's individual Śakti when struck by Mantra-śakti is rapidly developed, and then a strong active individual Śakti unites with Mantra-śakti to make the latter doubly powerful. It is because Mantra possesses this wonderful powerful. Power that a Jiva can, it is said accomplish that which appears impossible. Otherwise a Jīva could not achieve by his own effort the treasure which is worshipped even by Śiva. The Jaivī-śakti or the Śakti of a Deva (as such). With this Śakti or Śakti of a Jīva (as such) is transformed by the aid of Mantra into the Daivī-śakti he can accomplish that which a Deva can. Mantra is thus an aspect of the Divine Mother appearing through Mantra-Sādhanā with devotion to Her. It has been thus said (Tantra-Tattva II,45): "The string of fifty letters from A to Kṣa which are the Mārkās is Eternal, unbeginning and unending and Brahman itself." Thus great saying is the first of all Tantras. The realization of this Mantra-consciousness is Mantra-siddhi. If a Sādhaka attains perfect Siddhi in even a single Mantra he becomes possessed of the spiritual knowledge which is acquired by learning all Vedas. For Veda is the Pariṇāma or evolution of the Dhvani of Kula-Kuṇḍalinī in the body of Īśvara, and the Pariṇāma of the same in the body of the Jīva is Śabda. For Veda is Dhvani uttered by Brahmā and Śabda is Dhvani uttered by the Jīva. In that Śabda is every form of Mantra which is that which gives vitality to the Jīva. It is this Dhvani too which evolves into gross Śabda as uttered sound, the body of the Devatā. Siddhi in such Mantra is not gained so long as such Mantra is not awakened. It may be that the appearance of the Devatā is a fact or it is not a fact. But it cannot be said that the mere utterance of a Mantra is superstitiously supposed to effect any result, or that Japa of the Mantra is done with no other object than a mere vain and senseless repetition. The particular Mantra suitable for a Sādhaka is a matter determined by Cakra and othe calculations.

# Chapter 29

# THE GĀYATRĪ-MANTRA

The Gāyatrī is the most sacred of all Vaidika *mantras*. In it the Veda lies embodied as in its seed.. It runs: *Om. Bhūr bhuvaḥ svaḥ: tat savitur vareṇyaṁ bhargo devasya dhīmahi: dhiyo yo nah pracodayāt. Om.* "Om. The earthly, atmospheric and celestial spheres. Let us contemplate the wondrous Sole Spirit of the Divine Creator (Sāvitrī). May He direct our minds (that is, towards the attainment of *Dharma, Artha, Kāma,* and *Mokṣa). Om.*"

The Gāyatrī-Vyākaraṇa of Yogī Yājñavalkya thus explains the following words: *Tat,* means that. *(Tat* is apparently here treated as in the objective case, agreeing with *vareṇyaṁ,* etc., but others holding that the *vyāhṛit– Bhūr bhuvaḥ svaḥ–* forms part of, and should be linked with, the rest of the Gāyatrī treat *that* as part of a genitive compound connected with the previous *vyāhṛti,* in which case it is *teṣām).* The word *yat,* "which" is to be understood. (It may, however, be said that *yat* is there in *yo naḥ*). Savituḥ is the possessive case of Sāvitrī, derived from the root su, "to bring forth." Sāvitrī is, therefore, the Bringer-forth of all that exists. Bringing forth and creating all things, it is called Sāvitrī. The Bhaviṣ ya-Purāṇa says: "Sūrya is the visible Devatā". He is the eye of the world and the Maker of the day. There is no other

Devatā eternal like unto Him. This universe has emanated from, and will be again absorbed into Him. Time is of and in Him. The planets, stars, the Vasus Rudras, Vāyu, Agni, and the rest are but parts of Him." By ***Bhargaḥ*** is meant the Āditya-devatā, dwelling in the region of the Sun *(Sūrya-maṇḍala)* in all His might and glory. He is to the sun what our spirit *(Ātmā)* is to our body. Though He is in the region of the Sun, in the outer or material sphere, He also dwells in our inner selves. He is the light of the in the solar circle, and is the light of the lives of all beings. As he is in the outer ether, so also is He in the ethereal region of the heart. In the outer ether He is the Sun (Sūrya), and in the inner ether He is the wonderful Light which is the Smokeless Fire. In short, that Being whom the *Sādhaka* realizes in the region of his heart is the Āditya in the heavenly firmament. The two are one . The word is derived in two ways: (1) from the root *Bhrij,* "to ripen, mature, destory, reveal, shine." In this derivation Sūrya is He who matures and transforms all things. He himself shines and reveals all things by His Light. And it is He who at the final Dissolution *(Pralaya)* will in His form of destructive Fire *(Kālāgni)* destroy all things. (2) From *bha*=dividing all things into different classes; *ra*=colour, for he produces the colour of all created objects; *ga*=constantly going and returning. The Sun divides all things, produces the different colours of all things and is constantly going and returning. As the Brāhmaṇa-sarvasva says: "the Bharga is the *Ātmā* of all that exists, whether moving or motionless, in the three *Lokas (Bhūr Bhuvaḥ Svaḥ)*. There is nothing which exists apart from it."

*Devasya* is the genitive of Deva, agreeing with *Savituḥ*. Deva is the radiant and playful *(Lilāmaya)* one. Surya is in constant play with creation *(Sṛṣṭi),* existence *(sthiti),* and destruction *(Pralaya),* and His radiance pleases all. (*Līla,* as applied to the Brahman, is the equivalent of *Māyā). Vareṇyaṁ* =varaṇiyam or adorable. He should be meditated upon and adored that we may be relieved of the misery of birthg and death. Those who fear rebirth, who desire freedom from death and seek Liberation and who strive to escape the three kinds of pain *(tāpa-traya),* which are *Ādhyātmikā, Ādhidaivika, and Ādhibhautika,* meditate upon and adore the *Bharga,* who, dwelling in the region of the Sun, has in Himself the three regions called *Bhūloka, Bhuvar-loka and Svar-loka. Dhīmahī*=*dhyāyema* (from the root *dhyai*), we mediate upon, or lelt us mediate upon.

*Pracodayāt*=may he direct. The Gāyatrī does not so expressly state, but it is understood that such direction is along the *Cātur-varga,* or four-fold path which is *Dharma, Artha, Kāma,* and *Mokṣa* (piety, wealth; desire and its fulfilment, and Liberation.) the Bhargah is ever directing our inner faculties (Buddhi-Vṛtti) along these paths.

The above is the *Vaidika-Gāyatrī,* which, according to the Vaidika system, none but the twice-born may utter. To the Śūdra, whether man or woman and to women of all other castes it is forbidden. The Tantra-Śāstra, which has a Gāyatrī-Mantra of its own, shows no such exclusiveness; Chapter III, verses 109-111, of the Mahānirvāṇa-Tantra gives the *Brahma-gāyatrī* for worshippers of the Brahman; *"Parameṣvarāya vidmahe para-tattvāya dhīmahi: tan no Brahma Pracodayāt"* (May we know the Supreme Lord. Let us contemplate the Supreme Reality. And may that Brahman direct us.)

# Chapter 30

# THE GĀYATRĪ-MANTRA

## AS AN EXERCISE OF REASONING

The Society is called "Rationalistic". If its formation was meant to be merely a homage to one form of modern western thought, the title may be fairly correct. I think however that you had no intention of adding to the volume of imitativeness in this country, but by your action you wished to affirm the necessity of such reasonable thinking and practice as characteristic of the Ārya-Dharma, rightly understood and cleansed of all bad and useless accretion. There is always a difficulty, when English verbal labels are used to describe Indian philosophical and religious theories and practices. In fact such labels are a fertile source of confusion. I hear of a good suggestion to call it *Satyajñana-Sabhā* or a similar name.

Rationalism, in the sense of its technical opposition to Sensationalism, has no meaning in this country for those who believe that a child is born with his *saṁskāras*.

"Rationalism" in its more general sense involves, it has been said, the following beliefs: (1) Reason is the chief source and final criterion of knowledge. (2) Each individual must investigate and gain knowledge for himself, and must not merely submit himself to external authority. In other words he must do his own thinking. (3) As a result of this it is said that a rationalist must reject any alleged knowledge, the truth of which cannot be rationally demonstrated.

Upon such a statement a Vedāntist (I speak throughout of the Advaita-Vedānta) would ask what is the "Knowledge" here mentioned? If worldly (Laukika) knowledge is meant, then the Rationalist and Vedāntist are at one. Worldly knowledge is apprehended through the senses (Indriya). In its own sphere, reason is the chief source of knowledge and final criterion. So much is this so, that Śaṁkaracarya says that if even Veda were to contradict what is the subject of worldly proof (Laukika-Pramāṇa) it would not be Veda. In this sphere it is not a Pramāṇa, which overrides the testimony of the senses and inferences therefrom. The Yoga-Vāśiṣṭha (Bk. 2-- Ch. 18, VV.. 2-3) says:

*Api pauruṣaṁ ādeyaṁ śāstraṁ ced yūktibodhakaṁ*
*Anyat tvārsaṁ api tyājyaṁ bhāyam nyāyyaikasevinā.*
*Yuktiyuktum upādeyaṁ vacanaṁ bālakād api,*
*Anyat tṛṇaṁ iva tyājyaṁ apyuktaṁ padmajanmanā.*

That is, "Even a Śāstra of purely human authorship should be accepted if conformable to reason. Anything else (which is unreasonable) even though is the word of a Rṣi, should be rejected by one who follows reason. The word of a boy if reasonable should be accepted. Anything unreasonable should be rejected as of no more count than a blade of grass, even if it be uttered by the Lotus-born (Brahmā) Himself." On this subject read the whole of the

14th Chapter of Book II of the Mumukṣu-Khaṇḍa of this work which is a glorification fo Vicāra of reasoning.

But there is more than what is seen with the eyes. The mind admittedly exists, but it is not seen by the senses (Atīndriya). Again as to objects, scientific instruments enable the sense to perceive more than is presented to them in their natural state. These instruments thus effect a material extension of natural faculty. Then there are Psychic Powers *(Siddhi),* the subject of much study to-day in the West, but matters of long familiar practice in this country. Here the mind may operate independently of the gross bodily organs of sense, as also occurs in some cases of Hypnosis. These psychic powers are again extension of natural faculty. They are not supernatural, except in the sense that they are supernormal. They may, in any one individual, be natural or produced, but we do not reason ourselves into them. We can reason only upon whether they exist, and what they are and indicate. That is, we reason about them. In themselves they are peculiar mental faculties, by which the mind sees things or imposes itself upon and controls, or affects, others such as Clairvogance, Clairaudience, Hypnosis, Thought-reading, Telepathy and so forth. There is nothing unreasonable in all this. On the contrary an affirmation of their existence is reasonable and in accordance with the Vedāntic theory of Being upon which this paper proceeds. The only question about them is one of fact or proof. Do they exist or not? Nothing is more unscientific then to pronounce *a priori* against them and without investigation into the facts. Notwithstanding scientific bigotry (for there is a bigotry of science as of religion) psychical research is coming to be recognised as a useful form of enquiry.

Lastly, there is what is called sprititual or religious experience, which is of varying degrees and kinds, and is a knowledge of the nature (through an actual participation in Its being) of the excelling and infinite Principle which lies behind and manifests all phenomena. Professor James' celebrated work "Varieties of Experience" is one of the first essays in a field, which is only now commencing to be cultivated extensively. The possibility or fact of such experience cannot be said to be unreasonable. Such experience has been affirmed by all the great Religions, and by some of the great philosophies. If it is unreasonable, then the bulk of Humanity has been lacking in reason in all the past and in the present times. The question again here is one of fact and proof. Have such experiences taken place in fact? Are they real experiences or mere hallucinations? In the latter case why should they occur? The only direct and certain proof is the having of such an experience oneself. Probable proof may be had in various ways, such as the persistence and universality of such experiences, the nature of the truths said to be revealed by them and in particular the extraordinary effect which they have produced on the individuals who have had such experience, and (in the case of the greater experiences) the effect that they have produced on the world at large. To my mind it is a very shallow view which regards the effect produced on millions of past and present Humanity, by the Ṛṣis and Śākya-Muni of India, by Laotze, Jesus and Mohemmed, as the outcome of the hallucination of *Mahātmās* named and others. Which of these experiences, it may be asked, is true, or which one is truer than the others. This is too vast a question to be answered here. Let me however say this, that those who read these experiences with knowledge will find elements common to all together with some elements common to all together with some elements which seem to vary. As to these last let it be noted that just as in our ordinary life one man sees and knows more than another, so it is with spiritual experience, of which there are many grades. If two men are approaching a mountain, is the experience which one man has of it 50 miles distant untrue, because it differs from the experience of the other man who sees it at its foot? Do we not say that both are true, considering the position of each experiencer?

In India spiritual experience is called Veda, from the root "Vid" to know. It is experience in the limit, of which all others are gradual and partial reproductions. This may be primary, that is, an individual may himself have the experience, or he may accept the authority of those who have had such experience, for reasons I have slightly indicated but cannot develop here.

The Vedānta says that Reason is supreme in wordly *(Laukika)* matters open to our sense. By reasoning we may establish Laukika truth, but as regards what is not seen, such as the being of one Supreme cause of which the Universe is an effect, unaided reason can only establish probabilities and not certainty. Thus one may, with reasonableness, argue for or against Monism, Dualism, Pluralism and so forth. In this way mere reasoning may lead to contrary conclusions. And in fact what is more contradictory then the conclusions of Western philosophy with Realism (old style and new as propounded aby Mr. Bertrand Russell), Idealism (objective and subjective), Monism Pluralism, Panpsychism, Humanism, Pragmatism and the many other systems which jostle for men's custom in this philosophical Fair? It is matter of doubt whether modern metaphysic is any real advance on that of the greater among the ancients. In my opinion none is better constructed than the Six *Darśana.* The advance has been made in Science. But even here there is, dispute, both as to the facts observed and the theories based on them. For me, their greatest importance just lies in the fact, that the latest inferences corroborate the intuitively derived teaching of the ancient sages. Thus present scientific conceptions of the constitution of matter, and notably the break-down of the Atomic Theory, support the notions of Māyā, a single material basis of the Universe, and the existence of Ether which, as Ākāśa, was accepted in India when Europe had not passed beyond the socalled "four elements." Both science and Indian beliefs post an evolution of beings from the inorganic to the organic, and in the latter division, from plant to animal and animal to man. In India it has always been held that at here are no partitions or gulfs between the various forms of existence and that for instance the differnce between man and animal is not differnce of kind but of degree. Again from the new Psychology and Psychical Research, Vedānta gains support, as from theories touching the nature of mind as material force (as Herbert Spencer teaches) and as a power (the predominant ideas in "New Thought" literature), the extension of the field of Consciousness, dual personalities and various forms of psychical phenomena.

Nevertheless, so far as ultimates are concerned, neither Mataphysics nor Science can establish more than a high degree of probability; they may lead to the door of the shrine, but do not directly and unaided place the enquirer within. The Brahman or all-Pervader cannot be established by reason, because it is never an object of knowledge. The Śāstra says, one can only know Brahman by *being* Brahman and that is by spiritual experience. Its being and nature are taught by revelation. Revelation is not the speaking of any voice, divine or otherwise, from without. It is self-knowledge in its deepest sense and nothing more. The Vedāntist affirms that we can know ourselves, not only in our gross or physical aspect as being fair or dark, short or tall and so on, or In our subtle or mental aspect as perceiving and reasoning beings, but in our innermost essence as that of which both body and mind are manifestations. It may be the fact or it may not be the fact, but there is nothing unreasonable in the proposition as such. It is this Self-knowledge, attained by oneself in varying degrees, or accepted as the experience of others (Śruti), whose testimony we may, for reasons sarisfying to ourselves, accept, which renders certain that which to reason is only probable. Once Śruti is accepted, Reason can follow its teaching without violence to its own pronciples. What was before reasonable and probable is now both reasonable and certain. This must be so, unless we assume what is impossible, namely a divorce between rational and spiritual truth. Truth however is one and what is unreasonable must be rejected, whoever says it, "even if he be the Lotus-born."

It is not India who has denied the right of Reason. It is Europe who in the past has done so. But Europe has now, after fierce contest against Church tyranny and oppression (aided by the State) with its imprisonment, torture and burning at the State, largely achieved in the present the right of free-thinking. Had India been so opposed she might have been today more intellectually active. In the same way the political activity of Europe has been stimulated by the oppressive governance of its peoples. We westerners have had to fight for all the things of worth we have won.

Nowhere however has intellectual liberty been so authoritatively, and for such a length of time, recognised as in India. The word "Man" is derived from the root *Man,* which in Sanskrit means "to think". Man is *Manu*. Therefore man is "*The Thinker*". He is thus distinguished from the rest of the world by his *thinking*. What greater definition than this of our Āryan forefathers can be found? In no country in the whole world has there been more thinking than in India, which has been indeed a very hot-bed of speculation and divergent beliefs and practices: such as the Materialism of Chārvāka and the Lokāyatas, true atheists, men of the type of Ajitakeśakambalī, the opponent of Śākya-Muni, who denied that any Brāhmana, or any else, had discovered any truth concerning any other life than this, who said that man was made of the four elements and dissolved into the elements at death and had gone for ever; such again as the Sānkhyas, dualists and realists, affirming the realists, affirming the existence of Spirit, but holding a God as Governor of the universe unproved (Nirīśvara-Darśana); the Nyāyāvai-śeṣikas Pluralists, Realists affirming the existence of the Supreme Lord; Buddhist idealism (Vijñānavāda) and socalled "Nihilists" (Śūnyavādins); a Vedāntic Monism, qualified Monism, and Dualism in various theistic forms, Mimāmsakas, Jainas and every shade of thought imaginable.

In Vedāntic Sādhanā, Reasoning or *Manana* occupies, with *Śravaṇa Nididhyāsana,* a principal place. All the *Darśanas* particularly perhaps the Nyāya, are written to serve *Manana* or reasoning, and the Brahmasūtras, which the Vedāntic systems expound, are known as Vaiyāsikanyāyamālā.

As regards science, India has had its own great achievements which you will find recorded in part in Professors Brojendranath Seal's and Binoy Kumar Sirkar's works on the subjects. Up to the modern period India was more than the equal in this field of any other country. But undoubtedly, since that period, the palm for scientific thinking and experiment must be given to the West. Those who however imagine, that reasoning and freedom of thought are a distinctive appanage of the West are very ignorant of the history of their country. If one had to make the comparison, and one did make it over period, extending from say (to go no further ) 2000 B.C., the statement must be reversed in favour of India. No country has honoured Reason more, or given it greater freedom than India. The cultural restrictions in this country have been of a different kind, consisting in the social ordering of life, and in later times exclusion from knowledge by reason of artificial distinctions of caste. But those, to whom the book of knowledge was open, have always been able to think freely enough. When Europe was under ecclesiastical domination, the attempt was made to make every one think the same way in the manner laid down by Church authority. It is against this that European Rationalism protested.

I at first found a difficulty in choosing a subject to address to you out of the many which presented themselves, and had practically written a paper, with which I was not satisfied, because I could not put before you (as indeed I cannot even now) what I wished to say within the limits available to me, when, by something more than chance, I found amongst my old papers a note sent me some years ago on the Gāyatrī-Mantra, the holiest expression of the thought of India. I therefore restate its argument more summarily in words, and with some further additions of my own.

The Mantra opens and ends with the *Praṇava* or *Om*. This refers in the first place to the threefold aspect of the World-Cause in manifestation. That there is a cause (Mahāśakti) which, as the universal Self, contains the universe within Itself, is dealt with in the meditation which follows. Here both the Cause and Its manifestation are the object of thought. The Nādabindu indicates that causal state of the World-Power, prior to its threefold differentiation as represented by the letters A, U, M, which coalesce into *Om*. These letters stand for its working which is observable by all. For the first and second refer to present activities, as well as those in the past and future, of the *Mahāśakti,* as the Radical Vital Potential. M or Rudra as so observed is chemical action breaking down the combinations of matter. This is the disintegration of form. A (Brahmā) is the force which creates it anew by its ever rejuvenescent molecular activity, thus rescuing organised vitality from the process which are ever at work to consume (as "M") U (Viṣṇu) is the maintaining power which stabilizes matter which is only a relatively stable condition of energy, from which it appears, and into which it, at length merges. Looking at the sum total of manifested energy, Viṣṇu as Maintainer, through space and time is a theological statement of the doctrine of the general conservation of energy. The Mahāśakti, in Herself Perfect Consciousness (Cidrūpinī), is the threefold Powers of Will, Knowledge and Action and manifests in the building up, maintenance and disintegration of forms. What follows, as all else, is contained in *Om,* but some of its implications are developed in the rest of the Gāyatrī-Mantra *Om* considered as a sound *(Dhvani)* is approximate natural name of the first undifferentiated movement *(Sāmānya-Spanda)* of the stressing material cause (Prakṛti) of the universe. The primordial "Sound" or stress in the primordial functioning of the Brahma-Śakti.

Then follow the three *Vyāhṛtis—Bhūḥ, Bhuvaḥ, Svaḥ,* which are *Lakṣaṇa* of, that is, stand for, all the fourteen Lokas, though now in the (Vyāvahārika) world we are only concerned with the first three; Bhūḥ for Bhūḥ and the seven nether Talas, Bhuvaḥ for itself and Svah for Svah and the remaining upper regions up to Satya. The Lokas represent states of consciousness. Bhūrloka or earth is the state of normal experience. The Lokas above it are states of supernormal consciousness, and the Talas below are conditions of sub-normal experience. Objectively considered, matter becomes more and more dense as one descends from the high to the lowest Loka and thence to the Talas, and as the viel of matter is more or less dense, so the state of consciousness varies. The first five Lokas, from and including Earth, are those of the five forms of sensible matter, the sixth is that of Mind; and the seventh is the causal state of both Mind and Matter. Earth and the nether state are the gross body, the Lokas from Bhuvaḥ to Tapah are the subtle body, and Satya is the causal body of the great Purusa referred to in the Gāyatrī and worshipped in the Sun-circle *(Āditya-maṇḍala)*. The *Vyāhṛtis* indicate the Great Self which is indicated in *Om* prevades all the regions of the universe. How then do we get the notion of that Self and then experience it ?

In our ordinary condition of consciousness, the outer world is completely objective and stable and independent of it. It lies "over there" in the outer space entirely external to us, having apparently its existence in itself and of itself.

This state of consciousness is indicated by the first *Vyāhṛti "Bhūḥ."* This is our normal state. Our mind is Here. It is one thing Aham or I. The object, the *Idam* or "This" the Vimarśa-Śakti is there. It is another. But a little reflection reveals that these seemingly independent objects are for us bundles of certain qualities, which are so, only because they are sensed by the Senses which are constituted in a particular way. It is obvious that if our senses were not there, or if they were not seizing the object, there would be no sensation and no object. Again if the senses themselves were modified, the sense perceptions would also change. In that case the objects, which at first sight exist independently of our perceptions, would become something different from what they formerly were, as they would exhibit a different set of qualities. Thus the objective world is not really independent as we first thought, and the form it presents to us is due to the action of some objective force acting upon the subjectively sensuous character of the beings who perceive it. With such reflections the notion of objective stability wears off, and the world first assumes a mobile condition, in so far as it is seen that the objects, which at first seem to possess the qualities which characterise them, do so not only of themselves but also of ourselves. The conditon of mind in which this notion is firmly held is the second of the seven divisions or states of the Prathiva consciousness. All materially-minded thinkers, who look upon the objective world as independent of a subjective perceiver, are in the Bhūrloka.

The second condition of consciousness in which the subjectivity of the self first asserts itself, and the objective world loses its absolute and independent character and appears as dependent upon, influenced and modified by the subjective factor, is expressed in some forms of idealism. In such case though the subjective element is recognised, it is not ideal in the sense that it has its root wholly in itself, but it is objectively actual in the sense that it has its existence at least mainly in the external. The seer, seeing, and seen, are localised, in the outher space. As we proceed upwards, whilst the seen *(Jñeya)* remains external to us, the seeing *(jñāna)* is localised internally, until at length the seer *(jñātā* seeing *(Jñāna),* and seen *(Jñāna),* are all internalised, subjectified and unified. This *Jñāna-svarūpa* of the Supreme Consciousness is opposed to *Jñanavṛtti* or the limited and differentiated consciousness.

After the attainment of this second stage we pass to the third. We then ask, what lies behind the senses, wherein to a great extent the appearance of the external world depends? We then perceive that the senses do not apprehend objects unless attention, in the form *Manas* is bestowed upon them. The whole world, open at any moment to the senses, is impinging on them at every moment, but only that is perceived to which we pay attention. The Bṛhadārāṇyaka Upaniṣad gives good psychology when it says "I did not hear. My mind was elsewhere." But attention must be directed and willed. We learn then that behind the Senses there is some Self which directs its attention to a particular object, and so perceives it by the medium of the senses. There is thus no sense-perception without the co-operation of the attention of the Self. Therefore that world (considered apart from what it may possibly be in itself) is dependent both upon the senses and attentive mind of the self which is behind them. The attainment and habit of this thought is the third ascending stage of the Pārthiva consciousness.

We have thus attained a knowledge of the self. We next

reflect upon its nature. To the ordinary consciousness of the first wo states, the self either did not appear important, or seemed to be limited to the body and restricted within its scope. But reflection has now shown that not only is it unconditioned by the senses, but actually conditions them, giving them effective operation throught its power of attention. The self then appears uncontrolled by the physical body, self-luminous and overlapping the bounds of the physical senses. When this notion is reached the fourth stage of consciousness is attained.

The next question is -- what is the relation of the self, the senses and the objects? Are they each independent in their origin the one of the other, or is one the cause of the other two? They connot be independent of each other, for this would mean that either they had no relation to each other, or if there is any relation it is due to some fourth thing external to the others, which is the basis of their relation and apart from which they cannot be in relation. It is obvious that they are in relation to each other, and as such the ground of their relation must be either in, or outside, themselves. It is sufficient to say here that no fourth principle capable of holding them together and bringing them into relation is perceived. But logically the same resuld can be established for is a fourth principle bringing them into relation were assumed, which was dependent on soe one or other of them, the causal element would be still to seek, whereas if it were independent and still in relation ot the three, then the ground of this relation would have to be sought for in some fifth element and so on with *regressio ad infinitum.* We must then confine ourselves to the three and examine the nature of this relation.

The relation can be grounded only in that element out of the three which is independent of the others, for a dependent entity cannot have the ground of its relation to others within itself. The perceived objects are not idependent. For they require the senses to be perceived as objects of that character according to which we perceive them. The senses are not independent, for sense-perception requires attention of the Self. Objects in order to be objects must be perceived by the senses. Without the senses they are not objects for us. The senses are not operative sense without the attention of the Self behind them. On the other hand the Self does not cease to be the Self, when it is not attentively perceiving objects through the senses, as we see in the case of dream. The self in dream is cut off from the senses. Indeed it evolves both objects and senses. The Self in dream is cut off from the objective world, having nothing in it but ideas thereto. Yet it transforms for itself those ideas into outer objects and the sense which perceives them. What we see in dream is real while it lasts. Thus the Self is independent of the other two and has within itself the ground of the causal relation by which it evolves them. The firm and lasting consciousness which realises this is the fifth step in the ascending consciousness.

What then is the nature of the relation between the cause producing the objective world and the effect so produced? Is it a cause material in its nature, producing an effect external to itself, or an ideal cause working ideally upon itself to produce an effect? The cause cannot produce an effect which is really external to itself. Were this so, the dream-world of which we are creators would be external to the self which produces it. In that case it would not vanish with that state of consciousness which lies at the root of it. The objective world can only be ideally connected with its cause. Gradually the notion that the objective world is produced by a cause external to it is rejected, and the notion is accepted that the cause has the effect lying ideally wihin it, which is projected and externalised in the course of cosmic evolution. For when mind and matter are evolved each has levels really and (in the sense of impermanence) unreality. In its highest sense Reality = Persistence = Deathlessness (Amṛtatva) Ānanda, which is living unimpeded in the fullest measure, which is Ātma. And so Herbert Spencer on biological principles defines "pleasure" as the index of the unimpeded flow of vitality. What fully persists and is therefore fully "real" is the self. The firm establishment of this experience is the sixth consciousness. Just as the dream-world lies within the consciousness of the dreamer, who projects it into fancied objectivity, so the objective world of common *(Vyāvahārika)* experience lies within, and is projected by, the Consciousness of the socalled World --dreamer, who sums up in Himself all experiences. Is the world or its cause necessarily thus by virtue of the nature of the cause itself, or on account of some external fact? There is no material other than itself outside the cause which it takes within works upon, and puts forth. It might be thought that there was ideal connection with the objective world on the causal side, but that the root of the objective world upon which it operates was something lying elsewhere than in its inner being. But this is not so as the effect, the objective world, must necessarily be within the cause, otherwise it is not possible that it should be ideally connected with it. If the connection with the cause were something other than the constitution of the cause itself, there must been indication of what that something is and the nature of its connection with the cause. Moreover, if that something lies outside the cause, we we must suppose some medium connecting that something with the cause itself. And again the question would arise whether this connection was natural and necessary, or adventitious. If the latter, then what is it which brings about the connection? In this way we have a *regressio ad infinitum* unless we suppose the connection to be natural and necessary. It is reasonable then to hold that the objective world lies necessarily in its root the cause. Moreover, having arrived at the consciouness that the effect is ideally connected with the cause, it is more reasonable to hold that this connection is due to the constitution of the cause itself. When the entire objective world is viewed as necessarily lying within the cause, the seventh, or what we may call the Satya stage of the *Pārthiva* consciousness, is attained.

Up to this we have only dealt with the sub-divisions of the *Pārthiva* or earth consciousness, that is, experience as beings in the *Pārthiva* state elaborated by reflection to its highest point. By such reflection we reach the standpoint from which the whole universe is viewed as lying in a seed (Bija) form, ideally and potentially within its cause which is nothing but the Self.

Thus, one aspect of the grandeur of the Self as the potential cause of the entire universe is revealed. The *Sādhaka* has thus passed through higher and higher stages of the *Pārthiva* consciousness to the indwelling Spirit within it. His thus expanded consciousness bring forth the exclamation which is the Gāyatrī-Mantra, in which homage is made to the Supreme Power, which manifests in this and all other forms of experience and its objects in the Universe. Hence the word by which the *Sādhaka* denotes this indwelling Spirit is *Savitā,* or the Projector of the

It is however to be remembered that the strength of the force of the externality notion which commenced at the stage of Ether *(Ākāśa)* reached its greatest power in the earth principle *(Pṛthivī-Tattva)* of solid, ponderable, three dimensioned matter and in the *Pārthiva* consciousness. Therefore it is that *Savitā* the Producer, though really the Inner Self, it is itself, externalised as something placed out in space and hence we find it designated by Tat or That. This "Thatness" will, as we proceed, meet in one unity the Supremeness of the last stage. But it is the characteristic of the *Pārthiva* consciousness that it always tends to locate both the Seer and the Seen in outer space. The devotee to whose mental gaze the indwelling Spirit reveals itself, bursts forth into the Mantra: "Let us meditate on the adorable darkness-dispelling Spirit of the self-luminous all producing *Savitā,*" with the prayer that It may inspire and illumine our inward Reason. It is through this illumination of the Reason by the source of Reason, that the inner Reason which is our inner being sees and understands the entire universe and its principles. This *Savitā* produces the universe in accordance with the principles of Reason which are at base His own inner being *(Vicāracamantkritiḥ paramātmamayī),* and this production of His is revealed to us and realised by us in participation with the Divine Reason of His being. As we are, in our deepest ground, the Spirit which, in its outer aspect, is our limited releves and what is not ourselves; as our reason is an efflorescence of Its own enternal all-knowingness, so our outer reasoning is in conformity with the truth in its own sphere, and is illumined to pass beyond reasoning upon the objective world to an understanding of the rational vesture of the spirit, and then to the intuitive realisation of the Spirit Itself. This union of ours with the universal is shown by the fact that we, as so many individuals if we were to remain confined within our individuality, could never perceive the universe as common to us all. This common perception of the universe could not be achieved by us as individuals, but only as being one with the universal. And therefore in so far as we are the common perceivers of the universe, we are not individual but universal. Our individuality consists in our perception of the universe in so far as it differs from that of others. Thus, difference of perception which individualises us, is not based upon any inherent differentiating conditon in our essential being, but upon the externalising limitations, the result of particular Karma, which make it impossible for all to perceive everything at the same time to the same extent. This perception of the difference of the many, due to limitation, differentiates each individual from the other but it does not, and cannot differentiate him from the Indwelling Universal (here *Pārthiva)* which is the common ground all all. Thus the *Sādhaka* says that it is this *Savitā* or Indwelling Universal, which inspires the Reason of us all, both as individual and as universal and it is throught the Self-luminous Consciousness of this Most Glorious Self (known not only in *Samādhi*, but in and through every act of reasoning, its mental embodiment) that we are enabled to learn and understand the Truth *(Satyam)*. For it is *Satya* or the persistent Self Itself. The relation between the individual and the universal being thus grasped and it being realised that the individuality of the individual is only through the universal, we should then proceed to see what is the nature of this Universal which makes it project the univese as we see it around us.

Here we pass beyond the Gāyatrī Sādhanā into the subtle Ātma-sādhanā. The Vedāntist says that to such as truly see, whether with the eye of reason or intuition, the whole universe is perceived as originating from its source, as the Gaṅgā from the Himālayas, and at length returning thereto. Its source is in the Power of the Perfect Consciousness which is Śiva, which means the Auspicious and Good, the Brahman or all-Pervading. All which exist are Its varying forms existing in happiness so long as they are in Harmony with Him who is Bliss (Ānanda) itself. Power and Harmony— let us repeat these words day by day. Think continuously the Thought of Power and be powerful. Individual Power is small thing, but when it links itself to, or identifies itself with, the Supreme Power, it shows its mightness according to the degree of such harmony and union. Power however does not merely mean material force. The latter is only Power translated to the material plane. Power is also mental moral, spiritual Love is Power- the greatest of Powers. Everything in fact which exists is Power, which is the Mother (Āmbikā).

We may intellectually conceive this. But how to realise it? Here the Vedāntic practice *(Sādhanā)* is as profound as its theory. It says that man as body, mind and spirit is one whole. If one would understand and realise the Pure one must be that, both in body and mind *(Śuddhātmā)*. In the West it is commonly supposed that a man may arrive at or at any rate is competent to seek for, the truth by reason alone. Mere reason however is insufficient. A man may be deemed a philosopher in the west and yet lack in character and morals. This is not so in Vedānta which says that its doctrine cannot be perfectly understood, much less realised, unless the body and mind are made pure enough to approach the purity which that doctrine teaches. The whole being must be brought into harmony, so far as may be, with it. Thus it is understood and at length realised. The pure mind and body naturally think the thoughts which link man's mind with the universal Mind and the Universal Self of which it is the subtle form. Sādhanā varies according to the stages of development and therefore competency *(Adhikāra)* of man. But the highest of *Sādhanās* is *Karuṇā* or compassion. I took up recently an English novel, curiously enough called "The Rationalist." There I found the phrase "this new thing appearing on the horizon-the phenomenon of compassion which is now beginning to express itself in action." This "new thing" is as old here as the Vedas and the Buddha Gotama who ceaselessly taught it. Avoid giving pain. Allay it where it is. Yet the application of this principle is not so simple as is sometimes thought. The truly great of our race need no other power nor effort than to be themselves. By the mere fact of their own self-redemption, they redeem others. Others must at least strive to hold in view the ideal in the midst of the struggles into which their nature and circumstances may lead them. Mere apathy however is not Yoga. Yoga is unity with the Lord in the forms of His power as one's family, friends, people and the world at large. He is *Jagadbandhu,* that is friend of the World. We can each make effort to follow this Supreme Law and to extricate ourselves from the morass of merely selfish struggle. And as we sucessfully, according to our varying opportunity and capacity, do so, we will find that we make individual advance, a and that the power to impose our will on others increases. If each will, according to his capacity, so order his life that he does not cause pain to, and relieves the suffering of this great Body of the Lord which is the Universe, of which each is an infinitesimal part, then they will commence to really *understand.* The greatest cloud upon understanding is selfishness. The mass of men are still mere candidates for Humanity and must raise themselves to it. The meaning of Evolution is the liberation of the Spirit or Inner Self from all which obscures its essential freedom. This liberation is taking place in the gradual ascent from inorganic to organic being and the advance of organism culminating, for the present, in man as we know him. The highest humanity is that in which it and Divinity meet. In man the I principle is still being developed in present humanity. The end is perfection of the present "I," and then by stages its identification with the Universal "I", the *Pūrṇāham* which is the infinite Self. The *Sādhaka* thinks of this ascending or return movement repeatedly for *japa* on the Gāyatrī is necessary to correct the natural objective tendencies of thought. This is the true performance of *Sandhyā,* which literally means perfect *Dhyāna* or meditation, of which the Gāyatrī-Mantra is the soul.

Those who have not learnt the goal of evolution do not realise the necessity of Sandhyā. They have before their eyes only the present powers and capacities of man and think that his present possibilities on the lower plane should alone be realised. They think only of the fulfilment of desires, shutting their eyes to the purpose for which man exists in the world, namely, first harmony with the Active (Viśvātma-Śakti) and then union with the Unchanging Brahman (Cidrūpiṇī-Śakti). They fail to realise that the Reality, which underlies all phenomena, must also be in the deepest nature of man, and unless that Reality is known the deepest aspirations of Humanity cannot be fulfilled. From the earliest beginnings all earnest minds have sought the solution of the riddle of the universe. All types of thinkers whether materialists, idealists, or spiritualists, have supposed that there is some Reality, call it Matter, Mind,

Spirit, Brahman, God, Allah, what they will, which whilst eluding their mental grasp, is all the same there, though it cannot be comprehended by the mind in its fullness. It cannot only be there, but it must be *here* within the inmost nature of all, as one with the deepest inmost self. If so, man must not only study the objective universe, which he should do to gain knowledge of the external Śakti-aspect of this reality, but he must plunge deep into his own nature, for he can only realise it within and not without the self. Man's present existence is a mode of consciousness, ordinarily in the spiritual *Bhūḥ* Consciousness, or in the forms of a *Tala* Consciousness. The search is to find out the universal principle. Being in the lower order of evolution have not the "I" principle evolved to the level of *Vijñāna* or *Buddhi,* and therefore the reason and understanding must be developed. The greater portion of the work of evolution must be done by the individual himself, under the guidance of the divine principle of Reason, and if we do not wish to be left behind in the general progressive movement, we must give up all lethargy and the contentment which the animal (whether as beast or man) has with his present powers and capacities and their external environment. Man must seek to understand the meaning of life and its end, and looking beyond by the Eye of Divine Wisdom *(Jñāna-cakṣu)* endeavour to first intellectually grasp, and then to realise, that which is the Beginning, the Maintainer and the end of all the *Vācya-Śakti* of the Gāyatrī-Mantra.

# Chapter 31

## ĀTMA-SĀDHANĀ

### (YOGA BY REASONING)

I have in the previous article shortly indicated a form of Gāyatrī-Sādhanā given to me some years ago. Here follows the Ātma-Sādhanā which is taken up at the point at which the Gāyatri-Sādhanā ends.

Duality is inherent in the constitution of all manifested being. Therefore until man realises the whole (Pūrṇa-Brahman), that is, the Universe as one with its both immanent and transcending Root, there is an object whether the same is apparently wholly outside, and different from, and independent of the Self, or whether it is experienced internally as a mode of the latter's subjective existence. But the experience is of varying grades. For just as matter, objectively considered, becomes more and more gross from its first ethereal (Ākāśa) form to scientific, that is, ponderable matter, so when in the upward ascent of consciousness Matter has been withdrawn into itself and exists there as a mode of being, that mode becomes a more and more subtle expression of the principle whence all objectivity, whether externally respect or internally experienced is derived. At the stage of complete manifestation, that is, ordinary *Bhūḥ* experience, the object or "This" (Idam) is wholly outside, and independent of, the Self, the two being mutually exclusive the one of the other. Matter is then in the form in which we ordinarily sence it. We may remain at this stage which is that of objective science or go within and to the Root of all experience. If that Root is within then introspection can alone discover it. How? That which carries upwards or inwards is the will-to-know of a nature ever more and more purifying itself and thus gaining strength by its approach to the Almighty *Savitā* of all. This is prayer in its highest form. At each moment of attainment and advance we naturally render homage to the glory of the All-pervading Being, who gradually reveals His infinite Self, just as Linnaeus the great botanist fell on his knees when he first saw its objective expression in the form of the golden beauty of the flower of the wild Gorse. But the object, though it persists in experience until the attainment of the perfect Consciousness (Brahma-Svarūpa), is yet diversely realised as we proceed innerwards. In the first place it is brought from without to within the Self, and there experienced not as something different from the Self but as a mode of its own existence. Next as such it becomes less and less pointed and more diffused and is brought into closer and closer touch with the subjective being. This is effected by an intense and penetrating meditation at each stage of advance with a view to realise the subjective root of that stage. When the objective tendencies of thought are held in check, Consciousness of Itself more and more purely manifests.

In the *Pārthiva* consciousness, matter is in a fully pointed condition outside the Self until the Satya stage is reached. Even the Self appears as a concentrated objective point in space. At the Satya stage the notion is gained through reasoning that the entire universe must lie within the Self as its cause. Acting on this suggestion of the Reason, the Pārthiva consciousness turns back into itself, and for the first time as *Antarmukhi* is conscious of something within itself lying there in a pointed form. The pointedness remains, but the world is carried within the Self, where it is grasped as a mode of its own existence. The peaculiar consciousness is Rasa, which is the subjective root of what objectively appears to the Pārthiva consciousness as *Ap*. The external particularised location disappears. If the point is located outside, there is *Gandha*-- experience of matter in its Pṛthivī condition. Gandha, Rasa, Rūpa, Sparśa, Sabda are the various kinds of consciousness which in the evolutionary process are the subjective root of sensible matter and which on the full externalisation of such matter are the five different ways in which it affects the senses as smell, taste, sight, touch and hearing.

In *Rasa* experience the object is brought in closer relation with the Self, both by reason of its being placed therein, and of a lessened intensity of its pointedness to the self as compared with Gandha or Bhūh experience. With a lessening intensity of the Rasa experience, the latter is shifted from the inner to the outer and seems to be coming from outside less in the form of feeling than of intellection in the shape of general unqualitative and undifferentiated form. There is then the idea of something there all round the Self, affecting the subjective being by way of a superficially, instead of interiorly, felt experience. This is *Rūpa* experience, the subjective root of Agni who is the builder of forms. This is the last of the form *(Mūrtta)* division of Tattvas. The lessened intensity of the Rasa-feeling has necessarily the effect of setting consciousness on the surface of subjective being, and as the idea of space or co-existing externality-points is already there, this weakened. Rasa experience, being externally localised, spreads itself over the space and becomes the subjective root of the Rūpa consciousness. The Rūpa experience, when closely looked into and allowed to come very close to the subjective being, is experienced as Touch or *Sparśa,* the subjective root as Vāyu.This is not the touch produced by specialised form, for this is a sensation had only after the production of Agni. The experience may be compared to the perception in ordinary life of the thermal quality of objects. The subjective intensification of Rūpa, with its surface expansion, when concentrated into a point of the inner subjective being, produced the Rasa feeling which one located outwards was, as Gandha, the subjective root of the externalised objectivity of daily life. Rūpa affects the surface subjective being, whilst Sparśa again shifts experience into the inner, as the whole subjective being then responds to Sparśa as a whole. This Sparśa consciousness, which is objectively Vāyu, is when closely examined found to consist of externality idea-points spread over the surface of the subjective being, receding away as mere hints of outsideness, as compared with the something which is outside of Rūpa experience. This is Śabda experience, the subjective root of Ākāśa, the seed of all externalised or externally located world-phenomena. It persists as the deathless basis (Amṛta) of all manifestation downwards or outwards; into which all phenomena are resolved in their upward or inward course. The realisation of this is the Śabda consciousness.

The root of externality-consciousness refers back to its origin the inner mind (which projects the idea of mere outerness and which is its counterpart), the root from which the nation of externality arises as the tree from its seed. This internal-root which grows into Ākāśa is the Brahma-consciousness as the internal root will (corresponding on the Pārthiva place to the Manas) which lies at the root of all manifestation. Behind this is the "I am myself", which subjectifying itself as the "I am myself I" became the Cosmic Will. The former is *Cit* as the objectified self-consciousness. And from the fact that it is the starting point and internal correspondence of the objective world it may be called the *Bhūḥ* Consciousness of the internal ideal, the subjective region as distinguished from the Bhūh consciousness of external, actual objective region, the first Vyāhṛti in the ascending scale. But this Supreme Bhūh, being the terminating point of objectivity in the form of the Self as Universe cannot stand by itself. In must be the result of some assertion of consciousness which is not that of any other than Self-Being, as all other assertions or Vyāhṛtis of the external world are here transcended. Thus this assertion as "I am" may be called the *Bhuvaḥ* of the supreme objective region as distinguished from the Bhuvaḥ of the objective region lower down. And behind this assertion of self-existence as its root is the eternal subjective "I" (Aham) of the supreme *Savaḥ* as distinguished from the external objective "I" or individuality in the *Svah* lower down. This completes the field of assertion of self-consciousness behind which lies the entire consciousness (Cit) itself, that is, conciousness (Cit) *per se,* which whilst itself ever unchanged and unconditioned, is the source of all the changing forms of experience mentioned which again merge into it. This is Bliss itself (Ānanda) or Joy, or which the world is an expression in time and space, the Joy by which it is maintained and the joy into which the world re-enters, the

Universal Mother (like the earthly mother) clasping the child which She has produced to Her breast.

The "I" or Aham here of is not the limited "I" of Ahankāra which is only a gross and particularised reflection of the former in the Kāmakalā-vilāsa, the Supreme I (Aham) is very beautifully explained as the union (Sāmarasya) of its own infinite Self as Prakāśa with itself as Vimarśa-Śakti, which is a pure mirror (Darpaṇa) made of a mass of the Prakāśa Śiva's own rays. These are reflected back and the Pūrṇāhambhāva or the experience of the "I" as being all arises. That is the notion of Self had by reference to the Self which is then the Enjoy of Bliss. There is no other but the Self in the fullest purity and unlimitedness of both and is thus the supreme Aham. From this root "I", which is Kāma, the will to create and the collectivity (Samaṣṭi) of all the powers which constitute all manifested things, there burgeons forth the trunk, the branches, the leaves and fruit of the great Aśvattha tree which is the universe.

It is only when this Supreme Universal "I" is reached that it is possible to realise its eternal inwardness as Mahāśūnya, which is the Great Void in the sense that it nothing which thought can conceive or words utter. None of the higher stages can be realised until the next lower one is grasped. Before the universal I is reached, it is not possible to realise the "I-less" Cit or consciousness, as the veil of matter covers (though with decreasing thickness as we ascend) its Glorious Face. It requires a strong effort of subjective penetration to pass through this covering, dense as ponderable matter at its lowest end, to reach the Consciousness which lies behind, of which all forms are Its assertions. At the time of meditation, the entire thick veil of material (Pārthiva) existence must be gradually thinned by moving inwards according to the stages described; by reducing the crude and thicker form of consciousness into the subtle and more refined, till by gradual iner progress the subtlest point of the universal "I" which is the Lord (Īśvara) of Vedānta is reached. After this that which is the eternal and changeless ground of even this realised and then there is Kaivalya Mokṣa the ultimate Basis of all the Forms which have arisen out of Its self- assertion— the will to be many of which the Veda speaks. This is the great Self of the Vedānta. This is the Perfect Experience which is called the Supreme Love *(Niratiśayapremāspādatvaṁ ānandatvaṃ)*.

These forms of the Self can be broadly classified into the actual, objective or external which is the waking state (Jāgrat avasthā). The ideal, the subjective or internal, the assertional or the state of dream (Svapna) ; and the third the state of dreamless slumber (Suṣupti) which is the bare subjective standing by, itself not yet in active assertion, but having passed the equilibrium point about to assert itself, but for the time being having the assertion latent in it, lying there unperceived, but ready to shoot forth into assertion, at first qualitative, and then into perception, by reason of both qualitative and external manifestation. Herein all Ideas become merged and latent and thence project themselves into the ideal and thence again into the Actual in the course of the involution of the self into the Māyik covering which is the universe. The perfect consciousness, as realising all these three stage with all their difference and similarities, lies beyond them all, though it is one with all, supporting them by its own essential Being and Power (Śakti).They are its forms the forms of that consciousness which It is. It runs through all (Sūtrātmā) and unifies them all, but remains in itself unlimited and unconditioned, giving them both their separate existence, yet summing them up into its own life and Being, which comprehending all yet transcends them from the standpoint of its own Being in itself or Svarūpa. It is beyond all because it is infinite. It comprehends all in its supremely rich experience because it is the whole (Pūrṇa) It is Love because It is the Love of the Self for the self. It is Joy because all Love is that; but it is perfect also. It is the perfect Experience (Jñānasvarūpa) which thought achieves by a pure mind in a pure body. It is thus the Supreme Siddhi of all Sādhanā and Yoga.

*Oṁ Tat Sat.*